BROKEN
LADDERS

BROKEN LADDERS

Managerial
Careers
in the
New Economy

EDITED BY PAUL OSTERMAN

New York   Oxford
Oxford University Press
1996

Oxford University Press

Oxford   New York
Athens   Auckland   Bangkok   Bogota   Bombay
Buenos Aires   Calcutta   Cape Town   Dar es Salaam   Delhi
Florence   Hong Kong   Istanbul   Karachi
Kuala Lumpur   Madras   Madrid   Melbourne
Mexico City   Nairobi   Paris   Singapore
Taipei   Tokyo   Toronto

and associated companies in
Berlin   Ibadan

Library of Congress Cataloging-in-Publication Data
Osterman, Paul.
Broken ladders : managerial careers in the
new economy / Paul Osterman, editor.
p.   cm.
Includes bibliographical references and index.
ISBN 0-19-509353-4
1. Executives—Job descriptions.   2. Career development.
I. Title.
HD38.2.O88   1996
658—dc20   96-25776

1 2 3 4 5 6 7 8 9
Printed in the United States of America
on acid-free paper

Preface

This book grew out of my long-standing view that there is too little systematic research on the careers of white-collar employees. This concern has gained additional force as the widespread restructuring in recent years resulted in what appears to be considerable shifts in the terms of employment for all workers including managers. There was obviously much to be learned about what was happening inside firms to employees who had previously been sheltered from the vissitudes of the external labor market.

The Sloan Foundation has for some time supported a series of large-scale projects in which a group of researchers studied many dimensions of restructuring in various industries. Under the initiative of Tom Kochan, an effort was made to pull together what has been learned about human resources in those industries. One of the first fruits of this initiative was a conference I organized, with the support of the Sloan Foundation, on the evolution of managerial employment. In addition to representatives of the industry projects, we invited a few additional researchers and this book is a direct product of that conference.

Obviously thanks are due both to the Sloan Foundation and to Tom Kochan for helping to make this book possible. Another very large debt of gratitude is due to Susan Wright, who in her typical outstanding performance did a great deal of the organizational work on both the conference and the book. Karen Boyajian also contributed in important and essential ways to both the conference and the book. Conference attendees who did not contribute book chapters nevertheless helped improve the final product through their participation and thoughtful comments. In addition, John Van Maanen and Peter Cappelli made helpful comments on the introduction to this book.

Contents

About the Authors

STEPHEN R. BARLEY is an Associate Professor of Industrial Engineering and Engineering Management at the School of Engineering, Stanford University. He is also the editor of *The Administrative Science Quarterly*. He has written extensively on the social and organizational implications of new technology and the technical labor force since the early 1980s. He received his doctorate from the Organizational Studies Group at MIT.

ROSEMARY BATT is Assistant Professor of Human Resource Studies, Industrial and Labor Relations School, Cornell University. She received her B.A. from Cornell University and Ph.D. in human resources studies and industrial relations at the Sloan School of Management, MIT. She is coauthor with Eileen Appelbaum of *The New Workplace: Transforming Work Systems in the United States* (Cornell University ILR Press, 1994). Other articles have appeared in *The Journal of Policy Analysis and Management, International Contributions to Labour Studies of the Cambridge Journal of Economics,* and the *British Journal of Industrial Relations*. Her main research interests include innovative work systems, self-managed team systems, employee participation, and service sector productivity. Her current research focuses on organizational restructuring in the telecommunications services industry.

SARA L. BECKMAN is Co-Director of the Management of Technology Program at the University of California, Berkeley Haas School of Business, where she also teaches manufacturing and operations management, manufacturing strategy, and product design. Her primary research interests are in green design and manufacturing, product definition processes for software products, and the effects of vertical "disintegration." Prior to and concurrent with her involvement at the Haas School, Dr. Beckman worked for the Hewlett-Packard Company, most recently as director of the Product Generation Change Management Team. She holds B.S., M.S., and Ph.D. degrees from the Department of Industrial Engineering and Engineering Management at Stanford University and an M.S. in statistics from the same institution.

PETER CAPPELLI is Professor and Chair of the Management Department at the Wharton School, Co-Director of Wharton's Center for Human Resources, and Co-Director of the U.S. Department of Education's National Center on the Educational Quality of the Workforce (EQW).He has degrees in industrial relations from Cornell University and in labor economics from Oxford where he was a Fulbright Scholar. He has been a Guest Scholar at the Brookings Institution, a German Marshall Fund Fellow, and a faculty member at MIT, the University of Illinois, and the University of California at Berkeley as well as the Wharton School. Professor Cappelli's research for the EQW Center has examined changes in work and the effects on skill requirements, the contribution of workplace attitudes and behaviors to job related skills, and the effects on workforce skills associated with choices of employment practices. He is beginning a major study of work organization in financial services to understand why high performance work systems have been so slow to take hold in that industry, and he is heading a major study for the National Planning Association on the restructuring of the employment relationship.

RENÉE M. LANDERS is a Deputy Assistant Attorney General, Office of Policy Development, United States Department of Justice. Ms. Landers received her A.B. from Radcliffe College and her J.D. from Boston College Law School. From 1988 to 1993, she was an assistant professor of law at Boston College Law School. Previously she was an associate at the Boston law firm of Ropes & Gray and from 1985 to 1986, a law clerk to Edward F. Hennessey, the now-retired Chief Justice of the Massachusetts Supreme Judicial Court.

JOHN PAUL MACDUFFIE is an Assistant Professor in the Management Department at the Wharton School of Business, University of Pennsylvania. He received his B.A. degree from Harvard University and his Ph.D. degree from the Sloan School of Management at MIT. He also formerly held the Harman Fellowship in the Program on Work, Technology, and Human Development at Harvard University. Professor MacDuffie's research explores the relationship of technology, production systems, and human resource policies in manufacturing settings. His research has focused on the world automotive industry, through his involvement in MIT's International Motor Vehicle Program (IMVP). He has recently completed the collection of a second round of data for the International Assembly Plant Study (from a sample of 86 assembly plants representing 20 companies and 21 countries) in order to investigate the rate change in manufacturing performance over time, the diffusion of "lean or flexible" production systems through the industry worldwide, and the consequences for managers, workers, and unions.

K. C. O'SHAUGHNESSY recently completed his Ph.D. in Management at the Wharton School and is currently an assistant professor of management at Western Michigan University. His research focuses on the implications of strategy in the study of human resource management. Of particular interest is how organizational change and downsizing influence the performance of firms. Current projects include an analysis of changes in the skills of white collar employees and an analysis of the relationship between middle management compensation and the financial performance of firms. He is also involved in the Wharton Financial Institutions Center study of productivity issues in the life insurance industry.

PAUL OSTERMAN is Professor of Human Resources and Management at the Sloan School, MIT. He is the author of two books (*Getting Started: The Youth Labor Market and Employment Futures* and *Reorganization, Dislocation, and Public Policy*); the coauthor of *The Mutual Gains Enterprise: Forging a Winning Partnership Among Labor, Management, and Government*; and the editor of *Internal Labor Markets*. He has written numerous journal articles and policy analyses on topics such as labor market policy, job training programs, economic development, and poverty programs, and the organization of work within firms. He has also worked for the Massachusetts state government and consulted widely to government agencies, foundations, community groups, and public interest groups. He received his Ph.D. in Economics from MIT.

JAMES B. REBITZER is Associate Professor of Management at the Sloan School of Management at MIT. He is an economist specializing in the economics of employment relationships. His recent research has focused on professionals in professional service firms. His work has appeared in *The American Economic Review, Industrial Relations, The Journal of Public Economics, The Journal of Labor Economics, The Review of Economics and Statistics,* and *The Quarterly Journal of Economics.*

ELIZABETH (LIBBY) D. SCOTT is currently a Ph.D. student at the Wharton School at the University of Pennsylvania, studying Business Ethics and Human Resources. For more than ten years, she worked in various capacities in human Resources management, including equal employment opportunity, recruitment and selection, employee regulations, compensations, classification, and benefits. Most recently, she was Personnel Director for the Georgia Department of Labor. Her dissertation research examines the relationship between individuals' moral values and their job choices and opportunities.

LOWELL J. TAYLOR is Associate Professor of Economics and Public Policy at the H. John Heinz III School of Public Policy and Management, Carnegie Mellon University. He is a labor economist who has written widely on the theory of efficiency wages, immigration, minimum wages, and food stamp policies. His work has appeared in leading economics journals, including *The American Economics Review, The Journal of Public Economics,* and *The Quarterly Journal of Economics.*

MICHAEL USEEM is Professor of Management at the Wharton School and Professor of Sociology at the School of Arts and Sciences at the University of Pennsylvania. He is author of *Executive Defense: Shareholder Power and Corporate Reorganization* and of *Investor Capitalism: How Money Managers are Changing the Face of Corporate America.*

STACIA E. ZABUSKY received her Ph.D. in Cultural Anthropology from Cornell University. Her book *Launching Europe: An Ethnography of European Cooperation in Space Science* examines the local work practices of scientists and engineers who coordinate European space science mission for the European Space Agency. She is currently conducting a new ethnographic research project in the Netherlands, where she is studying how European expatriate professionals and their families experience and construct occupational, ethnic, and national identities while living and working for an intergrating Europe.

STACIA E. ZABUSKY received her Ph.D. in Cultural Anthropology from Cornell University. Her book *Launching Europe: An Ethnography of European Cooperation in Space Science* examines the local work practices of scientists and engineers who coordinate European space science missions for the European Space Agency. She is currently conducting a new ethnographic research project in the Netherlands, where she is studying how European expatriate professionals and their families experience and construct occupational, ethnic, and national identities while living in and working for an integrating Europe.

Introduction | I

PAUL OSTERMAN

America is reinventing how it works. Battered by international competition from the mid-1970s to the mid-1980s and chastened by lagging productivity, American firms invested heavily in new technology; experimented widely with workplace innovations such as self-managed work teams; climbed on the quality bandwagon, making Total Quality Management and customer satisfaction the new mantra; reengineered the structure of the corporation; and divested themselves of both businesses and employees that were not seen as "core." The result is that for nearly every group of employees the terms and conditions of employment have changed, in many cases quite dramatically. Whether these changes are on balance good or bad is by no means clear. For many workers, jobs require more diverse activities with more responsibility, the demand for skills is rising, and the rate of job creation has itself been impressive. Offsetting this are stagnating incomes for most Americans and insecurity even in the face of declining unemployment rates.

The historical record suggests that blue-collar and service workers will bear the brunt of economic insecurity. Managers have always appeared to be above the fray. They seemed immune from the business cycle because they were a "fixed factor" who were not laid off and rehired as the economy ebbed and grew. Perhaps their skills were too complex to risk losing or perhaps they were in the enviable position of planning the layoffs and hence protected themselves and their own. Even better, over the long run the demand for managers grew and this seemed sensible given the spread of large bureaucratic organizations, which by their very nature seemed to require more and more managerial expertise. Suddenly these good times have apparently ended. The current wave of reorganization and the reinvention of work have (assert many commentators) put managerial jobs at risk and changed the nature of managerial work as never before.

Daily headlines constantly signal these changes. In an article titled "Evolution of the Workplace Alters Office Relationships" the *New York Times* reported on a former Chase Manhattan Bank controller who does the same job he did last year in the same physical office but who is now an employee of AT&T because Chase outsourced his department's functions. The same article recounted the experience of an ex-IBMer who rents an office and is now a self-employed consultant. Indeed, IBM reduced its U.S. work force from 237,000 in 1986 to 130,000 in 1993. Many of the job losers were managers. A headline in the *Wall Street Journal* (May 4, 1995) reported that "Amid Record Profits, Companies Continue to Lay Off Employees," and the story led with Mobil Oil's second large round of headquarters cuts.

These events lead to the natural conclusion that the nature of managerial work is dramatically changing. Indeed, a range of observers has drawn just this conclusion. *Fortune* magazine reports that "The managers who come out best from this annealing fire will scarcely resemble yesterday's boss" (*Fortune,* April 4, 1994, p. 68) and, in more measured tones, Rosabeth Kanter writes:

> Bureaucratic-corpocratic assumptions about a steady, long-term rise up a hierarchy of ever more lucrative jobs give way to new realities and new expectations: long-term uncertainty, the need for portable skills, the likelihood of a stab at being in business for oneself. Climbing the career ladder is being replaced by hopping from job to job. Reliance on organizations to give shape to a career is being replaced by reliance on self. (Kanter, 1989, p. 299)

This book is designed to explain what is happening to the work and careers of managers. It is motivated both by the view that something has changed and by a skepticism that we really understand what has happened and why. Many of the assertions are based on fairly casual empiricism and a perhaps too-easy acceptance of the generality of a few dramatic cases. As we will see, both data and case studies suggest managerial work is indeed changing but that a bit more caution about the extent and nature of the transformation is appropriate.

Our uncertainty is not limited to *what* is happening but also extends to *why.* Is the story the simple one that competitive pressures have finally become severe enough to change managers from a "fixed" to a "variable" cost but little else is different? Or have technological change (e.g., the microcomputer revolution) or new ideas about the organization of enterprises fundamentally altered the nature of managerial work?

This book attempts to answer these questions. The chapters in the book examine concrete cases and provide evidence from a variety of perspectives: Chapters 4 and 5 examine the shifting situation of managers from the viewpoint of an entire industry: John-Paul MacDuffie on automobiles and Elizabeth Scott, K.C. O'Shaughnessy, and Peter Cappelli on insurance. Chapters 3 and 6 report on the impact of restructuring on managers at the level of specific firms with Rosemary Batt examining BellSouth and Sara Beckman Hewlett-Packard. Chapters 2, 7, and 8 take an occupational perspective: Michael Useem (senior managers), Stacia Zabusky and Steve Barley (technicians), and Renee Landers, Jim Rebitzer, and Lowell Taylor (lawyers, consultants, and accountants). Although chapters 7 and 8 are obviously not directly about managers, they examine occupations that can be thought of as bracketing managerial positions. Both are skill-based white-collar occupations whose evolution seems to foreshadow several trends that we observe for managers. In addition, chapter 8 explicitly addresses issues raised by the rising participation of high-level women in the labor market for managers and professionals.

The Framework for the Book

These are a number of different ways to think about managerial careers and the literature reflects this diversity. There has, for example, been considerable research that takes the individual as the point of analysis and examines his or her experience primarily using social psychology as the lens. The career studies pioneered by my colleagues Edgar Schein (1978) and John Van Manaan (1977) are strong examples of this tradition. Another perspective is the career development literature (see, for example, Hall, 1986) that asks about how firms might best identify, motivate, train, and promote managers.

The perspective taken in this book is rather different. Most of the chapters in the book examine shifts in the structural elements of managerial careers in what might be termed the "internal labor market" of managers. When researchers speak of internal labor markets, they refer to the rules and procedures that shape careers within the enterprise. These rules cover topics such as wage determination, mobility channels and job ladders, training, and employment security. For example, a classic description for many (though by no means all) occupations was that entry from the external labor market was possible only at the bottom of job ladders and mobility occurred up those ladders (and not across ladders). Wages were attached to job titles, not to individuals. In some settings, the firm made implicit commitments with regard to employment security, whereas in others the rule was hire/fire.

Thinking in terms of internal labor markets is useful because it enables us to describe the structure or framework within which careers evolve. Decisions made by individuals are made in the context of the opportunities and limitations posed by the overall structure. The nature of that structure varies across occupations and firms and a useful way of framing the discussion about restructuring is to think of it in terms of shifts in the internal labor market rules for managerial jobs. Thinking in these terms focuses our attention on the most important structural elements of careers and also gives us a way of thinking about variation across firms in those rules. This is because a good deal of the prior research on internal labor markets has studied both the determination of rules and the variation in rules across settings (see for example, Doeringer and Piore, 1972; Osterman, 1984; Pfeffer and Cohen, 1984; Baron, Davis-Blake, and Bilbey, 1986).

Taking an internal labor markets perspective on what is happening to managers does not imply that other lenses are unimportant or invalid. However, it does seem true that many of the perceptions, popular and otherwise, about the impact of restructuring on managers implicitly claim that the internal labor markets—the structure of managerial careers—have changed. It therefore seems appropriate to ask what the evidence says about managerial internal labor markets, then and now, and this is the goal of the chapters that follow.

What Managerial Careers Used to Look Like

To understand what has changed it is obviously sensible to start by describing the characteristics of the "old" internal labor market of managers. This is surprisingly hard to do. There is a large prescriptive literature on the best ways for firms to structure managerial careers but empirical descriptive and analytic material is much thinner. Nevertheless, it is possible to piece together from various sources a coherent description and the following represents characteristics of "traditional" managerial careers on which there is substantial evidence.

Managerial Careers Involved Movement Up a Well Defined Ladder

There are two points here: the existence of a ladder and the notion of moving up that ladder. Two large-scale analyses of longitudinal personnel data on managers reveal very clear and simple career patterns of movement up levels of the organization (Rosenbaum, 1984; Baker, Gibbs, and Holmstrom, 1994). In both cases, despite the mathematical possibility of numerous paths the overwhelming bulk of the sample actually followed a few well-trod routes. Ladders were well defined.

One implication of the clear ladders is that most movement was upward. Managers either were promoted or stayed where they were. Lateral shifts were rare. This pattern in the data confirms the observations of field researchers such as Rosabeth Kanter (1977) who reported that in her pseudonymous firm "Indisco" the rule was "Be promoted or perish. You are not really successful, or you do not mean much to the company, unless you get the chance to move on. Thus jobs and job categories were evaluated in terms of their advancement prospects" (p. 131).

Although both the Rosenbaum and the Baker, Gibbs, and Holmstrom studies were careful in their analysis of job *levels* neither paid attention to job *titles* and hence to the functional areas within which people worked. As a result neither study can tell us whether managerial careers played out entirely within functional areas (or "chimneys"), or whether an appreciable number of managers moved across areas as they rose in the organization. The case study evidence in the subsequent chapters suggests two dominant patterns. Most managers lived their careers within one functional area (careers were "highly regulated and functionally specialized" says Batt and "uni-functional" says Beckman). However, people being groomed for the most senior positions, the "fast-trackers," were likely to move across the chimneys as the firm sought to provide them with broad experience.

Managerial Employment Was Low Risk

All observers agree that managers did not face serious risk of layoffs. MacDuffie notes that in the automobile industry "there was no challenge to white employment security until the late 1970s" and this refrain is repeated in the other book chapters. The long-closed internal labor market of the old Bell System (with its nearly guaranteed job security) described by Batt is perhaps extreme but not different in kind than what was to be found for managers throughout the economy. In a similar vein, pay was not particularly at risk. MacDuffie's mid-level automobile managers lived "in a paternalistic culture that produced virtually automatic annual pay increases" and Useem's senior managers began the 1980s with the majority of their pay package in the base, not variable. In Hewlett-Packard, Beckman reports a strong policy, in the pre-restructuring period, of uniformity in pay and promotion policies throughout the firm. She also reports that pay was largely based on head count (and that head count seemed destined to grow indefinitely).

It is also worth noting that while layoffs were rare, turnover rates may have been considerably higher than the image promulgated by the term "the organization man." In the Baker, Gibbs, and Holmstrom data the rate of voluntary exist among managers was 8% to 10% per year and remained at this level even for managers with substantial tenure. Even more striking is the AT&T data provided by Bray and Howard. The authors followed a cohort of managers who joined AT&T, perhaps the most secure and career oriented of all firms, in 1956 (Howard and Bray, 1988). After the first eight years of employment 39% of the college-educated managers had left AT&T; while some of this may reflect problems in job matching, even between year eight and year 20 an additional 17% left (p. xi).

Managers Hired More Managers

A central aspect of managerial employment systems was the strong bias toward continually increasing managerial employment. This bias has deep roots. In 1929, American manufacturing firms employed 18 administrative workers per every 100 employees. By 1950 the figure was 24, by 1960 it was 29, and in 1970 it was 30 (Guillen, pp. 66, 82). In part, this reflected the impact of increased organizational size and the planning requirements that went along with this. However, there is clearly more to the story because, as David Gordon (1994) has shown, American firms are much more managerially intensive than are companies in other advanced nations. Table 1-1 uses International Labor Organization (ILO) data to examine the percentage of total employment that comprises "administrative and managerial workers." This category is uncomfortably vague but nevertheless useful for developing a broad-strokes analysis of the situation. The data demonstrate that America, in both 1980 and 1989, was far more managerially intensive than most other developed nations and was approached by only Canada, the United Kingdom, and Australia.

There may be a cultural component to this pattern but there are several additional explanations. We know that the most consistent finding in the executive compensation literature has been that managerial salaries rise with the size of the unit reporting to the manager (see, for example, Milgrom and Roberts, 1992). Perhaps, then, it is no surprise that managers hired more managers. The ethnographic literature on the politics of managerial employment also describes the strong temptation to create managerial fiefdoms by expanding the employment of subordinates (Jackall, 1988). David Gordon himself attributes the patterns to

Table 1-1. Percentage of Non-Farm
Employment in Administrative and
Managerial Occupations, 1989

Country	Intensity (%)
Australia	14.6
Austria	6.2
Belgium	3.0
Canada	12.9
Denmark	3.9
Finland	5.5
Germany	3.3
Japan	4.2
Netherlands	4.3
Sweden	2.4
United Kingdom	10.1
United States	13.4

Source: International Labor Organization, Yearbook
of Labor Statistics (calculated in David Gordon,
1994). The U.K. figure is for 1980; in that year the
figure for the United States was 11.5%.

high levels of conflict in American firms regarding work effort and job security
and hence the necessity to rely on higher levels of supervision, that is, more
managers.

What the Data Show About Change

A useful way to begin our examination of what has happened to managerial
careers is to review the available nationally representative data. Although these
data are too crude to capture much of what interests us, they nevertheless represent an important first cut at understanding recent trends and they can usefully
serve as a counterweight to claims made on the basis of casual observation. I will
examine data on four points: the number of managers employed in the economy,
the job tenure of those managers, unemployment experience of managers, and
compensation of managers.

Table 1-2 plots private sector "executive, administrative, and managerial
employment" as a percentage of the labor force from 1983 to 1994. These
particular years were selected because this is the period in which the census
occupational classification remained constant (i.e., to go back in time would
mean a slight, but potentially important, change in definition). It is apparent that
the 1980s and early 1990s did not witness a decline in the importance of managers in the economy; in fact there has been a slight increase. This pattern is
consistent with findings using other sources. For example, using the Census of
Manufacturing, Berman, Bound, and Griliches (1994) found that managers as a

Table 1-2. Managerial and Executive
Employment in the Private Sector as a
Percentage of Total Employment,
1983–1994

Year	Employment (%)
1983	10.1
1984	10.5
1985	10.9
1986	11.0
1987	11.3
1988	11.8
1989	12.1
1990	12.0
1991	12.2
1992	12.0
1993	12.4
1994	12.7

Source: Author's calculations from *Employment and Earnings*. The formula for the calculation is (executive, administrative, and managerial employment minus public administration) divided by total civilian employment.

percentage of the labor force in manufacturing increased from 27% in 1973 to 29.4% in 1987.

Although very suggestive, these data do have their limitations. The category "executive, administrative, and managerial" is quite broad (including funeral directors and construction inspectors as well as senior executives). Hence the trends may not be representative of the middle managers and senior managers that are our concern here. Nevertheless, there is certainly nothing in these data that suggests an erosion of managerial employment.[1]

If managerial ranks are not shrinking, it is still possible that the data demonstrate a change in the terms of their employment. There are two related ways to get at this. The first is to examine whether job tenure of managers (their longevity on the job) has changed. The second is to study the nature of their unemployment and layoff experience.

Several researchers have recently studied changing job tenure patterns of managers and, unfortunately, there is substantial controversy regarding the interpretation of the data. One approach is to employ census data that ask people to specify how many years they have been working at their current employer. The advantage of the census is that the sample sizes are very large. The disadvantage is that people seem to have trouble giving an accurate answer to job tenure questions (Brown and Light, 1992). The alternative data source is the Panel Survey on Income Dynamics, a longitudinal survey that tracked the same people during most of the 1970s and 1980s. The advantages are the longitudinal character of

Table 1-3. Job Retention Rates Based on Reports of Job Tenure with the Same Employer

	Current tenure group (years)			
	0–3 Years	3–6 Years	6+ Years	Total
	Retention rate (%)			
1983–87				
All	36	57	69	52
Professionals and managers	41	66	73	58
1987–91				
All	36	48	70	51
Professionals and managers	41	53	80	59

Source: Current Population Survey. Calculations by Diebold, Neumark, and Polsky (1994).

the survey and the simpler question that asked if the respondent was with the same employer as a year ago. The disadvantage is the sample size, which is much smaller than the census.

Table 1-3 shows the results obtained by Diebold, Neumark, and Polsky (1994) from the census. They calculated retention rates, which in principle are based on a ratio of the number of employees with, say, eight years' tenure to the number who reported three years' tenure in a survey five years later. In fact, these calculations are based on artificial cohorts because the census does not resurvey the same people; however if the sampling is done correctly this should not affect the results. If restructuring is changing the rules of the game for managerial job security, we would expect to observe this retention rate falling in the past decade. The categories used by Diebold, Neumark, and Polsky are not perfect for our purposes but they should nevertheless signal if substantial changes have occurred.

As an illustration, the first cell in Table 1-3 means that for all employees who had between 0 and 3 years of tenure with the employer in 1983 36% were still employed at the same firm in 1987 (the census changed its questions regarding tenure somewhat over the course of the various surveys and Diebold, Neumark, and Polsky have chosen years for comparison in which the questions remained constant).

The overall impression from these data is that for the labor force as a whole and for managerial and professional workers in particular there has been little change in retention probabilities. Whereas 58% of managerial/professional workers remained with the same employer between 1983 and 1987, between 1987 and 1991 the figure was 59%. There is certainly no evidence here of a collapse in careers for managers. By contrast, as past experience might lead us to expect, it is

Table 1-4. Occupational Stability (Based on Reports of Having Not Changed Employers)

	Occupational stability (%)		
	Managers	Professionals	Skilled Blue Collar
A. Number of Years in Which the Same Occupational Classification Is Reported			
1970s			
1–5 Years	42	32	44
6–8 Years	23	22	20
9+	33	44	34
1980s			
1–5	51	39	42
6–8	22	17	20
9+	26	40	35
B. Among Those Who Reported the Same Occupation in Nine or More Years, the Number of Times They Changed Employers			
1970s			
0–1 Changes	79	78	70
2–3 Changes	18	14	20
4+ Changes	1	7	8
1980s			
0–1 Changes	67	68	60
2–3 Changes	23	20	24
4+ Changes	9	11	14

Source: Panel Survey on Income Dynamics. Calculations from data provided by Stephen Rose.

blue-collar workers who took a hit during the same period: their retention chances fell substantially from 53% to 48%.

This conclusion is modified, however, for managers with three to six years of job tenure. In this group, which might be thought of as middle managers relatively early in their careers, there was a very dramatic fall in retention, from 66% to 53%. Indeed, this fall is larger than that experienced by blue-collar employees with the same tenure. We will see in several chapters of the book that middle level managers, not those at the top, are experiencing the greatest distress from restructuring and these data add support to that conclusion.

Table 1-4 shows the results from a similar exercise, limited to men, using the Panel Survey on Income Dynamics. These calculations, by Stephen Rose (1995) of the National Commission on Employment Policy, are somewhat different and are actually better structured for our purposes. The first panel shows the number of years in which a person who was a manager in at least one year was a manager (at any employer) over the decade. For example, among persons who were a manager at least once in the 1970s, 33% held that job title for 10 years. By contrast, among persons who were a manager at least once in the 1980s, 26% held that job title for 10 years. It is apparent that these calculations show an increase in occupational churning among managers in the 1980s and that this increase was greater for managers than it was for professionals and, surprisingly, for blue-collar employees.

In the second panel, the data are limited to persons who were strongly attached to the managerial occupation, that is, who held managerial job titles in at least eight of the 10 years in the decade. The panel then asks about the frequency with which these persons changed employers. Again, the data show a substantial decline in employment stability for managers although, in this case, the decline is more or less matched in the other occupations. Taken as a whole, the Panel Survey on Income Dynamics suggests considerable turbulence in the labor market for managers.

Another way to understand the experience of managers through the lens of national statistics is to examine their experience with unemployment and dislocation. During the recession of 1990–91 many commentators, influenced by the unending stream of corporate announcements about restructuring, claimed that we were experiencing the first "white-collar recession." Erica Groshen and Donald Williams (1995) examined this claim and found it incorrect: during the 1990–91 recession blue-collar unemployment rates remained much higher than white-collar ones, and while blue-collar employment fell by 3% no net white-collar jobs were lost (Groshen and Williams do not distinguish managers from other white-collar employees).

There were, however, some more subtle indications of a worsening of the position of white-collar employees. While their unemployment rates remained well below those of blue-collar workers, the gap was smaller than it had ever been and, in the subsequent recovery, white-collar unemployment fell more slowly than the historical record would have predicted. This is consistent with Henry Farber's finding that, during the 1990–91 recession, college graduates were much better off than blue-collar workers but nevertheless were 15% more likely to lose their job than they had in the 1982–83 recession (Farber, 1995).

Dislocation data on provide additional evidence that the situation of managers has worsened. The Census Bureau regularly conducts special surveys of worker dislocation, which is defined as permanent job loss due to plant closing, large-scale layoffs, or the elimination of shifts. Table 1-5 shows the percentage of occupational groups that experienced dislocation or permanent job loss over two periods.

It is apparent that even in the 1990–91 recession managerial displacement rates were below those of other occupational groups. However, it is also true that managerial displacement increased more rapidly than any group except administrative support (whose fate is presumably closely linked with that of managers). These findings are consistent with the research of Peter Cappelli (1992), who was the first to examine the experience of managers via the dislocated worker surveys. This sense of deterioration is reinforced by Lori Kletzer's finding that displaced managers who subsequently found new jobs experienced a larger earnings loss than did any other group of white-collar employees (Kletzer, 1994).

Table 1-5. Displacement Rates in Two Recessions (Number
Displaced as Percentage of Midpoint Employment Levels)

	Number displaced (%)	
Occupation	1979–83	1987–91
Managers	8.4	9.5
Professionals	4.9	5.1
Technicians	10.0	10.8
Sales	10.8	10.6
Administrative support	8.0	10.2
Non-white-collar	18.6	14.1

Source: Mishel and Bernstein, *The State of Working America, 1994–1995,*
p. 212. Washington: Economic Policy Institute, 1995.

A final perspective using national data is the earnings experience of managers. It is well known that earnings have stagnated in general. How have managers fared? Did they enjoy their traditional protection against adverse economic trends or did they share in the flattening of earnings? Did restructuring show up in the paycheck? Table 1-6 provides some answers based on the Current Population Survey. (These data do not include benefits. In fact, total compensation did rise more than just wages and, hence, inclusion of benefits would moderate the trends in the table but would not change the overall conclusion.)[2]

For the period 1979–93 managers, both male and female, experienced stronger earnings growth than did white-collar workers in general, blue-collar, and service employees. This pattern certainly does not suggest distress. However, in the more recent period, 1989–93, managers do appear to be taking a somewhat greater hit than other groups. For men, managerial pay declined more than white-collar pay in general, more than service sector pay, and—strikingly—almost as much as blue-collar pay. For women the pattern is less dramatic, but the latter period is still a relatively more difficult one for managers. The question, of course, is whether the weaker performance in the latter period is simply a readjustment to reflect the relative gains in the early years. Although the answer to this must await more data, the bottom line is, at the least, that managerial distress is not reflected in declining relative pay. This conclusion is reinforced by Stephen Rose's analysis of the Panel Survey on Income Dynamics, which found that managers who remained in their occupation throughout the 1980s experienced the largest earnings growth of any occupation (Rose, 1995).

Where does this review of the statistical evidence leave us? In at least some respects, the data do not suggest the kind of revolutionary change implied by much of the popular literature. Managerial employment has not fallen, indeed it has risen slightly. Unemployment and displacement rates of managers remain well below those of blue-collar workers. Earnings do not seem to have deterio-

Table 1-6. Percentage Change in Wages

	1979–89	1989–93	1979–93
Males			
Managers	6.7	−4.8	1.7
All white-collar	0.0	−3.4	−3.3
Service	−9.2	−1.8	−10.8
Blue-collar	−9.3	−5.8	−14.6
Female			
Managers	15.6	2.3	18.3
All white-collar	9.0	3.0	12.2
Service	−6.7	2.6	−4.2
Blue-collar	−3.9	−2.4	−6.2

Source: Mishel and Bernstein, *The State of Working America, 1994–1995,*
p. 119.

rated. Set against these sanguine findings, the census suggests that retention rates have fallen for middle managers early in their careers and the Panel Survey on Income Dynamics shows an even more dramatic increase in turbulence. Furthermore, on several dimensions managers took a greater hit in the past recession than previous recessionary episodes would have led us to expect. On balance, then, the evidence suggests a fraying around the edges of the previously secure managerial world. Whether this fraying will lead to an eventual collapse of the traditional structure cannot be predicted with these data and perhaps can be better addressed with the richer cases found in subsequent chapters.

What the Contributors Teach Us

The chapters that follow are varied both in their level of analysis and in the kind of data they use. Some focus on particular occupations whereas others examine an entire industry. Some use fieldwork whereas others draw on survey data. All share an effort to understand how the careers of managers are changing. The chapters are rich and it would be a disservice to try to summarize them here. However it is worthwhile to briefly review some central conclusions that cut across the cases.

The Nature of Restructuring

One clear message that emerges from the chapters is that the firms and industries represented in these cases experienced two quite distinct types of restructuring. In some instances, the restructuring simply involved cost cutting and downsizing. Other instances entailed significant transformations in how the work was done. MacDuffie describes an evolution in the auto industry in which initial responses to the crisis simply involved cost cutting while subsequently the introduction of lean production systems led to far-reaching organizational changes. Batt shows that in telecommunications the two tendencies are at war with each other within the same organization. Efforts to compete by improving service quality via teams and cross-functional systems run up against straightforward cost cutting. Both kinds of restructuring have some common implications (e.g., a reduction in managerial ranks) but in other ways the impact on skills, career opportunities, and morale is quite different. When restructuring simply involves cost cutting and downsizing, the content of jobs is not changed and managers gain little, in terms of wider responsibilities or broader skills, to compensate for the increased insecurity.

Job Security

It is clear in virtually every instance that managerial job security has been reduced by recent events. The insurance industry data used by Scott, O'Shaughnessy, and Cappelli demonstrate a substantial flattening of organizations with the disappearance of several layers of management. Sara Beckman describes the consolidation of manufacturing plants with the consequent loss of employment for some managers. In the survey of managers at her telecommunications company, Rose Batt reports that 92% said job security had decreased. Perhaps the only exception to this pattern is Michael Useem's finding that for CEOs the evidence is that, despite some highly publicized cases, dismissal rates have not risen over time.

Compensation

There appear to have been two major developments in managerial compensation. First, as is carefully documented in the chapter by Useem and confirmed by most of the others, the fraction of managerial pay that is contingent on performance has increased. Risk has gone up as firms seek to use compensation to more tightly align the incentives of managers with those of stockholders.

In addition to the changing composition of managerial pay the pay structure also appears to have been altered. Several of the chapters suggest growing inequality within firms as the pay of the most senior managers has risen more rapidly than that of those below them in the hierarchy. The "hardest" data on this are found in Scott, O'Shaughnessy, and Cappelli; Useem provides some additional evidence. One explanation is that as promotion becomes increasingly less likely due to reduction in managerial layers greater reward for those who do get promoted, and hence greater inequality, is necessary to maintain incentives. This prediction would follow from tournament models of career and pay (Rosenbaum, 1984; Lazear and Rosen, 1981). A less benign explanation is that senior management is looking out for itself and is able to use the smokescreen of restructuring to alter the pay structure in its favor.

Job Ladders and Skills

Although Sara Beckman reports that managers are confused about the impact of restructuring on their careers, one fact that emerges in all of the chapters is that upward mobility is much less probable than it used to be. Rose Batt tells us that promotions have virtually halted in her telecommunications firm and Scott, O'Shaughnessy, and Cappelli use their data to demonstrate an unmistakable flattening in the hierarchy of insurance firms.

None of the chapters suggest that lateral movement, across functions for example, is increasing to compensate for the loss of upward movement. What does appear to be true is that the nature of skills is changing. One trend is the growing importance of skills in dealing with organizations and people external to the firm. For senior management, according to Useem, this means a focus on external investors and relationships with boards. For manufacturing managers, Beckman suggests, there is an increased premium on capacity to work effectively with external suppliers. In addition, several of the chapters suggest required skills have become less functionally oriented and, in some senses, broader. Both Scott, O'Shaughnessy, and Cappelli and Rose Batt emphasize the growing importance of teams and the consequent premium on team skills. Useem argues that the rise of strategic business units means that senior managers, even those below the very top, are increasingly seen as general managers as opposed to functional specialists. MacDuffie's vivid description of lean production systems makes clear that automobile managers will need to be much more flexible, working in matrix organizations with multiple bosses, and at the same time having many more direct reports. These shifts put heavy emphasis on process skills and the Ford Motor Company expects these changes to be so profound that it is systematically offering personality tests to managers to help them assess their capacity to function in the new world.

Although career patterns and skills are clearly changing it is less clear whether managers are being "empowered" as much of the popular literature would have it. The managers surveyed by Batt do find that their individual jobs are broader and more interesting but they express a great deal of suspicion about the intentions of their employers. In addition, much of the reduction in managerial layers has occurred via the elimination of formerly independent operations and concentration of power in more central locations. This process is illustrated by Beckman's description of consolidation at Hewlett-Packard and is consistent with a description of events in a steel company provided by Prechel (1994). Prechel places heavy emphasis on the capacity of information technology to monitor and control the actions of formerly independent plant and production managers. Increased concentration of power is not consistent with the view that restructuring is empowering. It is also worth noting that there is no evidence in the cases of the kind of "intrapreneurialism" or free-floating independence that is sometimes celebrated by some of the more enthusiastic advocates of new organizational forms.

Senior-Middle Split

The firm is a political institution and politics, as Jeffrey Pfeffer has reminded us, plays an important role in structuring careers (Pfeffer, 1989). Several of the chapters provide evidence supporting this general proposition, specifically with respect to growing cleavages between senior and middle management. In the insurance industry, the earnings of highest level management grew much more rapidly than middle management. MacDuffie describes how, in the auto industry, the bonus system was deployed to protect the earnings of top management at a time when those further down the managerial hierarchy experienced stagnant earnings growth. Batt's survey shows that within her telecommunications firm middle management is skeptical of the intentions of top management and mistrustful of the direction of organizational change.

Why this divide has emerged is a question that is not fully resolved in the chapters. However, there are several clues. First, declining opportunities for upward mobility may reduce the sense of solidarity among different organizational levels. Now the steps are fewer and the gap between them wider and as a result mobility is reduced and identification with the top appears to be weaker. Middle managers may increasingly share as much in common with those below them as with those above. Second, the willingness of top management to increase their own pay at a time when middle management compensation is stagnating and job security eroding can only exacerbate the problem. While it is true that some economic models justify increasing top pay at a time when upward mobility is declining (because to maintain motivation it is necessary to raise the reward for success if the probability of success falls) it seems unlikely that this explanation is comforting for the lower level employees on the receiving end.

Organizations Are Ill-Equipped to Accommodate New Career Patterns

Two chapters directly address the impact of new career patterns within organizations. The chapter on technicians is important because, in many respects, the career patterns of technicians are similar to the emerging picture for managers. Instead of steadily moving up functional ladders, technicians survive by their wits and have craftlike careers. Their power and importance derives not from their location in a hierarchy but rather from their ability to deliver what the organization needs. Yet, as Zabusky and Barley vividly show, technicians get no respect from senior managers. Hierarchical organizations apparently do not know how to motivate or reward people whose careers are horizontal. This is not a hopeful sign given that managerial careers may increasingly resemble those of technicians.

There is a long tradition of research regarding the difficult situation women face in breaking into managerial ranks. More than 20 years ago, Rosabeth Kanter showed in *Men and Women of the Corporation* how the need of managers to have implicit and comfortable communication with their colleagues can lead to the exclusion from top ranks of persons considered "different." It seems clear that restructuring will place even more pressure on these relationships, perhaps to the detriment of women. First, the need for implicit communication will increase as informal teams play a greater role in doing the firm's business. Second, all observers agree that under new organizational arrangements demands on time rise, yet most firms have not thought through the implications of this in light of gender roles outside the firm. In many organizations, managers are assessed and promoted based on evidence of their commitment to the job. Since commitment is not directly observable, work effort (or work hours) is frequently used. This is very much the pattern in professional service organizations, such as law firms or consulting organizations, but is also common in other organizations. Landers, Rebitzer, and Taylor examine the impact of this practice in the light of the changing gender distribution of the managerial and professional labor force. It is apparent that reliance on work hours as a signal of commitment can lead both to a "rat race" (i.e., too many hours) and to a bias against female employment.

Summary

The foregoing material suggests that notable changes are indeed underway in the career structure of managers; however it is also apparent that the trends are not unidirectional. Indeed, two quite different tendencies appear in the data. Rose Batt characterizes the two directions as a conflict between cost cutting and empowerment. Another useful distinction is between centralization and decentralization. In the cost cutting/centralization model, local autonomy is reduced and layers of managers eliminated. This is made possible by concentrating more power in headquarters and making greater use of information technology and expert systems to manage.

The centralization/cost cutting model essentially represents an effort to perfect the traditional hierarchical model of organizations. It does not represent a fundamental shift in views about the purpose or structure of organizational forms. By contrast, the decentralization/empowerment model is based on a different vision of the firm, one in which organizational boundaries become diffuse (due to networks across organizations and teams within them) and in which managers have greater responsibility and discretion for managing these relations.

Explanations for the Transformation of Managerial Work

Although the new world of American managers is not as radically different from the old as some of the more fevered popular press reports might suggest, there have nevertheless been substantial changes. This section briefly reviews and assesses what the cases tell us about alternative theories of this transformation.

Throughout the postwar period, and probably before, managerial employment was steady and secure. Why has this changed? There are three possible explanations. The first argues that the costs of managerial slack simply became too great to bear. The second points to shifts in information technology. The third emphasizes changes in what might be termed organizational technology.

Agency Theory

An easy explanation for shifts in the terms of managerial employment is that competitive pressures have forced these changes on firms. Advocates of this argument would point to the difficult markets American firms have faced as international competitors have grown ever more successful. The logic is that profit squeezes have forced firms to rethink and reconfigure managerial employment. Superficially compelling as this argument is, it ultimately fails for the simple reason that there have been earlier periods of declining profitability for American firms, yet these did not lead to dramatic transformations in managerial work. Competitive pressure is surely part of the explanation but it must be interacted with new conditions or constraints.

We saw earlier that one of the characteristics of managerial career systems was that managers hired more managers. It is possible that this behavior was efficient but there are several reasons to doubt this. First, the evidence provided by David Gordon (1994) shows that American firms employed far more managers than did comparable firms in other nations, including nations with high levels of economic performance. Second, the incentives provided by salary rules (your salary is determined by the size of the unit reporting to you) created perverse incentives to increase managerial ranks. Finally, ethnographic accounts of managerial behavior, for example the classic book by Robert Jackall (1988), provide vivid evidence of empire building that seemingly had little to do with efficiency.

The tendency of managers to hire too many of their brethren is an example of what economists call an agency problem, that is, people in organizations acting in their own interests rather than according to the best interests of their principals (the firm's owners). Economic theory assumes that agents will, at least to some extent, act in their selfish interest unless their behavior can be perfectly monitored or unless there is an incentive structure that aligns their interests with those of their principals. Given the range of discretionary actions managers engage in and the size and geographic scope of American firms, perfect monitoring seems unlikely. Jackall's book is replete with stories of managers outrunning their mistakes, moving on long before their consequences are visible. Another example of agency problems is illustrated by a *Wall Street Journal* (April 26, 1994) story describing efforts by the Digital Equipment Corporation (DEC) to restructure its sales force. DEC wanted to devolve more authority to the people selling its product and instructed sales managers to implement this policy. However, the sales managers responded by firing salespeople and keeping their own jobs.

As already noted, however, agency problems alone cannot explain the recent shift in the fortune of managers because these problems are of long standing and have survived previous downturns. What may be new is reduced tolerance on the part of principals for excessive managerial agency costs. The source of this reduced tolerance must be explained and Michael Useem's chapter on the changing world of the most senior managers focuses our attention on shifting ownership patterns, in particular the growing importance—and impatience—of institutional investors. Institutional investors, and the related phenomena of corporate raiders, have left senior management less secure than at any time in memory and have seemingly reduced tolerance for agency costs, that is, for excessive managerial employment. Vickie Smith (1990, p. 14) quotes corporate raider Carl Icahn as saying his job is to eliminate "layers of bureaucrats reporting to bureaucrats."

Not all firms have experienced pressure from institutional investors or other types of mobilized owners, yet the restructuring movement is widespread. There are several possible explanations. Senior managers may fear that they too will come under investor pressure and hence they are engaging in precautionary behavior. There may also be an element of fashion or fad in restructuring, a type of behavior best explained by sociological models of mimicry and imitation (DiMaggio and Powell, 1983). On the other hand, there may be explanations distinct from agency and ownership considerations. These explanations take no position concerning the presence or absence of slack and agency problems but rather focus on "discoveries" that permit new organizational forms.

Information Technology

One way of thinking about what managers do is to argue that they process information and pass on the results to higher levels (Scott, 1981, p. 215). Technical developments that increase the effectiveness with which information can be processed may therefore reduce demand for managers. Clearly the explosion of distributed computer power in recent years lends considerable plausibility to this explanation.

It does not necessarily follow, however, that technical change that can substitute for managers will reduce their net employment. This is because the change may be so powerful that product price reductions will increase product demand sufficiently to offset the reduced use of managers for a fixed level of production. It is also true that some managers (for example, managers of information systems) are complements to computers. Nevertheless, what evidence we have suggests that increased computer power will lead to a fall in managerial employment (e.g., Osterman, 1986). In their chapter, Scott, O'Shaughnessy, and Cappelli describe how the spread of expert systems in the insurance industry has reduced the need for some categories of managers.

New Organizational Technologies

Greater efficiencies can be gained not simply through physical technology, such as computers, but also via new ideas and insights about how to organize people. There is good reason to believe that this is an important part of the recent story.

Much of the academic and management literature from the end of World War II to the mid 1970s can be read as a defense and justification of formal and fairly lengthy managerial bureaucracies. This was the central message of Chandler's (1977) explanation of the rise of the multidivisional firm and the role of management in extending the market (the "visible hand"). In sociology, Thompson's (1967) influential treatment of bureaucracy explained how in stable, predictable environments (which characterized the postwar economy until the mid-1970s) the planning and control function of management led to bureaucratic hierarchical forms. Similarly in economics, Williamson, Wacter, and Harris (1975) used a version of agency theory to explain that lengthy managerial internal labor markets were optimal because they provided the firm with a tool for limiting self-serving behavior. These explanations, and the organizational forms they implied, were widely accepted when the environment was stable. Whether firms functioned as well as the models implied is an open question. One of the managers interviewed in the 1970s by Rosabeth Kanter comments "We don't know how to manage these giant structures and I suspect that no-one does. They are like dinosaurs, lumbering on their own accord, even if they are no longer functional" (Kanter, 1977, p. 52). In fact, this informant might better have asked if the structures were optimal because the success of American enterprises in most of the postwar period seems to show that they were at least workable. However, as Scott and others have argued (Scott, 1981, p. 151; Aoiki, 1990), in unstable environments long-linked bureaucracy may not be the most efficient system. Surely from the mid-1970s onward, the economic environment facing American firms became increasingly unpredictable and this turbulence brought with it new ideas about how to manage organizations, many of which have been inspired by Japanese management practices. Production processes, both in manufacturing and in services, are being transformed via innovations such as total quality management and just-in-time production. Management itself is changing as ad hoc teams become more common and firms seek to break down traditional internal boundaries, such as those between design and manufacturing or between marketing and manufacturing. John-Paul MacDuffie describes in detail the implications of lean production systems for managers.

These organizational reforms taken as a whole appear to many observers to constitute a new model for organizing the firm, a new organizational technology. Some changes are even more radical as when, for example, the distinction between suppliers and customers is attenuated and suppliers actually operate on the premises of their customers. Changes like these will likely affect the nature of managerial tasks and influence career patterns as ladders become shorter, the organization becomes flatter, and boundaries of all kinds become permeable. In addition, to the extent that these reforms are more efficient, they will also lead to reduced managerial staffing levels.

Summary

Given the complexity of the world, it is unlikely that any one of these explanations can carry the day alone. Obviously, as the cases make clear, a mix of considerations lies behind the transformation of managerial work. However, it is striking how important what we have termed "organizational technology" is relative to the more standard explanations that rely on physical technology and agency costs.

A second important point is that the chapters do not all point in the same direction. Much of the internal labor market literature cited earlier is concerned with explaining variation across firms in their employment practices and these cases also show evidence of variation. Of course, the range of variation is not as great as in the economy as a whole since all of the firms and industries represented here are large. Furthermore, the constant in every case is the thinning of managerial ranks. Nevertheless, we might contrast the tendency towards centralization described by Beckman with the opposite tendency described by MacDuffie. The importance of information technology in reshaping managerial work in the insurance industry does not seem mirrored in the other cases. The transformation of managerial tasks under lean production seems more profound that the shifts described elsewhere. We lack sufficient observations to satisfactorily explain this variation but it is important to at least recognize that while there are similarities across the cases the story is not the same everywhere.

Conclusion

The chapters in this book make clear that the world of managers has changed. Insecurity is higher, promotions slower, the jobs are more complex, and the ranks are fewer. The chapters also make clear, however, that the story is not the same everywhere, and, in fact, there is variation even within the same firm. In addition, the more grandiose claims in the popular press seem to be belied by the data and the cases.

Taken as a whole, however, these developments seem to pose problems for organizations that they have not begun to address. Two of these problems are, first, whether the loss of large numbers of middle managers will eventually create new difficulties for organizations and, second, how to motivate the managers that do remain.

Agency theory suggests that we should celebrate the thinning of managerial ranks because there were too many of them. This perspective is strengthened if one thinks that information technology can substitute for the information processing function managers played. But what if managers did in fact do useful work that will now not get done? This work included interpreting top management objectives for people on the front line and reporting back to management the state of affairs at the point of production. Neither of these two tasks can be well accomplished with computers. Managers also created a level of certainty and uniformity about firm procedures and practices that can easily get lost in the new decentralized world.

The second challenge facing organizations is the impact of declining promotion opportunities and heightened insecurity on the motivation and performance of those managers who remain. There are several issues here. The first is how to motivate people who have been trained to believe that the sine qua non of success is upward mobility when the chances of that mobility have diminished sharply. The second issue is how to obtain commitment to the success of the organization when the organization itself has reduced its commitment to the individual. This problem is perhaps even more pressing for managers because so much of the managerial job involves internalizing the organization's objectives and values and transmitting these to others.

It is possible that high levels of fear in the economy will enable organizations to elude this problem for some time to come. It is also possible that the broader challenges of each person's job will be sufficiently compelling to offset the reduced attractiveness of the organization per se. We lack the research that would help us know the answer. Indeed, the impact of restructuring on commitment is an open, and very important, research question. What is clear, however, is that the risks are real and how they will be played out is as yet unknown.

Notes

1. Some evidence on this is provided by occupational projections produced by the Bureau of Labor Statistics. The Bureau predicts that between the years 1992 and 2005 "managerial and administrative" employment will grow by 24% whereas the entire labor force will grow by 21.8%. However, the Bureau also predicts that during the same period, the employment of "general managers and top executives" will grow by only 13.2%.

2. For all blue-collar workers hourly wages declined by 5.5% between 1989 and 1994 while total compensation declined by 2.0%. For white-collar workers the comparable figures were −.1% and +1.6%. (Mishel and Bernstein, 1995, p. 118).

References

Aoki, Masahiko.1990. "Toward An Economic Model of the Japanese Firm," *Journal of Economic Literature* xvii, no. 1 (March):1–27.

Bailyn, Lotte. *Living with Technology: Issues at Mid-career* (Cambridge: MIT Press) 1980.

Baker, George, Michael Gibbs, and Bengt Holmstrom. 1994. "The Internal Economics of The Firm: Evidence From Personnel Data," *Quarterly Journal of Economics* v. cix, no. 4, (November):881–920.

Baron, James, Alison Davis-Blake and William Bielby. 1986. "The Structure of Opportunity: How Promotion Ladders Vary Within and Among Organizations," *Administrative Science Quarterly* 31 (June):248–273.

Berman, Eli, John Bound and Zvi Griliches. 1994. "Changes In The Demand for Skilled Labor Within U.S. Manufacturing; Evidence From the Annual Survey of Manufacturers," *Quarterly Journal of Economics* cix, no. 2, (May):367–397.

Brown, James, and Audrey Light. 1992. "Interpreting Panel Data on Job Tenure," *Journal of Labor Economics* 10:219–257.

Cappelli, Peter. 1992. "Examining Managerial Displacement," *Academy of Management Journal,* 35, no. 1, (March):203–217.

Chandler, Alfred D., Jr. 1977. *The Visible Hand: The Managerial Revolution In American Business.* Cambridge: Harvard University Press.

Diebold, Francis, David Neumark and Daniel Polsky. 1994. "Job Stability in the United States," Working Paper no. 4859, NBER.

DiMaggio, Paul, and Walter Powell. 1983. "The Iron Cage Revisited: Institutional Isomorphism and Collective Rationality in Organizational Fields," *American Sociological Review* 48:147–160.

Doeringer, Peter, and Michael Piore. 1972. *Internal Labor Markets and Manpower Analysis.* Lexington Mass.: D.C. Heath.

Farber, Henry. 1995. "Are Lifetime Jobs Disappearing? Job Duration in the United States, 1973–1994," Working Paper, no. 341, Industrial Relations Section, Princeton University.

Gordon, David. 1994. "Bosses of Different Stripes: Monitoring and Supervision Across Advanced Economies," Working Paper no. 49 (January), Graduate Faculty in Economics, New School for Social Research, New York.

Groshen, Erica, and Donald Williams. 1995. "White Collar Employment and Unemployment After the 1990–91 Recession," mimeo (January), Federal Reserve Bank of New York.

Guillen, Mauro. 1994. *Models of Management.* Chicago: University of Chicago Press.

Hall, Douglas T., and Associates. 1986. *Career Development In Organizations*. San Francisco: Josey-Bass.

Howard, Ann, and Douglas Bray. 1988. *Managerial Lives in Transition*. New York: Guilford Press.

Jackall, Robert. 1988. *Moral Mazes; The World of Corporate Managers*. New York: Oxford University Press.

Kanter, Rosabeth. 1977. *Men and Women of the Corporation*. New York: Basic Books.

———. 1989. *When Giants Learn To Dance*. New York: Simon & Schuster.

Kletzer, Lori. 1994. "White Collar Job Displacement, 1983–1991," mimeo (March), University of California, Santa Cruz.

Lazear, Edward, and Sherwin Rosen. 1981. "Rank Order Tournaments As Optimum Labor Contracts" *Journal of Political Economy* xxxix:841–64.

Milgrom, Paul, and John Roberts. 1992. *Economics, Organizations, and Management*. Englewood Cliffs, N.J.: Prentice-Hall.

Mishel, Lawrence, and Jared Bernstein. 1995. The State of Working America, 1994–1995. Washington: Economic Policy Institute.

Osterman, Paul. 1986. "The Impact of Computers Upon the Employment of Clerks and Managers," *Industrial and Labor Relations Review*, 39, no. 2 (January):175–187.

———, ed. 1984. *Internal Labor Markets*. Cambridge: MIT Press.

Pfeffer, Jeffrey, and Yinon Cohen. 1984. "Determinants of Internal Labor Markets in Organizations," *Administrative Science Quarterly*, 29:550–572.

Pfeffer, Jeffrey. 1989. "A Political Perspective on Careers." In *Handbook of Career Theory*, Michael Arthur, Douglas T. Hall, and Barbara Lawrence, eds., 380–397. New York: Cambridge University Press.

Prechel, Harland. 1994. "The Economic Crisis and the Centralization of Control," *American Sociological Review*, 59, no. 5 (October):723–745.

Rose, Stephen. 1995. "The Decline of Employment Stability in the 1970's." Washington: National Commission on Employment Policy.

Rosenbaum, James. 1984. *Career Mobility In A Corporate Hierarchy*. New York: Academic Press.

Schein, Edgar. 1978. *Career Dynamics*. Reading, Mass.: Addison-Wesley.

Scott, W. Richard. 1981. *Organizations: Rational, Natural, and Open Systems*. Englewood Cliffs, N.J.: Prentice-Hall.

Smith, Vickie. 1990. *Managing In the Corporate Interest; Control and Resistance in An American Bank*. Berkeley: University of California Press.

Thompson, James. 1967. *Organizations In Action*. New York: McGraw-Hill.

Van Maanan, John. 1977. *Organizational Careers: Some New Perspectives*. New York: Wiley.

Williamson, Oliver, Michael Wacter, and Jeffrey Harris. 1975. "Understanding the Employment Relation: The Analysis of Idiosyncratic Exchange," *Bell Journal of Economics*, 6 (Spring):250–280.

Corporate Restructuring and the Restructured World of Senior Management

2

MICHAEL USEEM

During the late 1980s and early 1990s, hostile acquisitions, leveraged buyouts, and organizational restructurings remade the corporate landscape, for worse and for better. Plants closings, company mergers, and divisional downsizings shortened work careers and decimated employment communities. At the same time, process reengineering, flexible work methods, and streamlined hierarchies improved employee productivity and product quality. The two faces of restructuring, the devastation and the renewal, reshaped virtually all company investments and programs. The two faces also reshaped executive work. Senior management confronted more stressful work and less career security. They also faced less resistant work ranks and more generous compensation.

The changing world of senior management reflected this changing world of the corporation. Top managers could no longer lead quite so effectively through executive decree, as empowerment and participation undermined their traditional powers over the authoritative hierarchy. But they could also exercise more control over the work process, as accountability and information improved their monitoring powers over the delegated responsibilities. At the same time, senior management was more than victim and beneficiary of the new corporate order. Beyond any other single group, it bore responsibility for the remake. While the pressures and demands for change were usually not of their own making, executives did take the decisions on when and how to change. Senior management was thus both maker and recipient of the restructured corporate environment of the mid-1990s.

A host of organizational changes characterized the restructuring of the late 1980s and early 1990s, and three features affecting the executive suite stood out: (1) Firms pushed authority to succeed and fail lower in the company, leaving senior managers with fewer line decisions but more oversight responsibilities. They contracted headquarters, built strategic business units, and distributed operating information. (2) With responsibility devolved lower in the organization, executives invested greater time in grooming managers, and they applied more stringent, performance-based criteria in the promotion decisions. (3) Companies better informed their directors and shareholders, and executives devoted more resources to managing their relations with boards and owners. Other observers identified still other features of the "new managerial work," including greater emphasis on market globalization, strategic alliances, executive teamwork, and career management.[1]

This chapter concentrates on how these changes altered the world of company executives, the organization's seniormost five to 10 managers. The chapter is concerned with the promotion, compensation, and security of senior managers of major, publicly traded companies that generally appear among the rosters of the nation's 1,000 largest firms, whether ranked by sales, assets, or capitalization. It draws on a range of research studies, primary sources, data reanalysis, and personal interviews.

The Corporate World That Changed

To appreciate the altered world in which company executives now managed, it is useful to consider a somewhat idealized image of the large corporation before the deluge. Take the moment of its employment zenith at the end of the 1970s. The *Fortune* 500 companies had created employment for more than 16 million workers. The economies of scale had well served large firms, giving them a privileged place in a world where manufacturing clout, marketing reach, and vertical integration were still the formula. The nation's 500 great industrials had more than doubled their employment rolls in just 25 years. The growth engine showed no sign of slowing, corporate concentration no evidence of slackening. A 1976 article speculated on what the editors of *Fortune* magazine would do in the year 1998 when they could find no more than 479 companies to constitute their famous 500 list. Mergers, acquisitions, and the economies of scale had eliminated or decimated all but the nation's greatest corporations. Would the editors allow the cover of the annual *Fortune* 500 issue the literary license of preserving a trademark whose numbers no longer added up?[2]

If a classic form could be characterized, it was of a functionally defined hierarchy, with managers arrayed in tall lines of authority presiding over narrow spans of control. The central tendency was a seven-by-seven: seven layers of managers, each responsible for seven subordinates. No firm precisely fit any model, but many of the largest tended toward this one. Though the company had been a creature of the market, it had also learned how to tame the vagaries of the market. It would, for instance, create steady growth and stability by drawing a host of unrelated products under one tent. Such diversification allowed the peaks of momentarily prosperous products to fill in the momentary valleys of others. With the vagaries of the marketplace controlled, or at least buffered through sectoral diversity, company employment systems could achieve a stability unknown outside the public sector. Assured employment in American firms rarely reached the legendary standards of the Japanese lifetime employment model. Few American executives would echo Akio Morita, Sony's longtime chief executive, on the *first* principle of business ethics: "Management has the moral responsibility to nurture its employees." Yet for the some 25 million employees with the good fortune to find themselves inside the walls of the *Fortune* 500 manufacturers or *Fortune* 500 service companies, it would be a comfortable career of respectable income, solid benefits, and job security.[3]

While the Weberian ideal-type found near incarnation during the 1970s, its half-life proved surprisingly brief. Companies that had given rise to William Whyte's *Organization Man* and David Riesman's "other-directed" manager would also give rise during the 1980s to corporate raider Carl Icahn and buyout specialist Henry Kravis. Restructuring initiatives were launched by a brave, innovative few during the early part of the 1980s, but by the early 1990s the minority actions had turned into a majority. A 1992 survey of 530 companies revealed how far the restructuring had spread: three-quarters downsized during just the past year, nearly the same reorganized, and one-quarter divested, merged, or acquired other firms or divisions. Similarly, a 1991 study of 406 large companies found that one-third significantly reduced management staff; one-half laid off a substantial number of workers; one-half sold a business unit; and two-thirds shut down some company operations.[4]

The cumulative effect of a decade of such efforts transformed both what and how companies produced. Firms stripped away unrelated business areas, seeking to concentrate instead on their "core competencies." By 1990, the *Fortune* 500 largest manufacturers produced in only half the product sectors of a decade earlier. At the same time, many firms redesigned their remaining business areas, seeking to implant "high performance work systems." By 1990, half the *Fortune* 1,000 had introduced quality circles and self-managed work teams. Employment growth had also gone into reverse, with the 500 largest manufacturers steadily shedding workers after reaching a high-water mark in 1979, and the 500 largest service firms leveling off their growth in 1990. With the manufacturing nadir still not clearly in sight, the compilers of the *Fortune* 500 were not soon to face a day of reckoning.[5]

An important driver of the change was the growing muscle of institutional investors. Little noticed during the 1950s and 1960s, they moved into dominance by the late 1980s. Peter Drucker had offered prescient analysis. In his *Unseen Revolution* (1976), he warned that America's pension funds were rapidly growing and, in time, they would come to constitute a major force in the securities markets. Though their quiet accumulation of assets was then little noticed, Drucker argued that the implications would surely be noted one day. The book's subtitle warned what they might be: *How Pension Fund Socialism Came to America.*[6]

Little in the way of pension fund "socialism" came to pass in the years that followed. Though pension funds grew as anticipated, most beneficiaries retained no control over their assets, preventing any collective guidance that might have given them a socialist edge. Something more akin to pension fund capitalism, however, did appear. And with it came a parallel rise in the holdings and influence of four other kinds of investors: commercial banks, insurance companies, investment managers, and nonprofit endowments.

Institutional investors expanded their share of publicly traded stock, while individuals contracted their share. In 1965, individual holdings constituted 84% of corporate stock, institutional holdings 16%. By 1990, the individual fraction had declined to 54%, the institutional fraction had risen to 46%. A closer look at the 1,000 publicly traded companies with highest market value during the late 1980s reveals much the same trend. Between 1985 and 1995, as seen in Figure 2-1, the institutional share rose by more than a point per year, cresting over half in 1990. With the concentrating control over corporate equities came a concentrating focus on company performance. When firms did not measure up, investors pressed for organizational restructuring and strategic change; if they still did not perform well, investors pressed for director intervention and executive dismissal.

Institutional investors constituted a diverse lot. Some preferred to press distressed companies for change, others to sell distressed stocks instead. Some indexed much of their holdings, others actively managed their entire portfolios. Some followed long-term investment strategies, other churned their positions in response to momentary events. Some demanded that companies abandon poison pills and staggered boards, others demured. If an investor-pressure spectrum might be drawn, at one end would stand the activist public pension funds such as the $85-billion California Public Employees' Retirement System (Calpers); in the middle would stand mutual-fund and money-management companies such as the $435-billion Fidelity Investments; and at the other end would stand the inactivist private pensions of many corporations. A relatively small number of large investors led the charge against what they viewed as management inefficiencies, and a larger number followed their lead by voting with the activists. A substantial number also staunchly supported management.[7]

Intensifying international competition added to the momentum. Just as institutional investors were hitting their stride, so too were global companies. Both pressed American companies to become more competitive. Each could be unforgiving. Together they proved an unrivaled catalyst for improved product quality and workforce productivity. And only through an extensive reworking of the company's organization could management expect to improve the quality of its outputs at the same time it sought to lower the cost of its inputs. The relative salience of the competitive fray is evident in the 1992 restructuring survey. When asked to identify the factors motivating their restructuring, three-quarters of the 530 companies cited competitive pressure, the most frequently identified source of any.[8]

Corporate restructuring can thus be viewed in part as a response to demands from above for greater shareholder value—at the same time that competitive challenges from outside made it more difficult for firms to deliver that value. Other factors drove the restructuring as well, including information technologies, declining markets, and workforce quality. Some companies sought improved designs even in the absence of any external impetus. Still others resisted any change. Yet for a broad array of large, publicly traded corporations, the two pincers of investor demand and international competition fostered widespread restructuring agendas.

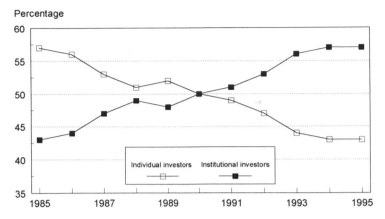

Figure 2-1. Percentage of Shares of 1,000 U.S. Largest Companies Held by Individual and Institutional Investors, 1985–95. *Source: Business Week.*

The Executive World That Changed

In response to investor and competitive pressures, senior management transformed their companies, and in so doing they also transformed their own worlds. They pulled up the ladders that had taken them to the top and dropped down new ladders requiring different climbing skills. Career success under the new rules required distinct work capacities and leadership strategies. Greater concern with shareholder value helped. So, too, did a proven track record of producing what contributed to it while laboring in what had become more competitive vineyards.

For those who mastered the new managerial skills and reached the corporate apex, staying there also required skills less familiar to their predecessors. The era of managerial capitalism allowed executives considerable latitude in setting their priorities. The era of investor capitalism would not. Managerial capitalism permitted executives to ignore their shareholders. Investor capitalism could not. Managerial capitalism created a world of shared contacts and clubs among its most powerful members. Investor capitalism did not.

Top managers under the reign of managerial capitalism had enjoyed the privilege of no longer having to "manage-up." They were the top. Having paid their dues by effectively "managing their bosses" during the many years on the way to the top, top managers could savor the moment when they had finally arrived. They no longer had, nor needed, a superior. Some of their contemporaries had earlier abandoned promising company careers to found their own ventures, driven by a long suppressed desire of wanting to be their own boss. For the stayers who reached the executive suite, they achieved much the same by other means. Having climbed so high that no rungs remained, they had become the undisputed masters of their own universe.

Investor capitalism, however, placed still another rung on the power ladder. More vigorous directors and more vigilant investors now often held the high ground, a notch above the company executives, no longer aside or below them. The chief executive and immediate associates were less fully their own masters, less determining of their own fate. Executive status remained high, executive compensation generous. But in contrast to their predecessors, many would no longer enjoy the perquisite of going to work in a boss-free environment.

Moreover, the hierarchies of power and career were no longer quite so coterminous. Traditionally, each upward step on the corporate ladder brought the rising manager more power. With exceptional talent, much diligence, and a little luck, aspiring managers could one day expect a shot at the topmost positions of corporate authority. Now, however, those who succeeded in reaching the executive suite faced still another power level—and one that would remain largely beyond their reach. Fewer might expect to go on their own board, as shareholders pressed for more outsiders. Virtually none could expect to join the ranks of those already perched on the ultimate, owners' rung. Having overcome all previous barriers on their upward ascent, senior managers now confronted their own glass ceiling, one they could peer through but not pass through. They would plateau on the penultimate rung.

The contrasts should not be overdrawn. Much of the managerial core was little different from what Gordon Donaldson and Jay Lorsch found in their 1983 study of *Decision Making at the Top,* or from what Rosabeth Moss Kanter revealed in her 1977 analysis of *Men and Women of the Corporation,* or from what Henry Mintzberg discovered in his 1975 ethnography of the "the manager's job." Chester Barnard's *The Functions of the Executive* (1938) and James March and Herbert Simon's *Organizations* (1957) remained enduring classics because they captured much of what senior managers in large organizations have always done, and probably will always do.

Still, the nature of work around many of these core activities acquired fresh definition. Outstanding performance was more fully rewarded, dubious achievements more harshly judged. Bolstering share price and raising dividends could make an executive wealthy. Falling short could eclipse a career. The ever present tension between managing stability and fostering change was no more resolved than ever. Yet the demands and rewards shifted toward the latter.

Executive Security

Traditionally, reaching the apex of the corporate pyramid was a career calling, a crowning achievement. With secure recognition of one's lifelong achievements, a secure financial future, and a secure hold on office, the successful executive could expect to "pass the baton" with proper ceremony and personal dignity. Other than the company's formal retirement age, little could be expected to interfere with the self-election of a retirement date. The executive suite seemed a secure perch from which one could eventually depart with a timing of one's own choosing and, not least, with one's reputation as well.[9]

The seemingly unprecedented dismissals of the chief executives of American Express, IBM, Apple Computer, Bank of Boston, Borden, Digital Equipment,

Percentage of 1,000 company CEOs

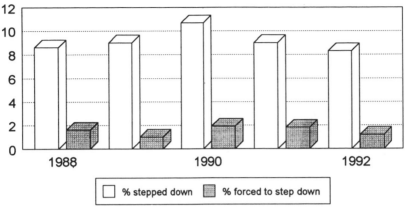

Figure 2-2. Turnover among Chief Executives of 1,000 Large Companies, 1988–92. *Source:* Andrew Ward, from *Business Week.*

Eastman Kodak, General Motors, KMart, and Westinghouse during the early 1990s, however, suggested that executive security could no longer be taken quite so much for granted. It would seem that more investor power over corporate decisions had come to mean less managerial power over corporate incumbency. Evidence on the seniormost management ranks, however, is equivocal. Consider turnover among the chief executives of the 1,000 companies ranked largest by market capitalization. From 1988 to 1992, one in ten of the CEOs annually left the list. Most of these departures remained voluntary retirements, but one analysis, drawing on a host of public sources to identify the forced retirements, found that about one in five departures could be deemed involuntary in 1988. During the next four years, however, there was little discernable movement in this fraction. Neither the rate of stepping down nor the rate of being forced to step down displayed temporal trend (Figure 2-2). A barebones demographic portrait of the chief executives of the 1,000 largest firms also revealed little change between 1986 and 1992: the CEO's average age (56), years with the company (21 to 23), and years as CEO (8 to 9) remained relatively constant (Table 2-1).[10]

The comparative stability of the executive office and instability of what lay below was partly a simple product of downsizing. In a period of workforce reduction, no position was sacrosanct on the organization chart save one: the chief executive. Many companies combined or abolished the duties of executive vice president, group vice president, and legions of middle managers. None closed the office of chief executive. The relative calm at the top but turbulence below is nevertheless perplexing. In an era of shareholder stress on performance, no position was more responsible than the chief executive. Accordingly, as the penalties for inadequate performance intensified, one might have expected to see more turnover at the top. In the political arena, for instance, U.S. Cabinet secre-

Table 2-1. CEO Years in Office, Age, and Salary and Bonuses for Largest 1,000 Companies, 1986–92

	Average years as CEO	Average years with company	Average age	Average salary and bonuses
1986	9	23	56	$651,000
1987	9	24	56	685,000
1988	9	23	56	787,000
1989	8	23	56	841,000
1990	8	22	56	868,000
1991	8	21	56	878,000
1992	9	21	56	984,000

Source: *Business Week,* various issues.

taries and British ministers come and go, often with cause, while their immediate subordinates, the senior civil servants, last a lifetime regardless of their bosses' failures.

The perplexing stability of the CEO may find explanation in the tradition of deflecting blame onto others, of embracing responsibility for what goes right and avoiding it for what goes wrong. In *Moral Mazes,* Robert Jackall discovered such behavior pervading several large chemical firms during the 1980s. It is also occasionally observed among elected officials, where Teflon seemed an apt metaphor for high blame-resistance. Evidence for widespread application in business comes from a study of senior management dismissal following a company's downslide in performance. Drawing on 67 semiconductor manufacturers from 1968 to 1989, the analysis compared firms whose chief executives were powerfully ensconced with those whose CEOs were less so. Powerful chief executives were those whose boards were less independent and whose stockholders were more dispersed. The study reported that performance downturns led more often to the dismissal of less powerful CEOs, less often of the more powerful. Moreover, performance downturns among firms with powerful chief executives more often led to the dismissal of the CEO's top managers, a kind of scapegoating for the chief executives' performance shortcomings.[11]

While CEOs appeared no more vulnerable during the early 1990s than the late 1980s, a longer time frame reveals heightened insecurity in recent years. A study of 114 industrial firms from 1960 to 1990 examined the likelihood of chief executive succession five years after taking office. Comparing those brought into the CEO's office in 1980 with those hired two decades earlier, the former were more than twice at likely to find themselves stepping down from office five years later. And for CEOs hired in 1985, the most recent year for which data were available, the prospects of turnover were even higher (Figure 2-3).

Powerfully ensconced or not, executives with mediocre performances records increasingly came under shareholder pressure to bolster returns or, failing that, to

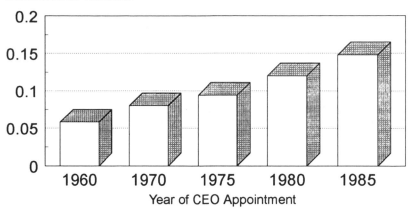

Figure 2-3. Likelihood of CEO Turnover during Fifth Year in Office among 114 Industrial Firms, by Year of CEO Appointment, 1960–85. *Source:* Ocasio (1994).

shake up their executive team. Investors communicated their displeasure with managerial incumbency in two ways. Most commonly, investors simply sold or bought blocks of stock in response to salient succession events. Less commonly but more often than in the past, investors rendered direct advice on what the succession should be or should have been. The first was the traditional, frequently applied medicine. The second was an untraditional but increasingly deployed strategy.

The rise and abrupt fall of a chief financial officer at Eastman Kodak and the subsequent fall of his boss are illustrative of both. Christopher J. Steffen had been hired in January 1993 to help turn around a company whose earnings and stock price had been sluggish. He was characterized as the "white-knight chief financial officer who could save stodgy Eastman Kodak." His publicized hiring was widely applauded by investors, and they delivered an explicit message to management. The company's stock price soared in the days that followed, adding more than $3 billion to the company's value. It seemed, however, that the board had imposed Steffen's appointment on a reluctant chief executive, Kay Whitmore, and despite the ministrations of antirejectionist therapy, the transplant failed to take. The CEO warned that the new CFO "will not last very long" if he "comes in here assuming he's the Lone Ranger." Whether assumed or not, the "three-billion dollar man" resigned within 90 days, leading investors to forward a second message. They dumped Kodak shares with vigor, driving the company's value down the next day by $1.7 billion.[12]

The second market message seemed to fall on deaf ears, however, as CEO Whitmore survived his CFO's departure and a stock sell-off. The California Public Employees' Retirement System (Calpers) and other public funds rendered public counsel, initially supporting the incumbent chief executive. A holder of two million shares of Kodak stock, Calpers met privately with the beleaguered CEO for some 90 minutes. He "needs to be given a chance," announced the Calpers general counsel, Richard Koppes, after the meeting, and the headlines the next day reflected the stay of execution. "Kodak's Chief Wins Support from Calpers," offered the *New York Times*. For the *Wall Street Journal*, the event summed to: "Kodak's Chief Gains Support from 2 Holders, Whitmore Assures Calpers He Will Make Changes to Boost Productivity."[13]

Calpers and other investors rendered further private counsel as well, going up to the board with their performance complaints. Three months later, the board finally forced the resignation of Whitmore himself. Large brokerage firms, including Lehman Brothers and Prudential Securities, immediately raised their stock recommendations to buy, and the company regained much of the value it had lost when Steffen resigned. "Getting Kay Whitmore out of there was a critical step in getting this company going in the right direction," offered a Prudential analyst. As a result, added a Dean Witter analyst, "the board's position and investors are now in alignment."[14]

Eastman Kodak's experience was symptomatic. A study of 480 large publicly traded companies in the early 1980s revealed that meeting analyst expectations was an act of CEO survival. When annual company earnings per share fall below analyst forecasts, the likelihood of CEO dismissal rises significantly higher. And, after the dismissal of an underperforming CEO, the research suggested, investors send a confirming note. Study of CEO succession at 235 large companies during the late 1980s reveals that stock prices generally react favorably to board-initiated replacements when company performance was poor.[15]

Not surprisingly, chief executives installed in the wake of investor-inspired coups seek not only to calm shareholders' fears but also to control their aroused expectations. The new chief executive of Eastman Kodak, George Fisher (formerly CEO of Motorola), thus asserted in late 1993 that Kodak would come in well below the analysts' earnings forecasts for 1994. The new chief executive of IBM, Louis V. Gerstner, Jr., (formerly CEO of RJR Nabisco) cautioned his investors soon after taking over in early 1993 that he would need time to mend the many ills of the past. And the new chief executive of Westinghouse Electric, Michael H. Jordan (formerly an executive with PepsiCo) said on taking office in mid-1992 that he wanted to reestablish credibility with shareholders "through consistency of financial results, avoiding major surprises and major disasters."[16]

Shareholder clamoring for a CEO's head, whether through stock sell-offs or direct entreaty, however, was not the same as obtaining it. Firms devised many ways to shield themselves well from direct constituent rule. Among the more widely deployed devices on the financial front was the poison pill, on the governance front was the staggered board, and on the director front was the noninde-pendent director. At best, these provided only partial protection, and sometimes they even backfired. A case in point of the latter was the much heralded addition of independent, nonexecutive directors to the board. Virtually all institutional investors favored such action. Yet, careful study reveals that the placement of inside managers on the board did not always provide the insulation that might have been expected. The study of the semiconductor industry found that it did: more inside directors reduced the likelihood of CEO dismissal. But the study of 114 large industrial firms from 1960 to 1990 found just the opposite. This counterintuitive result pointed to the importance of succession dynamics over executive loyalty. As a company fell from grace, a board was seemingly less reluctant to replace a faltering CEO if it perceived it has an experienced replacement capable of taking over. That perception was strengthened if a prospective inside candidate has already had opportunity to work closely with other board members as an executive director. In other words, by giving able lieutenants the visibility that comes with a director's seat, the chief executive was more likely to find himself replaced by one of them than if he had kept them all in the dark.[17]

Executive Promotion

Reaching the firm's apex was the product of a complex mix of career achievements, leadership qualities, and personal loyalties. The specific blend depended much on the most vexing company problems. If regulatory issues were paramount, executives who understand how Washington or state capitals work could have an edge. If manufacturing challenges were critical, those with production experience may push ahead in the competition for the top. If financial restructuring had been key, those with financial backgrounds gained the upper edge.[18]

Like the search for the origins of the universe, the quest for the generics of leadership is of enduring interest. But unlike competing theories on the universe origins, where evidence should ultimately vindicate one theory over others, competing theories on leadership foundations are sure to persist in uneasy coexistence, some applicable in some companies at some moments, others applicable in others at different moments. Corporate leadership is thus partially contingent. Certain core qualities are generic to most settings, others are unique to few. An executive's capacity to formulate a persuasive vision and to mobilize resources to achieve it would qualify as one of those universals. So, too, are capacities to set strategy, solve financial problems, and manage production or service delivery. But other capacities are more contingent on the era's specific blend of problems faced by the company.[19]

As investor power emerged as one of the era's critical contingencies for executives at many firms, working to assuage investor unrest came to be as important to the future of the firm as fixing failed strategy, securing external financing, or reengineering process. Those who did it best became more valued by the organization; those who could not master the new art of investor affairs became less valued. To those managers who worked well with investors went the kudos of success with a key constituency. To those who did not went the taint of displaying less than general management qualities.

Company stress on effective managerial work with investors varied from firm to firm. Within those companies most challenged by shareholder pressure, successful experience in managing shareholders became a more valued asset for the aspiring executive. Within those companies whose strong performance had kept investors at bay, experience in working with stockholders carried less weight. For both sets of companies, a demonstrated ability to produce shareholder value—or at least the divisional contributions to the company whole—constituted more of a career asset under the rules of investor than managerial capitalism.

Institutional investors closely followed those moments of executive succession, and on occasion even sought to shape the outcome. While the choice of the CEO was exclusively that of the board, investors often took great interest in the choice. The reigning executive's style, the anticipated tenure, and the successors vying for office all counted in the investor's appraisal. An approachable and credible executive with a compelling vision and effective implementation implied not only good leadership at the helm but also good organization below it.

At some companies, the owners' interest extended little beyond the chief executive and heirs apparent. At others, their gaze extended to other members of the company's inner circle. At still other firms, the attention focused as well on those who led the company's strategic business units. A highly centralized structure would draw attention to the chief executive and the two or three most powerful subordinates. A decentralized structure would also attract attention to those who presided over the largest operating units. Analyst concern concentrated on those in whose hands the company's present and future fate was believed to reside.

Several qualities among prospective executive successors stood out. The individual's prior performance record naturally topped the list. This could be tangibly gauged if the manager had served as the head of a large operating unit whose results were already well known to the investment community. If the successor had come up a financial or other functional stovepipe, however, performance evidence would be less transparent. A second quality concerned the strategic agenda that the manager would bring to the executive suite. A third quality was the extent to which the executive successor was also likely to bring a shareholder focus to high office.

A large, diversified-products company offered a case in point.[20] Its two executive vice presidents were both considered viable candidates to succeed the chief executive. The company brought both into all of its quarterly meetings with company analysts, and it increasingly involved them in informal company contact with investors. The chief executive explicitly fostered their involvement, in his words, "because that's part of the training program, if you will, for the next generation." As meetings with investors would close, the CEO would often say, "far more important than some of the things you're talking about here numerically are your meetings with [the two managers identified] as my potential successors." The chief executive was disappointed by the tepid response among some owners, but others were quick to embrace the proffered contact with both. The board's executive committee, all outside directors, regularly reviewed and compared the executive vice presidents' effectiveness with this outside world.

Company stress on effective executive work with investors varied from firm to firm. Within those companies most challenged by shareholder pressure, successful experience in managing shareholders became a more valued asset for the aspiring executive. Within those companies whose strong performance had kept investors at bay, experience in working with stockholders carried less weight. For both sets of companies, a demonstrated ability to produce shareholder value—or at least divisional contributions to the corporate whole—constituted more of a career asset under the rules of investor than managerial capitalism.

The importance of both qualities was evident in another large manufacturing company that faced both lackluster performance and hostile shareholders. Its chief operating officer, who had come up on the financial side of the firm, had worked extensively with inside managers and outside investors over many years. He had had ample opportunity to witness not only what the institutions had to say to the company, but also how his own managers managed their contact with them. For those aspiring managers who might one day serve as chief financial officer, treasurer, or comptroller, their conduct with shareholders was not among the paramount criteria. But it had come to carry a salience in the appraisal process. "Over the years," said the chief operating officer, "you observe their ability to project themselves" in meetings with institutional investors.

The simultaneous exposure to outside investors and top executives was particularly important for rising middle managers in this company, beleaguered as it was by a hostile shareholder environment. Assistant treasurers and assistant comptrollers would often join the company's many meetings with its large holders. Sometimes they sat in for their bosses, in other instances they were invited to take over from their bosses when topics moved into the technical or arcane. Whatever the purpose of their participation, their bosses made sure they did participate. Senior managers attending the meetings, often the chief executive or chief operating officer and one or more heads of the operating divisions, would field investor questions themselves at the outset. But then they would redirect the next query to the middle managers. Sometimes the subordinates would be too long-winded for their bosses' taste, regurgitating the detail they knew so well but beyond what any investor wanted to know. Afterward, they would receive constructive coaching. "We try to get them to sharpen a little bit," offered the chief operating officer, "to leave an impression with a few sentences instead of pages."

Regardless of the value of the meetings to either shareholders or the company, they provided a forum for management development, a "good training" venue for high potential prospects. Senior managers, observed the company chief operation officer, made it "apparent to their next-layer-down that this was something that they probably ought to develop some skills with." Executives rarely articulated the need explicitly. Nobody said "you've got to get your ass in gear and be able to handle these meetings." But like so many organizational challenges that are personally experienced, the need for swift mastery of the art of investor relations became self-evident.

Senior managers also learned which subordinates worked effectively in such meetings, particularly important for those moments when their bosses could not be present because of scheduling conflicts. The executives would request return appearances of those subordinates who, in the words of the chief operating officer, "seem to have the ability to convey ideas with an air of sincerity, understandableness and simplicity." Whoever attended, investor meetings provided a convenient if unacknowledged forum for management assessment. "It's a pretty good way to observe," concluded the chief operating officer, how the middle managers "react in terms of salesmanship, integrity and ability under hard questioning. . . . We've had a lot of opportunity . . . to measure people and how they perform."

Effective handling of company relations with major shareholders proved a managerial asset even in companies where the investor environment had not proven terribly troublesome. A major food-products company had been more trouble-free than most. The company nevertheless sought to bring investors into direct contact with many senior managers, not just the seniormost. This was partly to facilitate owners' familiarity with the managers, and partly to facilitate managers' familiarity with the owners. In the chief executive's words, the personal contact provided "good training" for those moving toward top management. It offered instruction in how to make an effective presentation to the stock analysts and money managers. And it offered insight into the minds of those with whom a rising manager would increasingly have to reckon. "Security analysts are by nature worried you're going to fall off a cliff," observed the CEO, and "I want our guys to hear about those huge chasms" toward which the analysts feared the company could veer.

In grooming senior managers for even higher level assignments, some companies invested explicitly in their education in the ways of investors. Such initiatives often included increased exposure to leading shareholders and company analysts. Careful study of Wall Street reactions to company actions helped. So also did experience in translating company results into language investors could understand and investor concerns into language managers could appreciate. This was evident at a broadcasting company, where the chief executive was grooming a division manager as a potential chief operating officer. Though not on the board, the division manager consulted with an outside director who held a large block of stock. He met with other major shareholders and studied how Wall Street operated. He confessed that he had much to learn about the investment world that owned the company, but, as part of his own career planning, he and the company had embarked on a program to do just that. He received the promotion.

Executive Compensation

Reaching the company apex brought greater insecurity than in the past. But it could also bring richer rewards. Compensation for chief executives grew steadily during the late 1980s and early 1990s, outpacing economic inflation, employee raises, and GNP growth. At the same time, the uncertainty quotient expanded as well. What had been fixed became more variable. Year-end compensation regardless of performance was transformed into bonuses and options requiring demon-

Percentage change

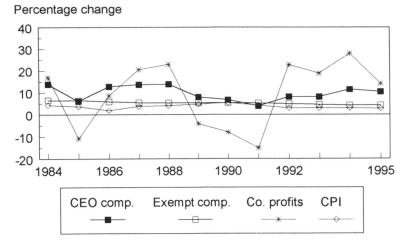

Figure 2-4. Annual Changes in CEO Cash Compensation, Exempt Employees Compensation, Corporate Profits, and Consumer Price Index, 1984–95. *Source:* William M. Mercer, Inc. (1996).

strated performance. And demonstrated performance came to take the more specific meaning of enhancing shareholder value.

For a decade, growth in executive compensation outdistanced most comparative baselines. This can be seen in a tracking of the cash compensation of the chief executives of large corporations from 1984 to 1994. During the 10-year period, the percentage annual increase in CEO compensation, including both salary and bonuses, exceeded that of the consumer price index during all years except one. CEO compensation also grew faster than of white-collar employees throughout the decade except for two years (1985 and 1991). In 1995, the consumer price index rose by 2.8%, white-collar salaries by 4.2%, and chief executive compensation by 10.4% (Figure 2-4).

The CEO's compensation grew faster even than that of the immediate subordinates. The average CEO compensation and the average compensation of the seven top officers of a panel of 45 large industrial firms were annually tracked by Hewitt Associates, a consulting firm, from 1982 to 1995. During this 13-year period, the average compensation (including benefits, perquisites, bonuses, and stock options) of the top seven executives rose from $455,000 to $1,459,000, a 221% increase. Across the same stretch, the average compensation of the chief executive officers climbed from $1,007,000 to $4,334,000, a 331% expansion (Figure 2-5).

The composition of the expanding executive pay pie, however, shifted from a fixed to a variable recipe. The proportion of pay "at risk" increased. The composition of the expanding at-risk slice also shifted from traditional measures of company performance to those tied more closely to shareholder value. The expanded variability is evident in the compensation of the top seven executives of

$ 1,000s

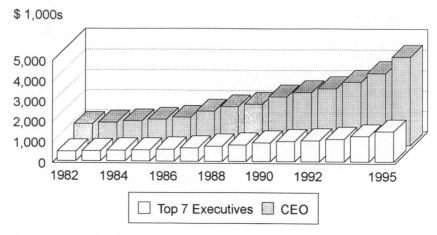

Figure 2-5. Total Compensation of CEO and Average Total Compensation of Top Seven Executives, 1982–95. *Source:* Hewitt Associates annual surveys.

the 45 large companies tracked from 1982 to 1995. Their compensation can be divided into a fixed portion, comprising salary and benefits, and two variable portions: short-term in the form of annual bonuses, and long-term in the form of stock options and other stock-based incentive schemes. In 1982, about one-third (37%) of top management's total compensation fell in the variable portion; by 1995, well over one-half (61%) had become variable. Virtually all the drop in the fixed fraction had been filled by long-term incentive pay, which rose from 17 to 40% of the compensation pie (Figure 2-6).

The trend line was even steeper for the chief executives. In 1982, two-fifths (41%) of the CEO's total compensation came from variable sources. By 1995, more than two-thirds (70%) did so. Again, the long-term component drove the change. Multiyear incentive compensation in 1982 constituted 17% of the CEO's income package. By 1995, the multiyear fraction stood at 47%, larger than any other source of income (Figure 2-7).

Another way to view it is to ask how a CEO might have lined up the major components of the compensation plan. In 1982, long-term incentives for the seven top executives of the 45 industrial firms on average equaled 27% of base salary; by 1995, they equaled 105%. For the CEO, the ratio of long-term to base pay rose 29 to 154%. A time series during the early 1990s for compensation of the chief executives of a larger and more diverse set of firms revealed a comparable growth in variability. In 1990, the average contingent income of the CEO's of 350 firms drawn from among the 1,000 largest constituted 61% of their total compensation. Two years later it had risen to 69% (Figure 2-8).

As companies increased the contingency of their senior managers' compensation, it should be expected that they also tightened its linkage to variability in shareholder wealth. This can be anticipated given the tougher marching orders from the investment community. Large shareholders were sure to look askance at companies that were "rewarding A while hoping for B" or, worse, rewarding A

Percentage

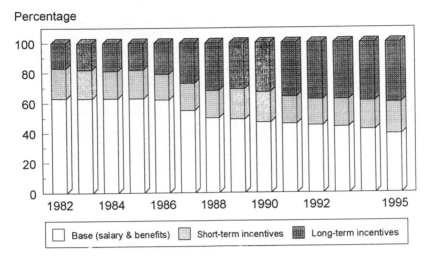

Figure 2-6. Percentage of Senior Management Compensation that Is Fixed or Variable, 1982–95. Data for top seven executives at 45 large industrial companies. *Source:* Hewitt Associates annual surveys.

while claiming B. Despite media, labor, and congressional criticism of the high levels of executive compensation, institutional investors expressed little concern over the amount. Successful portfolio managers and stock analysts themselves often drew pay packages that matched the best of the company executives.[21] What investors did despise were high compensation levels displaying little relationship to company performance or, worse, high levels that were contingent on

Percentage

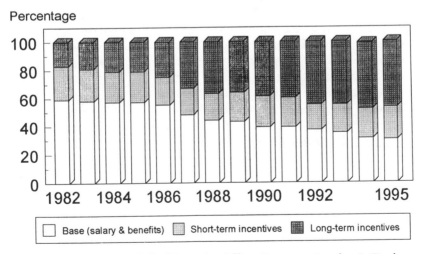

Figure 2-7. Percentage of Chief Executive Officer Compensation that Is Fixed or Variable, 1982–95. Data for 45 large industrial companies. *Source:* Hewitt Associates annual surveys.

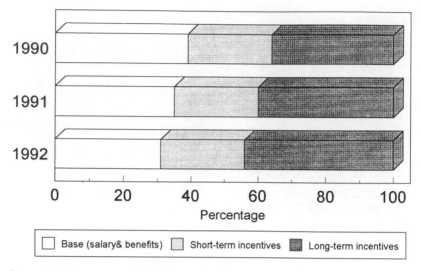

Figure 2-8. Percentage of Chief Executive Compensation that Is Fixed or Variable, 1990–92. Based on 350 companies among the 1,000 largest. *Source:* Towers Perrin (1992, 1993).

little except coming to work every day. And, for investors, the enduring measure of company performance was shareholder return, the combination of company dividends and stock appreciation that was the reason they had parted with their money in the first place.

The growth of long-term incentives in executive compensation suggested a shift in the desired direction since most such pay is built around share-based measures, above all stock options. A compact way to summarize the extent to which the variable fraction varies with changes in shareholder wealth is to examine shareholder pay-performance sensitivity for corporate chief executives. As developed by researcher Kevin Murphy, this sensitivity measure is defined as the extent to which a change in a CEO's compensation depends on a change in investor wealth. At issue is whether the chief executive's personal incentives mirror the company's investor objectives. If the CEO builds shareholder value by $1,000 over a given period, pay-performance sensitivity gauges the number of dollars the CEO adds to his or her own personal wealth at the same time. The greater the pay sensitivity, the greater the presumed CEO sensitivity to investor concerns.

Executive compensation is shareholder sensitive to the extent it includes stock-based incentives, cash awards driven by changes in shareholder return, and long-term nonstock compensation agreements contingent on movements in investor wealth. Analysis of data for the 1,000 largest firms ranked by market capitalization for 1991 and 1992 reveals that about half—56% in 1991 and 52% in 1992—of the pay-performance sensitivity was due to the CEO's personal stock holdings (rather than options to buy future stock). In 1992, utilities as an industry registered the lowest on the pay-performance sensitivity scale, with 113 firms displaying a median $0.61; in the communication industry, 27 companies did little better, with a median value of $1.41. At the other end of the sensitivity spectrum, 14 companies in health care displayed an average sensitivity score of $46.23, and 14 firms in entertainment and electronic media reached an industry-high average of $50.90. A typical utilities chief executive would be $0.60 richer for having made investors $1,000 wealthier, while the typical entertainment CEO producing the same result would be $51—or 85 times—richer.[22]

While extrapolation of trends from several proximate years should be treated cautiously, the slope of the line for CEO pay-performance sensitivity appeared to be steepening. The median figure for the 1,000 largest firms in 1991 stood at $5.44 per $1,000, while in 1992 it rose to $7.48. Both figures represented a substantial increase over an early sensitivity estimate. Using a similar approach but drawing on only the 250 largest companies (ranked by sales rather than market capitalization) in 1988, analysis revealed a median sensitivity of $2.59 (Figure 2-9).[23]

Analysis of other trend data yielded much the same picture. Of a set of large manufacturing firms surveyed by the Conference Board in 1982, four-fifths utilized stock-option plans to compensate their executives. By 1992, that fraction remained unchanged for manufacturers. But the decade proved a watershed for companies in financial services and even utilities. Two-fifths of a set of large financial-service companies surveyed in 1982 employed such plans, but by 1992 three-quarters did so. In 1982, one-fifth of a set of large utilities operated stock-option incentive plans for executives, but by 1992 half did so.[24]

The fuel in CEO stock options can be illustrated with the terms of appointment for the new chief executive of Eastman Kodak, who took office in December 1993, following the ouster of his predecessor by disgruntled directors and investors. The Kodak board recruited George Fisher from the chief executiveship of Motorola Inc., and in making the appointment granted him 7,190 Kodak shares at $63.19 each and 742,090 shares at $49.97. The new CEO could purchase the shares in 20% cumulative annual increments beginning in November 1994. Fisher also received 20,000 shares as a restricted stock grant that cannot be sold until he has been employed by Kodak for five years. The company issued the stock options on November 11, 1993, with Kodak stock trading that day on average at $63.19. If Kodak's share price had fallen below $59.97 when the option exercise time arrives, the options were worth nothing. To the extent the price was above this waterline, however, Fisher stood to gain handsomely. Compensation consultants estimated that the option package was worth, depending on the stock's movement, from $13 million to $17 million. The restricted stock grant was already worth $1.3 million at the time of issue, and it too would grow further as a function of the stock's price. As a further self-imposed incentive, Fisher purchased 107,400 Kodak shares outright just before taking office, tying up an additional $6.79 million of his own wealth in the company.[25]

If Eastman Kodak's shareholders did well, Fisher thus stood to do well, too. Or, restated to reflect the preferred causal order, if Fisher does well professionally,

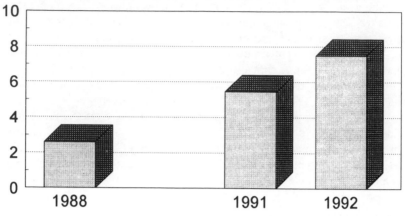

Figure 2-9. Shareholder Pay-Performance Sensitivity for Compensation of Chief Executives of Large Firms. *Source:* United Shareholders Association (1993), Jensen and Murphy (1990).

both he and investors and will also do well; if he does not, they will not. Prior to Fisher's appointment, by contrast, the pay of Kodak's CEO was one of the least investor-wealth contingent in the industry. In 1992, the pay-performance sensitivity estimate for Kodak stood at $0.61 per $1,000, on a par with the median for utility companies and ranking 925th among the nation's 1,000 largest firms. The CEO's salary and annual bonus stood at $1.46 million; his stock options were valued at $0.4 million. In 1992, Kodak shareholders saw their wealth (stock price plus dividends) decline by $1.89 billion, about 12% of total value. The CEO's own company-related wealth declined by $1.2 million. Had his pay-performance sensitivity stood near the 1,000-company average ($7.48), he would have instead suffered a personal loss of $14.1 million.[26]

Although high-powered incentives are now more evident in executive payrolls, the alignment of executive behavior with corporate purpose remains uneven. The pay-performance sensitivity is still modest at many companies. Also, even among those with higher sensitivities, pay practices sometimes operated to the contrary. When executive stock options became valueless because a company's share price had declined below that of the initial issue, firms occasionally reissued new options in place of those that had gone "underwater." The effect was to create a skewed performance-incentive distribution: contributing to company success was rewarded while failure went unchecked. Similarly, while annual bonuses appeared to be contingent on performance, the hurdles for receiving them were so low in some firms as to make them into a "thirteenth paycheck." Finally, as executives accumulated substantial personal wealth and negotiated rich retirement guarantees, the magnitude of their current performance incentives sometimes paled by comparison.[27]

Several developments during the early 1990s, however, were likely to press companies to further refine and tighten executive compensation around corporate objectives. Many institutional investors took the view that executive compensation should be so aligned, and they pressed companies to improve the linkage. TIAA-CREF, the $120-billion retirement funds for college teachers, issued a 1993 policy statement on corporate governance calling for increased board oversight of executive compensation and for rewarding executives "in direct relationship to the contribution they make in maximizing shareholder wealth." It urged a "pay for performance" system to ensure that company management responded to shareholder objectives.[28]

The U.S. Securities and Exchange Commission faciliated investor surveillance and pressure in 1992 by requiring that companies expand their proxy reporting of executive compensation practices. Four tables of data are now required: The first one must specify all forms of compensation of the five highest paid executives during each of the past three years. The second must list all stock options and appreciation rights granted the executives during the fiscal year. The third must identify all options and stock appreciation rights (gifts of cash or stock equivalent in value to the difference between a company's stock price at the grant and exercise dates) exercised by the executives during the year. And the fourth must detail all long-term performance incentives. The SEC regulations also require that the board report its views on executive compensation, how it sets the CEO's pay, and how it links CEO compensation to company performance.[29]

Boards themselves had taken steps to focus more effectively on compensation. According to a 1992 survey of 824 large companies, most major boards— 91%—had formed compensation committees to oversee and approve executive pay plans, up from 69% two decades earlier. Board compensation committees typically comprised only outside directors. Fewer than one in five (17%) included the chief executive, and almost half (47%) hired compensation consultants to assist their work. Moreover, director pay moved in the same direction as executive pay. Traditionally, corporate directors had received a fixed fee for services. It varied only to the extent that directors chose to participate in board affairs. Most companies dispensed their directors' fees according to how often the directors attended board meetings and the number of board committees on which they served. Some made virtually the entire fee contingent on attendance. The 1992 survey revealed that about three-fifths of the typical director's, compensation came from a fixed retainer, and much of the balance from per-meeting fees and committee assignments. Directors' compensation, however, was becoming increasingly contingent. The number of companies providing some director compensation in the form of stock rose sharply during the early 1990s, from under 40% in 1989 to nearly 80% in 1995 (Figure 2-10). A few firms, such as Scott Paper Company before its acquisition by Kimberly-Clark Corporation, moved to compensate outside directors solely through company stock.[30]

Chief Executives and Divisional Executives

Also in response to investor and competitive pressures, senior management at many companies transformed the relationship between the office of the executive

Percentage

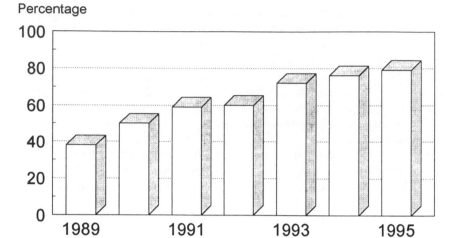

Figure 2-10. Percentage of Large Firms Offering Stock Compensation to Directors, 1989–95. *Source:* Towers Perrin (1993, 1994, 1995).

and divisional executives. The composition of the office of the executive—often composed of the chief executive, chief operating officer, chief financial officer, and general counsel—remained much the same. Its relations with the divisional heads, however, were much altered, and that in turn changed the nature of the work of all.

As companies restructured during the late 1980s and early 1990s, they increasingly defined their fundamental building blocks around products or services for internal or external customers. The traditional, large functional divisions created around development, manufacturing, and marketing gave way to numerous smaller divisions built around discrete products or services. ABB Asea Brown Boveri, a multinational manufacturer, grouped its workforce of 240,000 among some 4,500 profit centers.[31] The output-focused units tended to stress teamwork and downplay hierarchy. The product- or service-specific profit centers were, in turn, bundled into relatively autonomous operating divisions. Often termed strategic business units, these divisions each contained their own smaller versions of the major functional components that had previously stood as separate corporate entities, including development, production, and marketing.

The strategic business units, or SBUs, focused on common classes of products or services, and they acquired more responsibility for setting strategy and other policies than would have the functional divisions in the past. But companies also held them more accountable for results. With relationships to customers more clearly established, divisional executives acquired better information on their markets. With responsibility for decisions more clearly delegated, they also acquired greater power to act. And with accountability for results more clearly pinpointed and rewarded, they acquired stronger incentives to perform.

The number of SBUs varied greatly from firm to firm. DuPont grouped some 60 profit centers into a dozen business units. Xerox had created nine units, Bell

Atlantic 8, American Cyanamid 4, AT&T 19. Company nomenclature ranged as well, from strategic business units to business lines and operating divisions. Their relationships to headquarters also varied, some firms retaining more centralized functions than others. But they all shared a considerable degree of operating autonomy, giving the units and those who led them the feel of a quasi-independent business. Among large business units, the process replicated itself within, as divisional executives created autonomous subunits within their operations around distinct products or services.

The skill sets required of those heading these new, more autonomous business units differed in predictable ways from those who had run the traditional functional units. Those who had risen to the top of the functional divisions were professional specialists who had mastered their technical terrain, be it engineering, manufacturing, or marketing. Those who now sat atop the business units were management generalists who had working familiarity with engineering, manufacturing, and marketing. But they would also have to master planning, personnel, and finance. It was they, no longer the central office, who carried most of the operating authority and responsibility for meeting corporate objectives.

Several implications followed for the organization of senior management. First, the tier just below the office of the executive comprised general managers, not functional specialists. The chief executive would be less burdened by the problems of coordinating and linking diverse functional activities since most had been moved into or created within each of the divisions. Second, by virtue of the greater authority vested in the divisions, companies contracted their central staffing. The headquarters' offices of strategic planning and human resources became shadows of their former selves, with most staff reassigned into the business units. Third, companies could now more clearly link compensation for the second tier of senior managers to their own performance. Some firms created phantom stocks to do this, fictitious shares that mirrored a division's contribution to the company's shareholder value. Fourth, divisional executive security and promotion became more contingent on measurable performance, less dependent on proven seniority.

Finally, the office of the executive itself became less burdened by routine management concerns. With far greater authority vested in the divisions, SBU heads brought fewer problems to headquarters and sought less guidance. The chief executive and immediate associates accordingly allocated more of their time to general planning and financial issues. They also of necessity devoted greater time and care to the grooming and selection of the divisional executives. If the latter had far greater latitude to succeed and fail, it had become far more important to a company that the right people were appointed.[32]

The formation of strategic business units and the accompanying decentralization placed a greater burden on divisional presidents to perform as general managers. To the extent that the larger SBUs replicated the autonomous business-unit strategy down through their own organization, the next management tiers would have to possess much the same skill set, albeit for progressively smaller units. In other words, company restructuring had the effect of broadening the roles of executives at several levels, from functional specialists to management generalists. This may explain why so many graduates of the nation's leading business schools—about a third, for instance, from Stanford, Harvard and Wharton during the early 1990s—took their first positions with management consulting firms, up from a tiny fraction a decade earlier. It may also explain why executive education programs were devoted to general management more than functional programs.[33]

Company executives in Germany, Japan, and elsewhere experienced some of these same developments, though the tenor and texture varied considerably. Executive in most countries were pressed by the same intensifying international competition that had contributed to the restructuring of many American firms. But they also faced domestic capital markets and governance systems whose structure and evolution differed markedly from those found in the United States. Executives in both Germany and Japan enjoyed far greater insulation from investor pressures for improved performance. The tenure of senior managers in Germany and Japan thus appear more secure, executive promotions more certain, compensation less contingent.[34]

A sharp increase in U.S. investments abroad during the mid-1990s, however, could eventually threaten that security. Until the 1990s, American investors had generally avoided international investments. By one analysis of 1989 holdings, American investors placed 94% at home. During the early 1990s, however, U.S. investors overcame much of their shyness about international investing. The net purchase of non-U.S. stocks soared in 1991 and 1993. With less than $10 billion net non-U.S. purchases through most of the 1980s, net purchases in 1989 hit $17 billion. In 1991 they reached $35 billion, and in 1993 they totaled $68 billion. As U.S. investors insert their moneys into other national economies, they are also likely to insert themselves into other companies' management as well. In time, executives in other countries may restructure their firms and face restructured worlds in ways and with results akin to what transpired in the United States. The changes will not be identical because of distinct national traditions. But they may be inexorable, given the steadily accumulating assets and powers of American institutional holders and their 1990s penchant for international investments.[35]

A House Divided

The institutions of American capitalism have been superb at absorbing rising groups, at transforming *nouveau riches* into *ancien classes*. In recent decades, few enduring divisions could be identified within the higher circles of the large-firm business community. Outliers appeared here and there—isolated firms and executives with virtually no ties to other large firms or other executives. And of course senior managers took strongly divergent positions on matters of public policy and partisan politics. But the underlying networks are generally inclusionary, caring little about executive background and much about current achievement. The shared networks stemmed from what researchers sometimes term "structural equivalence." While executives of Sun Belt and Rust Belt industries, of oil and auto companies, of insurance and defense firms brought diverse views to high office, they confronted problems generic to management anywhere.[36]

Management challenges, however, stood in sharp contrast to those of investors, where meeting payrolls gave way to maximizing investments. Investors and executives stood on opposite sides of a formal fissure, a source of structural nonequivalence. With less commonality, less mutuality, and less reciprocity, the American business community had fractured, its house divided.

The long-time manager of the Vanguard/Windsor fund, John Neff, exemplified one side of the divide. With assets of more than $10 billion in early 1994, the Windsor fund invested heavily in a small number of companies (67 at the start of 1994). Its positions, as a result, were large: $699 million in Citicorp, $558 million in Aluminum Company of America (Alcoa), and $510 million in Bankers Trust. John Reed of Citicorp, Paul O'Neill of Alcoa, and Charles Sanford, Jr., of Bankers Trust naturally took considerable interest in John Neff, and he in them. After all, he had tied up 6.2% of his 380,000 shareholders' hard-earned money in a bank under John Reed's leadership, 5% in a manufacturer under Paul O'Neill, and 4.5% in the bank led by Charles Sanford. But while Reed, O'Neill, and Sanford frequented the well-traveled inner circles of the business community, they were unlikely to encounter Neff in any. He moved in worlds far removed from those of the executives whose corporate assets he held and oversaw.

Company executives traveled in worlds far less removed from one another. They came to know each other through service on their governing boards and Business Roundtable committees. They joined in fundraising for the United Way, deserving hospitals, and favored charities. They served together on advisory bodies, mayor's commissions, and campaign committees. They frequented the same clubs, sometimes the same schools, occasionally the same islands. Although business circles in the United States never acquired the singular culture, common vision, and sharp boundaries that characterized top management in some nations, they did acquire a sense of mutual familiarity, an acquaintanceship that was either personalized or, at worst, no more than once or twice removed. Business executives, in short, worked in circles that crisscrossed and interlaced. The feeling of kindred spirit did not achieve a consciousness of class that characterized banking in Britain, manufacturing in France, or wealthy families in some emerging economies. But it did acquire a sense of shared experience and mutual concern.[37]

Vanguard's John Neff would not be part of that. Nor would the chief executive of Calpers. Nor would most others who presided over the mushrooming assets of public pensions and investment companies. A journalist would characterize Neff in 1989 as one of America's great financial figures but one virtually invisible to the nation's higher circles. "He is little known outside the investment community because he is modest, gray, and unspectacular. . . . He doesn't get into the newspapers, least of all the gossip columns. Main Line society has never heard of him." Yet he had emerged as one of the nation's moving powers: "He is one of the most eminent financial figures in the country," noted the observer."[38] In the past, dominant financial figures would have found their way into the nation's higher circles where business, government, and celebrities enjoyed ready access and mutual familiarity. The new financial eminences, by contrast, displayed little interest in such inner byways. Nor did charter members display much interest in bringing them out of the cold.

Some large investors had never been in the cold. Those presiding over the nation's insurance companies, bank trust departments, and private pensions had already been very much a part of the higher circles. Citicorp and Bankers Trust are counted among the nation's premier institutional investors. In a 1994 ranking of the 300 largest money managers, Bankers Trust stood 3rd ($187 billion under management) and Citicorp 22nd ($74 billion under management).[39] Alcoa executives presided over a pension fund with more than $3.7 billion in assets. For those toiling in these vineyards, the inner circle was tangible and familiar. John Reed served as outside director on the boards of United Technologies and Philip Morris; Charles Sanford on the boards of Mobil Oil and General Re; Paul O'Neill on the board of General Motors. All participated in a range of professional, nonprofit, and charitable activities. O'Neill, for instance, served as a trustee, director, or member of the American Enterprise Institute, Business Council, Business Roundtable, California State University Foundation, Conference Board, Gerald R. Ford Foundation, Hudson Institute, Institute for International Economics, John F. Kennedy School of Government of Harvard University, Manpower Demonstration Research Corporation, and RAND Corporation.[40]

But for those presiding over the nation's public pension funds and investment companies, the two largest pillars of the fivefold institutional family, the worlds diverged. Their networks tied into a host of professional circuits, such as the New York Society of Security Analysts and the Association for Investment Management and Research. Few, however, found their way into the traditional watering holes of the inner circle. For them, such byways were socially distant and professionally irrelevant. The worlds of the Business Roundtable and Bohemian Grove, and the atmosphere of familiarity, mutuality, and clubiness that they and kindred organizations engendered, were to be avoided. Intimacy clouded judgment, familiarity obscured analysis. Succumbing to either was a surefire way to lose clients and shortchange beneficiaries. Social distance, not proximity, would be their measure of professionalism. The result was a kind of fault line, a cleavage between those who managed money and those who managed companies, an enduring divide between those who had money and those who made money.

Conclusion

Corporate restructuring redefined the nature of executive work. More executive compensation is at risk, and it is more contingent on the creation of investor wealth. Senior managers experience intensified pressure to achieve steady financial growth, and higher risk of personal loss or dismissal if they fall short. They are expected to produce more with less, they are held more accountable for doing so, and they expect more from others.

During the era of managerial dominance, reaching the summit of the corporate pyramid provided an unimpeded view. For the newly ascendant executive, the landscape slopped down as far as one could see. No other summits blocked the commanding vista. The successful manager could savor the view in all directions, knowing that all lay below.

As the managerial era closed, however, the landscape acquired other imposing features. As if a geological eon had been compressed into moments, other pyramids appeared almost overnight. Their foundations resided not on the production of wealth, but on the possession of wealth. Their summits rose so swiftly and so high that few executives had anticipated during their own long climb to the top that they might find a disappointing view once there. But the corporate top was now dominated by still higher and now unattainable summits. In the mountaineer's parlance, executives had mounted a "false summit." Moreover, they could see no way across to the truer peaks. To reach those heights would have required a long career ascent on an entirely different slope. With both the route and the view thus blocked, the executives of necessity made the best of a now diminished vista.

Even on their own, now diminished peaks, some managers felt the perch far more perilous. Or at least the process of reaching the summit had become so. Trend evidence confirmed that companies had thinned their middle- and upper-management ranks. Yet other evidence also confirmed that boards were no more likely to forcibly evict their chief executives. For all of those in and around the corporate apex, however, personal rewards came to depend less on incumbency, more on inventiveness. Companies transformed fixed income into variable compensation, secure paychecks into contingent options. Company performance and personal accountability became more important, service length and lofty title less so.

A layer down in senior management, corporate restructuring brought changes in work and rewards as well. Narrow functional skills were expanded to general management skills. With more autonomy to make decisions, business-unit presidents were also expected to make them well and to be judged and compensated accordingly. In holographic fashion, the complete repertoire of business skills, experiences, and rewards were replicated at the business-unit levels and then, in turn, at the subunit levels and beyond. Top executives could focus more on corporate strategy and financial oversight. The next tier could act more like business owners.

Notes

The chapter draws on the author's book, *Investor Capitalism: How Money Managers are Changing the Face of Corporate America*. For helpful comments and suggestions the author thanks Paul Osterman, Jeffrey Pfeffer, and other participants in a 1994 conference for this book's authors.

1. See, for example, Roomkin, 1989; Kanter, 1989; Hirsch, 1993; Galbraith, Lawler, and Associates, 1993; Kiechel, 1994.

2. *Fortune* magazine, various annual issues reporting the *Fortune* 500 and the *Fortune* Service 500; Tobias, 1976.

3. Morita, 1988.

4. Wyatt Company, 1993; reanalysis of data reported in Johnson and Linden, 1992, and Useem, 1993.

5. Wyatt Company, 1993; Davis and Stout, 1992; Davis, et al., 1994; Lawler, et al. 1992; *Fortune* magazine, various annual issues reporting the *Fortune* 500 and the *Fortune* Service 500.

6. Drucker, 1976.

7. Useem, et al., 1993; Useem, 1996, Chapter 2; *Institutional Investor,* 1994.

8. Wyatt Company, 1993.

9. Sonnenfeld, 1988.

10. Ward, 1994; various annual *Business Week* issues on "The Corporate Elite."

11. Jackall, 1988; Boeker, 1992.

12. Rigdon, 1993, p. 1; Rigdon and Naik, 1993, p. 3; Rigdon and Smith, 1993.

13. Cowan, 1993; Rigdon and Naik, 1993.

14. Holusha, 1993a,b, p. 49; Randall, 1993, p. 1; Rigdon and Lublin, 1993.

15. Friedman and Singh, 1989; Puffer and Weintrop, 1991.

16. Holusha, 1993c; Norton, 1993; Hays, 1994.

17. Boeker, 1992; Ocasio, 1994.

18. Fligstein, 1990; Forbes and Piercy, 1991; Ocasio and Kim, 1994.

19. Pfeffer, 1991; Smoot and Davidson, 1993.

20. I had interviewed the senior managers of this company and several others mentioned in the text as part of a study reported in Useem, 1996.

21. Senior analysts at 30 investment companies surveyed in 1993 averaged $425,000 to $500,000 in annual compensation, and some earned close to $1 million (reported in Santoli, 1994).

22. United Shareholders Association, 1993.

23. Jensen and Murphy, 1990; United Shareholders Association, 1993.

24. Buenaventura and Peck, 1993.

25. Bounds, 1993.

26. United Shareholders Association, 1993.

27. Crystal, 1991.

28. TIAA-CREF, 1993.

29. Yerger, 1993.

30. Bacon, 1993; Worrell, 1993; Collins, 1994.

31. Taylor, 1991.

32. These changes are chronicled in Useem, 1993, pp. 57–128. See also Galbraith and Merrill, 1991; Golden, 1992.

33. Information from the placement offices of the Harvard Graduate School of Business Administration (Office of Career Development), Stanford Graduate School of Business (MBA Career Management Center) and the Wharton School of the University of Pennsylvania (Graduate Division Career Development and Placement).

34. Gerlach, 1992; Roe, 1993; Charkham, 1994.

35. French and Poterba, 1991; United Nations, 1993; Securities Industry Association, 1994.

36. Baltzell, 1962, 1964; Burt, 1980, 1983; Useem, 1984; Mintz and Schwartz, 1985; Mizruchi and Schwartz, 1987; Christopher, 1989.

37. Useem, 1984.

38. Train, 1989, p. 138; see also Eaton, 1994.

39. *Institutional Investor,* 1994.

40. Company records.

References

Bacon, Jeremy. 1993. *Corporate Boards and Corporate Governance*. New York: Conference Board.

Baltzell, E. Digby. 1962. *An American Business Aristocracy*. New York: Collier Books.

———. 1964. *The Protestant Establishment: Aristocracy and Caste in America*. New York: Random House.

Barnard, Chester Irving. 1938. *The Functions of the Executive*. Cambridge: Harvard University Press.

Boeker, Warren. 1992. "Power and Managerial Dismissal: Scapegoating at the Top," *Administrative Science Quarterly* 37:400–421.

Bounds, Wendy. 1993. "Kodak Gives Fisher Options to Purchase 750,000 of Its Shares," *Wall Street Journal*, December 20, B2.

Buenaventura, Maria Ruth M., and Charles Peck. 1993. *Stock Options: Motivating Through Ownership*. New York: Conference Board.

Burt, Ronald S. 1980. "Models of Network Structure." In *Annual Review of Sociology*, Alex Inkeles and Neil J. Smelser, ed. Palo Alto, Calif.: Annual Reviews.

———. 1983. *Corporate Profits and Cooptation*. New York: Academic Press.

Business Week. Various editions of the annual issue on "The Corporate Elite" and the annual issue on "The *Business Week* Top 1000."

Charkham, Jonathan. 1994. *Keeping Good Company: A Study of Corporate Governance in Five Countries*. New York: Oxford University Press.

Christopher, Robert C. 1989. *Crashing the Gates: The De-Wasping of America's Power Elite*. New York: Simon and Schuster.

Collins, Glenn. 1994. "Scott Paper to Pay Directors in Stock," *New York Times*, August 31, D3.

Cowan, Alison Leigh. 1993. "Kodak's Chief Wins Support from Calpers," *New York Times*, April 6, D4.

Crystal, Graef S. 1991. *In Search of Excess: The Overcompensation of American Executives*. New York: Norton.

Davis, Gerald F., and Suzanne K. Stout. 1992. "Organization Theory and the Market for Corporate Control: A Dynamic Analysis of the Characteristics of Large Takeover Targets, 1980–90." *Administrative Science Quarterly* 37:605–633.

Davis, Gerald F., Kristina A. Diekmann, and Catherine H. Tinsley. 1994. "The Decline and Fall of the Conglomerate Firm in the 1980s: De-Institutionalization of an Organizational Form." *American Sociological Review* 59:547–570.

Donaldson, Gordon, and Jay W. Lorsch. 1983. *Decision Making at the Top: The Shaping of Strategic Direction*. New York: Basic Books.

Drucker, Peter F. 1976. *The Unseen Revolution: How Pension Fund Socialism Came to America*. New York: Harper & Row.

Eaton, Leslie. 1994. "The Kids Managing America's Money," *New York Times*, May 22, sec. 3, pp. 1, 6.

Fligstein, Neil. 1990. *The Transformation of Corporate Control*. Cambridge: Harvard University Press.

Forbes, J. Benjamin, and James E. Piercy. 1991. *Corporate Mobility and Paths to the Top*. Westport, Conn.: Quorum/Greenwood Publishing Group.

French, Kenneth, and James M. Poterba. 1991. "Investor Diversification and International Equity Market," *American Economic Review* 81:222–226.

Friedman, Stewart D., and Harbir Singh. 1989. "CEO Succession and Stockholder Reaction: The Influence of Organizational Context and Event Context," *Academy of Management Journal* 32:718–744.

Galbraith, Craig S., and Gregory B. Merrill. 1991. "The Effect of Compensation Program and Structure on SBU Competitive Strategy: A Study of Technology-Intensive Firms," *Strategic Management Journal* 12:353–370.

Galbraith, Jay R., Edward E. Lawler III, and Associates. 1993. *Organizing for the Future: The New Logic of Managing Complex Organizations.* San Francisco: Jossey-Bass.

Gerlach, Michael L. 1992. *Alliance Capitalism: The Social Organization of Japanese Business.* Berkeley: University of California Press.

Golden, Brian R. 1992. "SBU Strategy and Performance: The Moderating Effects of the Corporate-SBU Relationship," *Strategic Management Journal* 13:145–158.

Hays, Laurie. 1994. "Market Psychology, Salesmanship Raise IBM Stock From Ashes," *Wall Street Journal,* September 15, A1, A4.

Hewitt Associates. 1994. Personal communication of data. Lincolnshire, Ill.: Hewitt Associates.

Hirsch, Paul M. 1993. "Undoing the Managerial Revolution? Needed Research on the Decline of Middle Management and Internal Labor Markets." In *Explorations in Economic Sociology,* Richard Swedberg, ed. New York: Russell Sage Foundation.

Holusha, John. 1993a. "Kodak Stock Drops After Officer Quits," *New York Times,* April 29, D1, D5.

Holusha, John. 1993b. "Eastman Kodak Chief is Ousted by Directors," *New York Times,* August 7, pp. 37, 49.

Holusha, John. 1993c. "At Kodak, Lower Expectations Begin with Stock," *New York Times,* December 16, D1, D6.

Institutional Investor. 1994. "America's Top 300 Money Managers," July:113–56.

Jackall, Robert. 1988. *Moral Mazes: The World of Corporate Managers.* New York: Oxford University Press.

Jensen, Michael C., and Kevin J. Murphy. 1990. "CEO Incentives—It's Not How Much You Pay, but How," *Harvard Business Review* (May–June):138–153.

Johnson, Arlene S., and Fabian Linden. 1992. *Availability of a Quality Workforce.* New York: Conference Board.

Kanter, Rosabeth Moss. 1977. *Men and Women of the Corporation.* New York: Basic Books.

Kanter, Rosabeth Moss. 1989. "The New Managerial Work." *Harvard Business Review,* (November–December):85–92.

Kiechel, Walter, III. 1994. "A Manager's Career in the New Economy," *Fortune* (April 4):68–72.

Lawler, Edward E., III, Susan Mohrman, and Gerald Ledford. 1992. *Employee Involvement and Total Quality Management: Practices and Results in Fortune 500 Companies.* San Francisco: Jossey-Bass.

March, James G., and Herbert A. Simon. 1957. *Organizations.* New York: Wiley.

Mercer, William M., Inc. 1994. Personal communication.

Mintz, Beth, and Michael Schwartz. 1985. *The Power Structure of American Business.* Chicago: University of Chicago Press.

Mintzberg, Henry. 1975. "The Manager's Job: Folklore and Fact," *Harvard Business Review* 53 (July–August):49–61.

Mizruchi, Mark S., and Michael Schwartz, eds. 1987. *Intercorporate Relations: The Structural Analysis of Business.* New York: Cambridge University Press.

Morita, Akio. 1988. *Speaking Out.* Tokyo: CBS/Sony Group Inc.

Norton, Erle. 1993. "Westinghouse Names Jordan to Top Posts," *Wall Street Journal,* July 1, A3–4.

Ocasio, William. 1994. "Political Dynamics and the Circulation of Power: CEO Succession in U.S. Industrial Corporations, 1960–1990," *Administrative Science Quarterly* 39:285–312.

Ocasio, William, and Hyosun Kim. 1994. "The Rise and Fall in Subunit Power and the Decline of the Financial Conception of Control in Large U.S. Manufacturing Firms, 1981–1992." Cambridge: Sloan School, MIT.

Pfeffer, Jeffrey. 1991. *Managing with Power.* Cambridge: Harvard Business School Press.

Puffer, Sheila M., and Joseph B. Weintrop. 1991. "Corporate Performance and CEO Turn-over: A Comparison of Performance Indicators," *Administrative Science Quarterly* 36:1–19.

Randall, Eric D. 1993. "Kodak Chief's Exit Good for Stock, Bad for Staff," *USA Today,* August 9, 2B.

Riesman, David. 1950. *The Lonely Crowd: A Study of the Changing American Character.* New Haven: Yale University Press.

Rigdon, Joan E. 1993. "Kodak's Chief Gains Support from 2 Holders, Whitmore Assures Calpers He Will Make Changes to Boost Productivity," *Wall Street Journal,* April 6, A4.

Rigdon, Joan E., and Joann S. Lublin. 1993. "Kodak Seeks Outsider to be Chairman, CEO," *Wall Street Journal,* August 9, A3, A14.

Rigdon, Joan E., and Gautam Naik. 1993. "Kodak's Financial Officer Quits in Rift with Chief." *Wall Street Journal,* April 29, A3, A6.

Rigdon, Joan E., and Randall Smith. 1993. "Kodak's Chairman Reassures Investors, Prom-ises to Sell a 'Major Asset.'" *Wall Street Journal,* April 30, A4.

Roe, Mark J. 1993. "Some Differences in Corporate Structure in Germany, Japan, and the United States," *Yale Law Journal* 102 (June):1927–2003.

Roomkin, Myron J. 1989. *Managers as Employees: An International Comparison of the Chang-ing Character of Managerial Employment.* New York: Oxford University Press.

Santoli, Michael. 1994. "The Hunt is on for Research Analysts," *Wall Street Journal,* May 27, B4f.

Securities Industry Association. 1994. *1994 Securities Industry Fact Book.* New York: Securi-ties Industry Association.

Smoot, George, and Keay Davidson. 1993. *Wrinkles in Time.* New York: Morrow.

Sonnenfeld, Jeffrey A. 1988. *The Hero's Farewell: What Happens When CEOs Retire.* New York: Oxford University Press.

Taylor, William. 1991. "The Logic of Global Business: An Interview with ABB's Percy Barnevik." *Harvard Business Review* 69 (March–April):91–105.

TIAA-CREF. 1993. "TIAA-CREF Policy Statement on Corporate Governance." New York: TIAA-CREF.

Tobias, Andrew. 1976. "The Merging of the 'Fortune 500'," *New York Magazine* (December 20):23–25, 49, 67.

Towers Perrin. 1992. *Perspectives on Management Pay* (July). New York: Towers Perrin.

———. 1993. *Perspectives on Management Pay* (August). New York: Towers Perrin.

———. 1994. Personal communication. New York: Towers Perrin.

———. 1995. Personal communication. New York: Towers Perrin.

Train, John. 1989. *The New Money Masters.* New York: HarperCollins.

United Nations. 1993. *World Investment Report: Transnational Corporations and Integrated International Production.* New York: United Nations.

United Shareholders Association. 1993. *Executive Compensation 1,000.* Washington, D.C.: United Shareholders Association.

Useem, Michael. 1984. *The Inner Circle: Large Corporations and the Rise of Business Political Activity in the U.S. and U.K.* New York: Oxford University Press.

———. 1993. "Management Commitment and Company Policies on Education and Training," *Human Resource Management Journal* 32:411–434.

———. 1996. *Investor Capitalism: How Money Managers Are Changing the Face of Corporate America.* New York: Basic Books.

Useem, Michael, Edward Bowman, Craig Irvine, and Jennifer Myatt. 1993. "U.S. Investors Look at Corporate Governance in the 1990s," *European Management Journal* 11 (June):175–189.

Ward, Andrew. 1994. Personal communication. Atlanta: Emory Business School, Center for Leadership and Career Studies.

Whyte, William H. 1956. *The Organization Man.* New York: Simon and Schuster.

Worrell, Kay. 1993. *Corporate Directors' Compensation, 1993 Edition.* New York: Conference Board.

Wyatt Company. 1993. *Best Practices in Corporate Restructuring.* New York: Wyatt Company.

Yerger, Ann. 1993. "SEC Pay Disclosure Rules Produce Results," *Corporate Governance Bulletin* (May/June):21–26.

From Bureaucracy to Enterprise?

3

The Changing Jobs and Careers of Managers in Telecommunications Service

ROSEMARY BATT

In response to technological change and product market deregulation, longstanding U.S. telecommunications firms are radically restructuring their business strategies and organizations to improve competitiveness. While the popular and business press as well as academic researchers have focused attention on the dramatic changes occurring in the collapse of industry boundaries, megamergers, and the rise of new strategic alliances, they have largely ignored how these structural changes are profoundly altering the employment and careers of employees. In the Bell operating companies, where bureaucracy is seen as *the* major obstacle to competitiveness, managerial workers have become a significant target of reform because they are equated with bureaucracy and historically comprised approximately a quarter of the workforce.

This chapter analyzes how organizational restructuring is affecting managerial labor markets—the jobs, careers, and employment levels of line managers in Bell operating companies. It addresses a series of questions: How does organizational restructuring affect both employment levels and the nature of managerial work—the division of labor between the managerial and nonmanagerial workforce? How does it affect the career trajectories of lower and middle level managers? Are these changes leading to a loss of managerial power and a convergence in the working conditions of managerial and nonmanagerial workers? Or, conversely, do managers stand to gain from the flattening of hierarchies and devolution of decision making to lower organizational levels? Who wins and who loses in the process? Do new organizational cleavages and conflicts arise as a result?

The chapter's central argument is that a new vision of organization has taken hold—one that replaces "bureaucracy" with "enterprise." This vision is found both in management and academic literature and in corporate offices. But the vision entails sharp contradictions that have unintended consequences: new cleavages between lower and middle level managers on the one hand, and top managers on the other. The new vision relies on two competing approaches to

55

organizational reform. The first approach begins with human resources and relies heavily on decentralizing management to lower levels. It draws on ideas from organizational behavior, strategic human resources management and industrial relations, and total quality. It views competitive advantage as emanating from entrepreneurialism and innovation at the point of customer contact. According to this logic, lower and middle managers have new, dynamic roles to play; their jobs must be redesigned to give them more opportunities to be creative and more autonomy to make decisions to meet customer needs. Supportive human resources practices include training in new skills (human resources management, business, marketing) as well as incentives (career opportunities, employment security, compensation) to inspire organizational commitment. The approach attempts to simulate small business enterprise in large firms.

The second approach begins with technology and engineering. It focuses on realizing scale economies through systemwide innovations. Organizational consolidations, new applications of technology, reengineering, and downsizing are all vehicles for enhancing efficiency and cutting costs. Rather than relying on decentralized discretion, this macro approach privileges the centralized decisions of top managers, consultants, and engineers—decisions that ripple through organizations to lower levels. Changes in the design of jobs and human resources practices flow *as a consequence* of new technologies and organizational restructuring. Because companies cannot make prior commitments to job enhancement or employment security, the two approaches are often in conflict. The central question is whether or how the two approaches can be reconciled.

In the case of the former Bell system companies since divestiture in 1984, the second logic has dominated the first for at least two reasons. First, top management views bureaucracy as the most serious obstacle to competitiveness (in contrast to manufacturing firms that view mass production modes as relics to be discarded). Second, advances in new digital and fiber optic technologies allow companies to reap even greater scale economies than they have in the past. The integrated nature or "systemness" of the telecommunications services industry makes centralization and consolidation an attractive approach to industrial organization. These centralized approaches have undermined the entrepreneurial and job enhancing approach to quality service that total quality theorists and others advocate. Top management has created contradictions for lower and middle managers along several dimensions. First, while new performance systems evaluate middle managers on the basis of broad customer service measures, top managers are judged by shareholders on the basis of narrower financial criteria. Second, while middle managers now have greater authority and responsibility for meeting performance goals, they lack the necessary control over budgets and operational decisions needed to get the job done—control that "real entrepreneurs" or owners of small businesses have. Third, they have heavier workloads with fewer financial or promotional rewards. Fourth, while their new role requires increased discretionary effort, creativity, and commitment to the firm, firms have simultaneously decreased their long-term employment commitments to managers. In the past, the AT&T system created a seamless web of loyalty that rose through seven layers of management, with all employees unified around the goal of public service. In the present, the incentives and rewards for top management are at odds with those offered to lower level managers, who feel resentment and a sense of betrayal.

This argument draws on evidence from extensive qualitative field research and quantitative data collection in several regional Bell operating companies. It uses the results of a comprehensive survey conducted in 1994 of 330 lower and middle level line managers in one operating company. The survey asked employees how work organization and human resources practices were changing and how these changes affected their jobs and careers.

This chapter reviews the dominant literature that has shaped the corporate thinking on restructuring and briefly describes the telecommunications industry context—the way the old system worked and how and why it is crumbling under the weight of technological change, national deregulation, and globalization of markets. The chapter also examines how changes in business strategy and structure at the firm level are reshaping the employment levels, jobs, and careers of lower and middle level line managers.

Theoretical Perspectives

Two quite different views of the outcomes of corporate restructuring for managers have emerged in the last decade. On the one hand, the popular and business press provide numerous anecdotes of unemployed managers who are victims of corporate downsizing (Fisher, 1991; Cowan and Barron, 1992; Zachery, 1993). Researchers note the "collapse of internal labor markets" for managers and the growing similarity of employment conditions for managers and workers—for example, in the decline in managerial employment security. Researchers have also identified the loss of power and authority of supervisors when firms introduce employee participation or self-managing teams into production-level jobs (Klein, 1984; Schlesinger and Klein, 1987).

On the other hand, the same press carries images of the new manager, the "product champion" and innovator: corporate restructuring gets rid of bureaucracy and frees up middle and lower level managers to be more entrepreneurial. Participatory management allows managers to gain from workers' creativity; self-managed teams free up managers from administrative chores. These conflicting views also arise in different strands of the business school and academic literature. The arguments grow out of a rejection of bureaucratic organization and mass production as incongruent with global markets that demand low cost, high quality, reduced cycle time, flexibility, and innovation.

The excellence literature, for example, argued for making all managers into entrepreneurs (Peters and Waterman, 1982; Peters and Austin, 1985; Peters, 1987). In stark contrast to the dominant literature of earlier periods that focused on top managers as the sole source of creativity and innovation (Barnard, 1946; Drucker, 1967; Mintzburg, 1973; Kotter, 1982), writers in the 1980s argued for loosely coupled organizations with "lean staff" that would create room for innovators across layers and departments of management. By recreating marketlike conditions inside large organizations, or "small in large organizations" (Drucker,

1988), managers would have greater incentives to initiate change and would take greater ownership over their productive units. The resource mobilization litera- ture, spearheaded by Rosabeth Moss Kanter, went further in arguing that middle managers were the real source of innovation in large firms (1982a, 1982b, 1983). New managerial ladders could provide greater opportunities—a shift from nar- row, functionally based careers to a variety of ways of making it to the top (Kanter, 1984).

Another stream of literature, the strategic human resources management literature, called on management to link their business strategies and human resources strategies to improve performance (Tichy, Fombrun, and Devanna, 1982; Beer, et al., 1985; Dyer, ed., 1988). Business school faculty and manage- ment consultants emphasized performance-enhancing human resources policies (training, participation, and compensation) (e.g., Lawler, 1986). While the "con- trol to commitment" strategy (Walton, 1985) originally focused more on the nonmanagerial workforce, the ideas apply equally to the treatment of managers as employees.

Economists and compensation specialists developed a complementary argu- ment in the "new economics of personnel" literature which called for "mar- ketlike" pay systems in large firms to improve incentive structures. This involved reducing the percentage of fixed-base pay or salary while increasing at-risk pay and linking an individual's pay to his or her contribution (pay-for-performance) (Gerhart, Milkovich, and Murray, 1992; Lazear, 1992; Shuster and Zingheim, 1992).

Industrial relations scholars additionally pointed to the need for middle managers to stop fighting over grievances and to learn to negotiate with union leaders in joint productivity-enhancing committees. Where unions existed, there was a greater likelihood of successful and broad-based adoption of performance- enhancing innovations by the workforce if union leaders embraced the experi- ments (Kochan, Katz, and McKersie, 1986).

Reengineering and macrorestructuring approaches, by contrast, called for systemwide analysis of work processes and the elimination of all redundant work, no matter what the consequences for jobs and human resources practices (Ham- mer and Champy, 1992).

Some argue that these alternative approaches provide a basis for a unified new vision of organization—from a "bureaucratic culture" to an "enterprise cul- ture" in the firm (Ray, 1986). But researchers have rarely examined the vision in light of empirical reality—the competing claims that alternate approaches to reform make on managerial employees. As argued above, the reality of this change is often contradictory and may be summarized as follows. First, there should be fewer managerial jobs and opportunities for promotion. Second, the jobs that remain should be more interesting and challenging. Third, the ones that remain should be more contingent on productivity and accountability, offering less income and employment security. The scant empirical literature on the changing nature of managerial jobs and careers also suggests mixed results for firms and managers (See Fulop, 1991 for a review) as well as wide variation in the outcomes (Heckscher, 1995). Managerial jobs may be more interesting, but there are fewer of them, and they no longer carry implicit long-term contracts and employment or income security. For managers, some may benefit and rise quickly; others may lose their jobs; others may both benefit and lose along different dimensions of their jobs and careers—having more powerful but more stressful jobs, more challenging but less stable careers. The challenge for empirical research is to untangle how these themes play out for differently situated managers—in different industries, corporate settings, managerial levels, functional areas, and professional occupations—distinctions that have rarely been made in the managerial literature.

Managerial Jobs in Telecommunications Services: 1950–1980

The AT&T bureaucracy and the managerial jobs that occupied it grew dramatically between 1950 and 1980. Managerial jobs grew in absolute numbers by 50% between 1950 and 1960, by 60% between 1960 and 1970, and by 47% between 1970 and 1980. By contrast, despite the overall expansion of the AT&T market, nonmanagerial jobs rose by only 4.6% in the first decade, 23% in the second, and 2.7% in the third. Automation eliminated low-skilled work. The proportion of managers in the total AT&T workforce grew from 13.5% in 1950 to 29.4% in 1980. The ratio of all managers to all nonmanagers at AT&T was 1:6.3 in 1950 and 1:2.4 in 1980. Table 3-1 compares the relative growth of managerial and nonmanagerial jobs.

There are two probable explanations for this transformation. The most important concerns AT&T's strategic response to increased regulatory oversight in the post–World War II period, which put pressure on the company to cut costs and reduce rates while expanding universal service. Regulators required detailed performance measurements and accountability. AT&T attempted to meet cost-minimization requirements through the logic of mass production: using electromechanical technology to reap scale economies, improve productivity, and lower costs in the provision of a high volume standardized product (voice transmission). But most jobs in telephone service were not susceptible to Taylorism or machine-pacing—only operator jobs were. By contrast, the network infrastructure or wireline required (and continues to require) a highly skilled and autonomous field staff; and the business office provided customized service through "universal service representatives" until the early 1980s. Those jobs that could not be machine-paced were heavily supervised, and this pattern is evident in the variation in spans of control for managers across occupational groups. In one representative Bell operating company, for example, by 1980 the ratio of first-line supervisors to workers was 1:6 in network crafts, 1:8–10 in customer services, and 1:20 in operator services.

A second factor contributing to the increase in managers was the growth of independent unionism and the threat of strikes in the post–World War II period, which led AT&T to seek ways of shifting work out of the bargaining unit to staff managers or "subject matter experts; this strategy has accelerated in the post-divestiture period, according to trade unionists.

Despite the growth in bureaucracy, productivity in telecommunications ser-

Table 3-1. Growth of Managerial Workforce at AT&T: 1950–90

	1950	1960	1970	1980	1984	1990
AT&T Bell						
Managers	70,630	105,833	169,401	248,562	111,432	115,851
Nonmanagers	446,129	466,795	574,534	589,939	267,568	137,920
Total employees	516,759	572,628	743,935	838,501	379,000	253,771
Managers as % of Total	13.7%	18.5%	22.8%	29.6%	29.4%	45.7%
Ratio of Managers to Non-managers	1:6.3	1:4.4	1:3.4	1:2.4	1:2.4	1:1.2
% Change over prior period:						
Managers		+49.9%	+60.1%	+46.7%	−55.2%	+ 4.0%
Nonmanagers		+ 4.6%	+23.1%	+ 2.7%	−54.5%	−48.5%
Total employees		+10.9%	+33.2%	+ 9.7%	−55.3%	−33.0%

Source: *Bell System Statistical Manual 1950–1980*. AT&T Comptrollers' Office, June, 1982. New York, pp. 701–708, in Keefe and Boroff (1994, Table 1). The figures for 1950 to 1980 are for the Bell System, excluding Bell Labs (research and development) and Western Electric (manufacturing). The 1984 and 1990 figures represent AT&T's total U.S. operations following divestiture, including manufacturing but excluding NCR.

vices (measured as employees per 10,000 access lines) grew by 5.9% per year between 1967 and 1988—over five times the average rate of 1.1% for the non-farm business sector—and 10 times the rate of 0.8% in services (Waldstein, 1988, Table 4, U.S. Department of Labor, 1990:10–12).

Managerial Jobs

In contrast to the literature on managerial labor markets that views the flexible deployment of managers as a *raison d'etre* for their employment security (Osterman, 1988), most management jobs in the Bell system were highly regimented and functionally specialized. They resembled much more the Taylorism of industrial labor markets than the breadth commonly associated with managerial or salaried labor markets. There were seven layers of management leading up to officers in the operating companies and at AT&T. The primary role of supervisors and managers was to monitor and enforce work discipline. Standard operating procedures set at the top created relatively nonthinking managerial jobs that required implementing policies down the chain of command, enforcing discipline, and funneling numbers back up. The top-down, command and control management style at AT&T has led several observers to compare it to the military. For example:

> AT&T is to the Bell System what a general staff is to an army, and AT&T seems somewhat proud of the parallel. A company writer calls the military-modeled

general staff "the greatest contribution to the art of management" of the first half of the twentieth century; pridefully he notes that AT&T adapted for its own use many of the staff concepts developed by Frederick the Great, Von Steuben, and Napoleon. . . .

A traffic manager in the smallest of Bell offices reports to the traffic manager directly above him in the next largest office area to district to regional to operating company and ultimately to 195 Broadway ["AT&T's Pentagon"]—just as an Army G-1 officer has counterpart from battalion level all the way up to the Defense Department. . . . (Goulden, 1968, p. 17)

AT&T transfers men as freely among the operating companies as the U.S. Army does among its divisions (Goulden, 1968, p. 22).

The military culture may also have been enhanced by AT&T's frequent recruitment of veterans, a rich source of experienced people with radio, communications, and electronic skills. In addition, in the post–World War II period, management by numbers became the norm, and to many, an obsession. The Bell system measured the performance of managers as the aggregate of the performance of workers under them. If top management demanded better numbers, middle and lower managers felt squeezed and, in turn, pressured workers.

Detailed measurement systems were at least in part a response to federal and state regulators who increasingly sought to gain control over rates and service quality. State public utility commissions (PUCs), for example, set performance standards for network operations, from the length of time to repair a service outage to safety standards required during routine installation and repair. Each functional department in the telephone companies developed its own system of record keeping and internal performance measures as demanded by the state PUCs, and these measures were unique to the functional specialization of the department. The company tended to emphasize quantitative measures or output per unit input—tasks per day for network crews or seconds per call or call-waiting time for operators or customer service representatives. But PUCs also emphasized quality and service—in network, for example, the repair of service within a 24-hour period. Moreover, in the telephone service industry, quantity and quality of service are closely linked because good service is timely service. In customer services, for example, average waiting time is a key indicator of service quality because customers place heavy emphasis on quick response in judging service quality. As one long-time manager in the Bell system commented, ". . . the telephone company has always been obsessed with quality, probably too much so. For example, we used to require that a customer call be answered in two rings. That was our own internal measure, but maybe we didn't really need that—and it was expensive."

The system of functionally specific measures reinforced separation and "turf" competition between managers in different departments. Maximizing efficiencies in one department, however, often undermined efficiencies in another. Maximizing tasks per day in network, for example, creates incentives for network craft workers to find quick fixes to problems; but such quick fixes may result in repeat calls for repair attendants and construction work to repair the deteriorated network. Functionally based measurement systems, therefore, created managers that were "efficiency-minded," but narrow in perspective, and this often resulted in overall inefficiencies. As companies began to mechanize record keeping and measurement systems in the 1970s and 1980s, they simply computerized the inefficiencies in the old system.

Because the PUCs were so important in setting rate structures and perfor- mance requirements, the telephone companies geared their managerial structure towards meeting the demands of the PUC. The state telephone company presi- dent held the most important political position as an official reporting to the PUC. Regulatory was viewed internally as playing a public relations role, massag- ing the interface between the telephone company and the members of the PUC as well as state politicians who periodically voted on rate hikes.

AT&T's concern for public image translated into a corporate emphasis on employee involvement in community service, such as for example, "The Pi- oneers," which involved thousands of volunteers from Bell companies in commu- nity service activities. Employees were expected to play leadership roles in com- munity organizations such as the Jaycees, and those who did so were looked on favorably for their leadership potential.

A detailed account of AT&T's attempts to manipulate public opinion in its favor traces the company policies to the 1910s and 1920s:

> Every employee in the Bell System is considered a potential public relations representative. Telephone company employees, as a class, are gracious and ac- commodating. This is no accident. The uniformity of behavior is the result of design. Employees are selected and trained by the company as public relations agents, because it is believed that through constant cultivation of public sympa- thy, telephone companies will have less trouble in getting increased rates and in opposing adverse legislation. (Danielian, 1939, p. 281)[2]

While this research captures the cynical side of AT&T's manipulation of public perceptions, many employees took seriously their public service mission and participation in community affairs. For example, a study by Howard and Bray portrays telephone company managers as responsible public servants who took pride in their work. "Compared to managers in other organizations, they were more emotionally stable but less daring and more bound by rules. As managers of a government-controlled monopoly, they were less 'dollar' conscious in a propri- etorship sense, but assumed social responsibility for the service the telephone business provided and had a real sense of obligation to the community" (Williams and Peterfreund, cited in Howard and Bray, 1988, p. 36). In a questionnaire administered by Howard and Bray, these managers consistently scored high in terms of their pride in their jobs and their overall job satisfaction (Howard and Bray, 1988, p. 132).

Internal Labor Markets

Internal labor markets in the Bell system—the formal and informal rules govern- ing managers' jobs and careers—reflected the company's bureaucratic and func- tionally specialized organization. Career ladders were long and vertical. As early as 1910, AT&T began encouraging loyalty through "The American Plan," (company-paid pensions, sickness and disability benefits, employee stock options, and an organization of retired and long-service employees). The company had seniority-based benefits and career ladders filled almost exclusively from within by the 1920s (Schacht, 1985, p. 35–36). The Bell System recruited first level supervisors either from the rank and file or from the external labor market. Management positions above first level were filled exclusively from within. Managers received considerable training, much of which was designed to socially and psychologically separate them from workers. Those promoted from within were particularly encouraged to break all social ties with former coworkers. A former AT&T employee noted that people came into the system at a young age, received "heavy socialization" into their managerial role, and lost a sense of themselves in a system that demanded "total selfless loyalty."[3]

Workers who were promoted from the ranks had at least a high school education and could expect to rise to lower or middle level management in their respective functional specialties: male network craft, female office workers in the business office or operator services. External recruits were usually college-educated, and tended to be placed in positions dispersed throughout the organization (Plant, Commercial, Engineering, Accounting, Traffic). They were expected to climb higher, and a select group was "fast-tracked" and chosen to be groomed for top management, which involved assignments across departments plus midcareer training or executive development courses. The Bell System provided generous educational allowances and tuition aid for college courses and beyond, and many employees availed themselves of these opportunities in order to gain promotions.

In their longitudinal study of AT&T, managers Howard and Bray (1988) document the advancement of college- and non-college-educated males through management ranks from 1956 to 1976. The modal level of achievement for non-college-educated managers was a level two management position, while that of college-educated managers was level three. In Howard and Bray's sample of 422 managers (274 college and 148 non-college-educated), between 5% and 10% of non-college-educated workers were promoted each year (depending on the year). By contrast, between 15% and 25% of college-educated managers received promotions in the same period (Howard and Bray 1988, p. 128–129).

Most careers in the Bell system, however, did not resemble a professional development track. Workers were promoted from within because as supervisors, they had an intimate knowledge of the technology and job requirements—of which standard operating procedures were important, for example, and which were obstacles to getting the job done. Most managers capitalized on job specific formal and informal knowledge, living out their careers in the same department or subdepartment. In this setting, informal sponsorship or paternalism was extremely important for ensuring movement up the ranks. If a subordinate was particularly skilled and reliable, this sponsorship not only facilitated upward movement, but discouraged lateral mobility. Some employees say that "good performers" were penalized and became "stuck" because superiors depended on them.

What is significant about this portrait is that once divestiture and downsizing began, managers with long histories in the Bell system and deep, functionally specific knowledge had few occupational alternatives outside of the system. The skills and knowledge accrued in a Bell system "career" were not portable. Those who left the system often retired and/or retrained for entirely new occupations.

In summary, managerial lives in the Bell system were a mixed blessing. Jobs were regimented and relatively uncreative, but had an important public service mission. The system clearly created middle-class jobs and management opportunities that otherwise would not have been available for a population dispersed in small towns, cities, and rural areas across the country. The system provided lifetime employment security unlike that provided by other large corporations because AT&T had a guaranteed rate of return and was not seriously affected by business cycle fluctuations.

Technology Change, Deregulation, and Restructuring: 1980–1994

At divestiture in 1984, the Modified Final Judgement (MFJ) allowed AT&T to participate in deregulated equipment and long distance markets, but divested AT&T of its 22 local telephone companies that were consolidated into the current seven regional Bell operating companies (RBOCs) and that retained their monopoly position in local services. AT&T downsized rapidly, eliminating over one-third of its domestic workforce in the first six years following divestiture but expanding the relative proportion of managers to 54% (Keefe and Batt, 1996). It restructured into business units based on market segments, invested heavily in new digital technologies, and began implementing total quality management. Employee morale plummeted (Keefe and Batt, 1996).

The regional Bell companies moved more slowly, reducing the workforce by attrition, and investing in those unregulated markets that the MFJ allowed—such as information services, cellular, and international services. Cost pressures on phone companies increased from the late 1980s on, however, as local access carriers (LACs) such as Metrofiber and Teleport constructed local fiber loops in metropolitan areas and skimmed the more lucrative business customers. Large institutions, such as schools, hospitals, universities, and utilities, developed their own private networks and reduced reliance on phone companies. And cable companies, wired to roughly 65% of households nationally, were perched to enter the local residential market as soon as legislation permitted. The anticipated deregulation of local services in the 1990s led the RBOCs to accelerate their efforts to cut costs through consolidations, downsizing, and reengineering of business processes. The 1996 Telecommunications Act deregulated all markets, so that long distance companies, cable companies, and other carriers could provide local services and the Bell companies could enter long distance.

The resulting changes in business strategy and structure in the regional Bell companies are summarized and presented in Table 3-2. First, companies shifted from a public service mission shaped by engineers and regulators to a sales-maximizing mentality shaped by finance and marketing departments, and oriented toward Wall Street. Second they shifted from a standardized high-volume

Table 3-2. Telecommunications Services Business Strategy
and Production Organization

Components	Old System	New System
Capital market	Regulated by FCC, State PUCs	Partially regulated: Sensitive to stock market
Pricing mechanism	Regulated: Cross-subsidized (local/long dist.) (resident/business)	Partially regulated: More competitive "Incentive-based" "Cost-based"
Product market	Standardized: Voice	Differentiated: Voice, data, video, image
Technology	Lead, copper transmission; Analog, mechanical switching	Fiber optic transmission; Digital switching
Competitive advantage	Low cost, scale economies	Cost, quality, customer service
Business strategy	Universal public service, "Engineering driven"	Segmented service markets, "Market driven"
Management structure	Vertical Bureaucratic Centralized	Horizontal Entrepreneurial Dual: region/local
HR/IR	Centralized	Dual: regional/local

product market (voice) to a differentiated product market (voice, enhanced services such as voice messaging, data, video, image). To support this shift, they invested heavily in fiber cable and broadband integrated services digital networks (ISDN) to allow them to carry high speed data, voice, video, and imaging and remain technologically competitive.

To respond to new competitive conditions, Bell operating companies developed organizational strategies that have the unintended consequence of sending contradictory messages to employees. On the one hand, micro level experiments are designed to increase employee participation and decentralize decision making so that employees can improve customer service. On the other hand, macro strategies that centralize decision making, streamline the organization, and reduce costs dominate and often undermine local initiatives. While companies reengineer and downsize to eliminate bureaucracy, they request increased employee commitment and discretionary effort to enhance service quality. Managers on the regulated side complain that they are asked to do more with less, while they observe companies shifting resources to expand their activities in lucrative nonregulated markets such as information services, cellular, and international services.

Similarly, companies are centralizing some functions while decentralizing others. On the side of centralization, companies are taking advantage of scale economies to consolidate and standardize operations at the regional level (from what was the state or local telephone level). Additionally, they have created regional business units defined by market segment (residential, small business, large business). The difficulty with the business unit structure in telecommunications is that the network infrastructure serves all segments; critical decisions regarding choice of technology and operational standards that would be controlled by the business unit in most other industries are under a separate regional entity because of the "systemness" or integrated nature of the network.

At the same time that companies have created regional corporate entities and regional business units defined by market segment, they are attempting to decentralize decisions regarding customer service, quality, and work organization to the local or "district" level (analogous to a plant in manufacturing). This idea comes from quality and excellence theorists that "empowering" managers to "get close to the customer" is the key to continuous improvement in service quality.

In summary, the direction of change is to hollow out the old state telephone companies, with key operational decisions shifting either up to the regional corporate or business unit entity or down to the "district" or local managerial level. This has created tensions between local and regional, lower and top level managers over operational decisions.

Implications for Managerial Jobs

The implications of these changes in business strategy and structure for lower and middle level managers can best be understood through a detailed study of one representative Bell operating company that draws on qualitative and survey data. Since the early 1980s, this company like other Bell companies began experimenting with participatory management practices, beginning with the union-management Quality of Worklife (QWL) program in 1980 that sought to do away with AT&T's traditional military command and control approach. The changes for managers stressed new *behaviors* rather than new *skills* in the technical sense of the term. Management training emphasized a "softer" approach, listening rather than dictating skills. Managers had to learn to discuss and negotiate with employees and union leaders over problems as they arose, rather than only in the context of grievances. In the course of the 1980s, the QWL program grew and gave way to more extensive employee involvement, and later a total quality program in which lower-level managers tapped the ideas of workers to improve customer service. In the mid-1980s, the company began experimenting with the use of self-managed teams (SMTs) as a next step in managers "letting-go;" where teams were introduced, a first-line supervisor now had the role of "coach" and was supposed to lead rather than command, inspire rather than demand obedience.

At the same time that participatory experiments were occurring, the company was centralizing, consolidating, and downsizing. Between 1984 and 1990 the company consolidated the old telephone companies into one regional entity, merging executive positions, human resources, regulatory, labor relations, and finance into one corporate organization and standardizing the network technology across the region. Overall workforce reductions of 25% occurred through attrition and an early retirement buyout for managers. Serious efforts to cut the managerial force began in the 1990s, leading to a reduction of 23.5% of managers by 1993. Approximately 50% left through early retirement buyouts, another 40% through transfers to other subsidiaries, and another 10% by other programs to provide early exit or extended leaves. These voluntary reductions rippled through the organization, leaving random holes in staffing levels.

While the company surpassed its goal for reducing management ranks, at least some managerial positions were subsequently refilled by promoting non-managerial workers into lower-level management positions. By 1993, when top management decided that downsizing was not occurring at a quick enough pace (line and staff managers still comprised 24.5% of the workforce, and the ratio of first-line supervisors to workers was 1:5.9), the company announced an across-the-board 10% downsizing, forcing involuntary separations among managers and attrition among nonmanagers. At least one out of seven management levels was to be eliminated. The forced reductions broke with the company's tradition of employment security and sent shock waves through the organization. The company announced an additional downsizing in 1995–96.

Across the Bell companies, interest in self-managed teams has often focused on their importance as a vehicle for downsizing. With roughly 50% of management staff at the first-line supervisor level, companies view self-managed teams as vehicle for dramatically cutting indirect labor costs. Managers in different companies have expressed similar experiences: "We lost so many management jobs that they backed into it [SMTs]"; or "This experiment [SMTs] was viewed as 'my toy.' Now that we're downsizing, it's being taken seriously." In another company, a network supervisor said the objective was ". . . increased span of control. Traditionally in my area it was 1:5. The company wants to go to 1:30. There's no way to supervise this many, so the duties of the supervisor have to change." The change to self-managed teams is also facilitated through new technologies that electronically monitor the flow of work. This is true not only in services where information systems track the call handling of operators and customer service representatives, but in network where handheld computers now allow field technicians to record work as they complete it.

Supervisors who have learned to become coaches appear to like the job better because they are freed up to get out in the field more and do less paperwork. Because their work involves more coordination and less direct disciplining and supervision, their jobs look more like those of middle managers, and in this sense they are enhanced. By contrast, first-line supervisors who continue with traditional responsibilities express frustration over their jobs because administrative tasks are heavy and downsizing has led workloads to increase. A company-sponsored survey of network supervisors found that only one-third of respondents were satisfied with their jobs; another one-third said they would return to craft jobs if given the opportunity. But even among supervisors who have at least some self-managed teams under their jurisdiction, the workloads appear daunting. According to one such supervisor, "My span of control has tripled . . . I work 14 hours a day, five days a week. . . . I'm fully accountable if anything goes wrong. Supervisors now spend 60% of their time doing paperwork. High stress.

Performance is slipping some. We used to make two or three visits a day to each worker. You'd go out and find out how he's doing. Now I see each worker once a week."

The company in this case study used the experience from self-managed teams to redesign supervisors' jobs and reduce their administrative work from roughly 60% of their time to 10%. Under the piloted job redesign, coaches would spend 50% of their time in the field training and developing workers. The job redesign was not implemented, however, because of more macrolevel organizational restructuring.

In the survey conducted for this study, despite the fact that SMTs are clearly equated with fewer supervisor jobs, there was surprisingly broad-based support for the idea.[4] Sixty-eight percent of all network managers and 85% of customer services managers supported their use. Moreover, the support was higher among firstline supervisors (71%) who, according to conventional literature should have the most to lose, than middle managers (57%).[5] Regardless of whether managers had direct experience with these teams or not, approximately three-quarters saw the benefit to teams in the increased cooperation and sense of ownership over work that members have.

For middle level managers responsible for local or district level operations, the company used total quality concepts to create small, cross-functional business units known as "district operations councils," in contrast to the past when middle managers had little discretion and reported through department hierarchies to state-level officials. The district operations councils, local geographic units established at divestiture and made up of local managers from different departments, had functioned in the 1980s primarily as vehicles for public relations, employee involvement in community affairs, and the telephone company's interface with the regulatory environment. Local managers maintained departmental turf and interacted little beyond monthly council meetings. Under the total quality program, the new role for the district operations councils is to improve service quality, maximize revenues, and control costs. Legislative and regulatory concerns became secondary; coordination of community activities was discontinued. Councils took responsibility for initiating quality action teams to solve particular problems or initiate workplace innovations such as self-managed teams. Newly revised customer service reports provided data at the local level, rather than at the state level as had previously occurred. While the district operations councils still do not constitute profit centers, they come much closer to the concept of cost centers than historically.

Conceptually, this reform represents a change not only from centralized to decentralized, and functional to more collaborative ways of operating, but from a focus on *public* service to *individual customer* service, from actions such as community service that present the collective face of the company, to actions designed to respond to individual customer service requirements or complaints. For middle managers, this requires a shift in skills away from the regulatory environment and toward business, marketing, and human resources management. More importantly, some managers believe the new mission runs counter to the moral and ethical principles on which their public service careers were built. This reaction was evident in qualitative interviews with managers as well as in their survey responses; for example, while 86% of all managers said their work gave them a sense of accomplishment, only 40% agreed with top management's strategic direction for the company; and only 29% said that their values were similar to those of the company.

Another dimension of change was the inclusion of local union presidents in the district operations councils. In order to gain union support for the quality program, top management negotiated a multitiered partnership structure with the regional union leadership, and then mandated that all middle managers should work with their local union counterparts. This design was to overcome the historic problem that one top manager described, "We always seem to jump over the middle manager." While some local presidents had begun participating in that portion of the council meetings pertaining to the joint Quality of Worklife program, the new mandate was for them to participate in the regular monthly business meetings of the district council.

The responses of middle and lower level managers to survey questions concerning the changing nature of their jobs and skills is consistent with much of the above description of organizational change[6] (see Table 3-3). The overall picture that emerges from survey data is of managers in the midst of a transition to a more decentralized and participatory culture along some dimensions of work, but constrained and frustrated by top management decisions with respect to cost cutting and downsizing.

Ninety-three percent of all managers said the skills needed for their jobs were changing, but the kinds of new skills varied significantly by managerial level. Over 60% of lower-level managers in customer services cited technical (computer) skills as the most important new ones, whereas 75% of middle managers cited "soft" skills in leadership, general management, quality, and labor relations. The pattern was similar but less pronounced in network, where 53% of lower managers ranked new technical skills in first place and 60% of middle managers ranked soft skills as the critical new ones.[7]

With respect to the decentralization of decision making, the evidence shows that middle and lower level managers are experiencing more discretion, but diffusion is uneven. On the one hand, over 55% of all managers said that their discretion to make decisions to meet customer needs had increased in the last two years; and consistent with this pattern, a substantial minority (47% of network and 42% of customer services) said that the amount of supervision they receive had decreased in the same period. On the other hand, a majority (53%) also said that bureaucratic rules and procedures continued frequently to obstruct their ability to meet customer needs. Moreover, with respect to changes in control over tasks and work pace, responses were relatively evenly divided between those who experienced greater control, less control, and no change.

Surprisingly, however, and contrary to the image that exists of managers in a large bureaucracy with little discretion over their jobs, 59% of all managers said they had complete or "a lot" of control over the tasks, procedures, and pace of their work, and these responses did not vary significantly by department. This is surprising because historically customer service jobs are viewed as more con-

Table 3-3. Managerial Perceptions of Changing Participation and Discretion

Job Dimension	All line managers	All network managers	All customer service managers
	(% of positive responses to questions)		
Middle managers:[a]	N = 41	N = 31	N = 10
Have substantial control over*			
Quality programs	82	79	84
Labor relations	76	75	77
Training	64	71	58
Capital allocations	54	43	61
Have *increased* control over**			
Training	20	21	19
Quality programs	60	63	58
Labor relations	47	42	52
Have *decreased* control over**			
Capital budget	57	57	55
Lower-level managers:[b]	N = 290	N = 199	N = 91
Have susbstantial control over*			
Tasks	59	59	58
Procedures	58	57	61
Pace of work	59	58	62
Have *increased* control over**			
Customer service	56	56	55
Tasks	34	34	27
Pace of work	29	30	25
Middle and lower managers	N = 331	N = 230	N = 101
Have participated in**			
Quality teams	46	45	48
Crossfunctional teams	44	44	46
Problemsolving teams	51	49	55
QWL teams	28	26	35
Support use of SMTs**	72	68	85
Support union participation:**			
In total quality	92	92	93

*% of positive responses to yes/no question.
**% of positive responses to question (1–2 on 5-point scale).
[a]Third level managers
[b]First and second level managers

strained and easily regulated than network jobs that are more widely decentralized and require flexibility to respond to the local outside network environment. While this difference may exist among frontline workers, it does not seem to carry over into lower and middle level managerial jobs.

The evolution of a more participatory culture is also evident: three-quarters of the managers surveyed had participated in at least one form of collaborative or problem-solving team: quality action, QWL, cross-functional, or problem-solving team; 10% had participated in all four. Participation, however, increased by management level, even after controlling for tenure. In other words, although there is a growing collaborative or participative culture, it is more available to those higher up in management. These patterns did not vary significantly by department. The differences in participation rates across levels of management are reflected in different levels of satisfaction expressed by managers concerning their involvement in decision making: whereas 72% of middle managers in network were satisfied with their participation, only 55% of lower managers were satisfied. The pattern is similar in customer services, although the overall rates of satisfaction are higher. In sum, managers show great interest in increased decision-making responsibility.

They are also highly supportive of the new partnership with the union, contrary to the conventional wisdom concerning middle management resistance to labor-management participation. Ninety-two percent of all managers said they supported union participation in total quality, 86% said it was critical to the success of total quality, and 75% said it was necessary for the success of self-managed teams. Over 90% of district managers said that local union presidents participated in monthly district council meetings; and 53% also invited them to regular staff meetings.

Among middle-level managers at the district level, evidence of increased discretion is mixed. On the one hand, they indicate they have considerable (complete or a lot of) control over decisions regarding quality (82%), human resources practices such as training beyond what is required by the company (64%), and industrial relations (76%). A majority (60%) say that their control over quality has increased over the last two years, and a substantial minority (47%) also note an increase in their authority over labor relations matters. On the other hand, in network where district-level managers are responsible for managing their capital budget, the majority (57%) say they have only some or little control over these budgets and 57% say that this control has declined in the last two years. Many of these managers experienced cuts in their capital and training budgets in 1993 and 1994. Some are resentful and view their budget cuts as financing investments on the nonregulated side of the business.

For the majority of managers at all levels, downsizing has had a significant effect on workloads and staffing levels. Ninety-three percent of all managers said their workload had increased over the last two years, and this response did not vary significantly by department or managerial level. Sixty-three percent of all managers (68% of network and 52% of customer services) said they worked 10 hours or more each day, and over 60% said they had more overtime or take-home work than they wanted. Sixty percent (64% in network and 51% in customer services) said they were always or quite frequently understaffed. These higher workloads are reflected in increased spans of control. Seventy-two percent of all managers say that their span of control has increased, with a significantly greater percentage (82%) in customer services than in network (67%). Almost 40% of those with enlarged spans of control now supervise 3 to 5 additional workers; another 37% manage between 6 and 15 additional workers. Traditionally, the standard size of work groups in network was 6 workers, and in customer services, 10 (see Table 3-4).

Changing Internal Labor Markets

Downsizing has also, at least during this period of transition, reduced overall mobility throughout management. Although job ladders on paper have not changed, movement has halted. In 1990, for example, approximately 5% of managers were promoted to higher pay grades, a fraction of what existed in the 1950s through 1970s when Howard and Bray did their study. Moreover, approximately the same number of managers were promoted in 1990 as in 1991–93 combined; and the very small number of new managers hired from the outside in 1990 was still over twice the combined total of new hires for 1991–93. Gender-based occupational segregation has historically reduced lateral mobility and continues to do so: while 31% of the managers in the sample were female, they were concentrated in customer services (71% female) and underrepresented in network (14%).

Interviews with managers indicate that downsizing also reduces requests for lateral transfers: managers don't want to risk losing their "sponsorship" and joining a new department where they will be the new person, a relative unknown to a new supervisor who will evaluate them. Interviewees also related stories of managers reluctant to take advantage of opportunities for midcareer educational programs or international experience for fear that ("out of sight, out of mind") their departments would have learned that they were dispensable, their jobs would have been eliminated, and they would face less attractive job prospects or the necessity to relocate in order to have a job at all. In response to survey questions, 92% of managers said job security had decreased, 89% said that opportunities for promotion had declined, 80% said that opportunities for mobility had decreased. A large minority (38%) said they had had to relocate in the past three years as a result of organizational restructuring.

Finally, the company introduced a new managerial performance evaluation and compensation system that ties jobs more closely to external market conditions and links pay to performance. It reduces managerial job classifications from 3,600 to 2,000, largely by eliminating departmental distinctions and creating short descriptions of broad responsibilities rather than detailed lists of specific tasks. The new compensation plan shifts from a salary-based plan built around internal equity to a variable-based system linked more closely to the external market. Rather than moving to broadbanding with a number of gradations in each band, the company expanded the number of pay grades from eight to 15, a change that allows the company to more accurately link internal rates with external variation. To promote pay-for-performance, the company moved from more or less across-the-board increases to a forced distribution system. In the past, virtually all managers received a top rating in a three-point scale and, therefore, gained the maximum amount in annual pay raises available. Under the new system, managers receive between 80% and 120% of their grade, but a forced distribution means that supervisors will be forced to differentiate more between high and low performers among their subordinates. In addition, 10% of

Table 3-4. Managerial Perceptions of Workloads and Career Opportunities

Job Dimension	All line managers	All network managers	All customer service managers
	(% of positive responses to questions)		
Middle and lower level managers[a]	N = 331	N = 230	N = 101
Workload has changed:			
Larger span of control**	72	67	82
Work 10+ hours/day	63	68	52
Increased workload**	93	92	97
Too much overtime*	61	60	64
Frequent understaffing*	60	64	51
Opportunities have declined:**			
Vertical promotions	89	92	82
Lateral transfers	80	83	74
Employment security	92	91	93
Have been forced to relocate**	38	41	33

*% of positive responses to question (1–2 on 5-point scale).
**% of positive responses to yes/no question.
[a]First, second, and third level managers

salary continues to be at risk (an innovation since divestiture), with group pay-outs dependent on financial and service performance.

In summary, managers show mixed reactions to the dramatic changes in their jobs and careers. While they like their jobs and the opportunity for greater participation in decision making, they are highly dissatisfied with opportunities for advancement and corporate leadership more generally. Whereas less than 20% are satisfied with their employment security or opportunities for advancement, 78% are satisfied with their jobs and 68% with their participation in decisions. They appear to be a hard-working and reliable workforce. Eighty-four percent reported having zero absences in 1993. Most score high on commitment variables: 61% say they are willing to work harder for the company, 60% say they are proud to work for the company, and 56% say they are loyal. By contrast, they see a gap between themselves and top management. Only 31% agree with top management's resource allocation decisions, only 29% believe top management is committed to quality, and only 19% think that top management considers employee interests in making organizational decisions. In other words, while they feel committed to the organization, they are critical of top management's commitment to them (see Table 3-5).

Conclusions: Implications for Internal Labor Market Theory

Managers in the old Bell system grew up in internal labor markets that closely resembled the classic industrial ladders described by Doeringer and Piore (1971).

Table 3-5. Managerial Perceptions: Satisfaction, Commitment, Attitudes Toward Top Management

Job Dimension	All line managers	All network managers	All customer service managers
	(% of positive responses to questions)		
Middle and lower managers	N = 331	N = 230	N = 101
Are satisfied with:*			
Participation in decisions	68	65	75
Job	78	77	80
Sense of accomplishment	86	83	90
Job's use of skills	81	79	86
Career opportunities	17	12	28
Benefits	73	66	92
Pay	83	77	97
Company	70	64	94
Are committed to company:**			
Willing to work harder for company	61	56	72
Are proud to work for company	60	53	74
Feel loyal to company	56	52	66
Had zero absences in 1993	84	87	78
Have similar values	29	24	44
Are satisfied with top management:*			
Strategic direction	40	31	58
Resource allocation	31	22	53
Commitment to quality	29	26	38
Consideration of employees	19	15	28
Demographics:			
% Female	31	14	71
% White	88	92	77
% age 41–50	63	58	73
Education: means	Some college	Some college	Some college
Tenure: 21 years or more	77	80	67

*% of positive responses to question (1–2 on 5-point scale).
**% of positive responses to yes/no question.

Companies are in the midst of redefining those markets to simulate external marketlike conditions in an enterprise culture. A useful framework for comparing the past and future models is along four critical dimensions: job definition, deployment, employment security, and wage rules (Osterman, 1987, 1988). This comparison is outlined in Table 3-6. In the past, jobs were defined narrowly and functionally; managers had a small span of control and limited discretion. Technical skills were emphasized, and lower and middle level managerial jobs focused

Table 3-6. Implications of Organizational Change for Managerial Internal Labor Markets (ILMs)

Components	Old ILM	New ILM
Job definition	Rigidly defined, narrowly functional	Broader, cross-functional
Span of control	1:6	1:15–30
Discretion	Very limited	Greater in areas of customer service, HRM/IR
Skill requirements	Specific functional and technical	Technical plus general management, leadership, HR/IR
Training: Lower/middle	Company provided technical training plus college tuition	Company provided technical training plus quality, business, leadership training; tuition aid
Training: Upper	Company paid executive education	Company paid executive education; more stress on finance, marketing, industry analysis
Deployment	Internal recruitment	Internal & external recruitment
Internal mobility	High: nonmanager to mid-manager 1st level to top-manager	Low: nonmanager to 1st level 1st level to midlevel
	Vertical/functional	More lateral, external: "forced lateral transfers"
	High occupational segregation by gender	High occupational segregation by gender
Employment security	Cradle to grave	Contingent on skill and performance
Wage rules	Salary-based + automatic annual raise	Variable-based + 10% at risk + contingent raise

heavily on monitoring workers and reporting up the chain of command. A commitment to internal recruitment shaped deployment strategies, and vertical mobility was high: nonmanagerial workers could aspire to lower and middle level positions; college-educated recruits to first-level supervisory positions could count on long careers in middle and top management. Company-provided training was of high quality, and company-paid tuition supported college education for managerial advancement. Wages and benefits were generous.

Under the new system, lower and middle level managerial jobs are broader, focused on providing quality service, and intended to involve more cross-functional collaboration. Spans of control are double or triple what they were in the past, allowing managers less time for traditional supervisory tasks. While self-managed teams absorb some supervisory functions, electronic tracking replaces manual reporting. The evolution to a new coordinating or coaching role has been identified as a significant change by researchers studying firstline supervisors in other contexts (Manz and Sims, 1987; Schlesinger and Klein, 1987; Klein, 1988). In this sense, the job of first-line supervisors stands to be enhanced, but the ranks will be pared down. For middle managers, greater discretion is occurring in some areas (notably in customer service, quality, human resources management, and industrial relations), but not others (control over resource allocation).

Training systems for managers, already quite developed and well funded in the old Bell system, do not appear to be undergoing dramatic change. Changes appear to be more in the thrust of training in new areas such as knowledge of business, marketing, and the industry; and management and leadership skills. There are much greater changes in deployment: in the greater use of external recruitment for middle and upper management positions and in the decline in vertical mobility. While the notion exists that more lateral mobility will occur across the organization, current downsizing has dampened most movement over-all, and it is unclear how long this will continue. The radical departure from the past is in what may be termed "forced lateral movement"—either due to consolidations and relocations of offices or transfers to other nonregulated growth subsidiaries as a means of ensuring continued employment. Continuity with the past exists in continued high levels of occupational segregation by gender. Employment security is now contingent on skill and performance; wage rules create variable rather than fixed pay and income security.

What is the significance of these changes for firms and managers? Do these new practices achieve the goal of creating an enterprise culture that is more suited to new competitive markets? The long, vertical career ladders of the past created two central benefits: first, they preserved the skill base in the industry through continuity in the training and development of technicians and professionals; second, they built loyalty and commitment through job and income security. They sacrificed creativity and breadth. Companies are attempting to undo the worst excesses of bureaucratic behavior by altering internal labor market rules to favor an enterprise culture. While gaining participation they may be losing the goodwill of managers.

One of the effects of the new enterprise culture is to create a new cleavage—between lower and middle managers on the one hand and top management on the other. Other researchers have noted the contradiction in constraints imposed by top management in the context of also promoting "entrepreneurialism" (Donaldson, 1985). Researchers studying the restructuring of British Telecom also found evidence of this contradiction: the devolution of authority to middle managers turned out to be more rhetoric than reality and created high expectations among middle managers who were subsequently demoralized when the reality turned out to be far less than that promised (Colling and Ferner, 1992). Middle managers in the old Bell system companies talk openly of their resentment toward top management—who on the one hand ask middle managers to be more committed and creative than ever in improving quality and customer service; but on the other hand, who cut the resources needed for these managers to accomplish this goal. On the one hand, middle managers say they are told they have new power to make quality improvements in work processes; on the other hand, companywide reengineering teams announce process changes without the input of middle and lower managers. On the one hand, middle managers are told to create an ongoing learning organization; on the other hand, they have no certainty that they will lead those organizations in the near future.

The extent to which these contradictions undermine quality improvements or firm competitiveness remains to be seen, as does the extent of change in internal labor markets that actually occurs. While company policies governing internal labor markets have changed, actual changes in practice are lagging. The regional Bell companies, for example, have been slow to implement forced separations even when they have been officially announced. While external recruitment is occurring to a greater extent than in the past, these companies will maintain a strong commitment to internal promotions. While new performance management systems have been announced, the systems of the past were intended to differentiate "higher" and "lower" performing employees, but as implemented did not. Changes in job design and human resources policies are difficult to implement because their implementation often depends on managers who stand to lose in the process. Thus, this study captures organizations in the midst of transition, but the end point is still unclear; and it may fall far short of the lean and nimble entrepreneurial player that is envisioned in current management theory.

Notes

This chapter was prepared for the Conference on the Changing Careers of Managers, Sloan School, MIT, July 20–21, 1994.

1. Interview with labor relations manager, regional Bell operating company, August 11, 1993.

2. Company-paid dues to such organizations totaled $4.8 million between 1924 and 1935 (Danielian, 1939, p. 284). In a speech at a Bell system conference in 1921, for example, then president of AT&T Thayer stated: "Membership in such organizations as the United States Chamber of Commerce, National Labor Organizations and National Farmers Organizations, etc., local Chambers of Commerce, Rotary Clubs, etc., and civic organizations of every description, improvement societies, neighborhood groups, church clubs, consumers' leagues, etc. afford unusual opportunities for establishing contacts with the leaders in general public activities and those who are molding public sentiment" (Danielian, 1939, p. 285–286).

3. Jeff Keefe, personal communication, August 15, 1994.

4. It should be noted that this survey was conducted in 1994 when "involuntary separations" of managers had been announced, but not yet implemented. Anecdotal evidence in 1996, with the company in the midst of major downsizing and reorganization, suggests that managers' attitudes have deteriorated significantly.

5. Comparing managers who do and do not have direct experience with self-managed teams, 90% of those with experience supported their use; but even among those

without experience, 51% favored them. Asked directly whether self-managed teams undermine the authority of firstline supervisors, 70% of those with experience said rarely or never, compared to 45% of the managers of traditional groups.

6. The data in Tables 3-3, 3-4, and 3-5 consist of 331 line managers in two core departments—network and customer services. About two-thirds of the respondents are from network and one-third from customer services, reflecting the relative size of the workforce in each of these departments. The survey asked three levels of managers in each department (middle, lower middle, and first line) a series of questions concerning changes in the job characteristics, skill requirements, work organization, and human resources practices in the firm.

7. Surprisingly, over 50% of managers said that opportunities for training had not changed, and over 70% said that more training was not a high priority; most managers responded that their training was adequate. Two interpretations are plausible: this may reflect the fact that the old Bell system companies have historically invested heavily in training (historically 3.5% of payroll in this company); alternatively, it may be that managers are reluctant to admit their skill deficiencies.

References

Barnard, Chester. 1946. *The Functions of the Executive.* Cambridge: Harvard University Press.

Beer, M. B., Spector, P. Lawrence, D. Mills, and R. Walton. 1985. *Human Resource Management.* New York: Free Press.

Colling, Trevor, and Anthony Ferner. 1992. "The Limits of Autonomy: Devolution, Line Managers, and Industrial Relations in Privatized Companies," *Journal of Management Studies* 29(2):209–227.

Cowan, Alison Leigh, and James Barron. 1992. "Executives the Economy Left Behind," *New York Times,* November 22 Section 3, page 1.

Danielian, N. R. 1939. *A.T.&T.: The Story of Industrial Conquest.* New York: Vanguard Press.

Doeringer, Peter, and Michael Piore. 1971. *Internal Labor Markets and Manpower Analysis.* Lexington, Mass.: D. C. Heath.

Donaldson, L. 1985. "Entrepreneurship applied to middle management: a caution," *Journal of General Management* 10(4):5–20.

Drucker, Peter. 1967. *The Effective Executive.* New York: Harper & Row.

Drucker, Peter. 1988. "The coming of the new organization," *Harvard Business Review* 66(1):45–53.

Dyer, Lee, ed. 1988. *Human Resource Management: Evolving Roles and Responsibilities.* ASPA/BNA. Washington, D.C.: Bureau of National Affairs.

Fisher, Anne B. 1991. "Morale Crisis: Job satisfaction among middle managers is hitting new lows. What's an employer to do?," *Fortune* (November 18) 70–80.

Fulop, Liz. 1991. "Middle Managers: Victims or Vanguards of the Entrepreneurial Movement?," *Journal of Management Studies* 28(1):25–44.

Gerhart, Barry, George Milkovich, and Brian Murray. 1992. "Pay, Performance, and Participation." In *Research Frontiers in Industrial Relations and Human Resources.* David Lewin, Olivia Mitchell, and Peter Sherer, eds. 193–238. Industrial Relations Research Association Series. Madison, Wis.: IRRA Press.

Goulden, Joseph. 1968. *Monopoly.* New York: G. P. Putnam's Sons.

Hammer, Michael, and James Champy. 1992. *Reengineering Work: A Manifesto for Business Revolution.* New York: Warner Books.

Heckscher, Charles. 1995. *White Collar Blues: Management Loyalties in an Age of Corporate Restructuring.* New York: Basic Books.

Howard, Ann, and Douglas Bray. 1988. *Managerial Lives in Transition: Advancing Age and Changing Times.* New York: Guilford Press.

Kanter, Rosabeth Moss. 1982a. "The Middle Manager as Innovator," *Harvard Business Review* 59 (July–August):95–105.

Kanter, Rosabeth Moss. 1982b. "Power and Entrepreneurship in Action: Corporate Middle Managers." In *Varieties of Work.* P. L. Stewart and M. G. Cantor, eds., Beverly Hills, Calif.: Sage.

Kanter, Rosabeth Moss. 1983. *The Change Master. Innovation for Productivity in the American Corporation.* New York: Simon and Schuster.

Kanter, Rosabeth Moss. 1984. "Variations in Managerial Career Structures in High-Technology Firms: The Impact of Organizational Characteristics on Internal Labor Market Patterns." In *Internal Labor Markets.* Paul Osterman, ed. Cambridge: MIT Press.

Keefe, Jeffrey, and Karen Boroff. 1994. "Telecommunications Labor-Management Relations: One Decade After the AT&T Divestiture." In *Contemporary Collective Bargaining in the Private Sector.* Paula Voos, ed. 1994 IRRA Research Volume. Madison, Wis.: IRRA Press.

Keefe, Jeffrey, and Rosemary Batt. 1996. "United States," in *Telecommunications: Worldwide Restructuring of Work and Employment Relations,* Harry Katz, ed. Ithaca, N.Y.: Cornell University Press. (forthcoming).

Klein, Janice. 1984. "Why supervisors resist employee involvement," *Harvard Business Review* (September–October):87–94.

Klein, Janice. 1988. *The Changing Role of First-Line Supervisors and Middle Managers.* U.S. Department of Labor, Bureau of Labor-Management Relations and Cooperative Programs. BLMR 126.

Kochan, Thomas, Harry Katz, and Robert McKersie. 1986. *The Transformation of American Industrial Relations.* New York: Basic Books.

Kotter, John. 1982. *The General Managers.* New York: Free Press.

Lawler, Edward. 1986. *High Involvement Management.* San Francisco: Jossey-Bass.

Lazear, Edward P. 1992. "Compensation, Productivity, and the New Economics of Personnel." In *Research Frontiers in Industrial Relations and Human Resources.* David Lewin, Olivia Mitchell, and Peter Sherer, eds. 341–380. Industrial Relations Research Association Series. Madison, Wis.: IRRA Press.

Manz, Charles, and Henry Sims. 1987. "Leading Workers to Lead Themselves: The External Leadership of Self-Managing Work Teams," *Administrative Science Quarterly* 32(1):106–129.

Mintzberg, H. 1973. *The Nature of Managerial Work.* New York: Harper and Row.

Osterman, Paul. 1987. "Choice of Employment Systems in Internal Labor Markets," *Industrial Relations* 26(1):46–67.

Osterman, Paul. 1988. *Employment Futures: Reorganization, Dislocation, and Public Policy.* New York and Oxford: Oxford University Press.

Peters, Thomas. 1987. *Thriving on Chaos.* London: Macmillan.

Peters, Thomas, and Nancy Austin. 1985. *A Passion for Excellence.* London: Collins.

Peters, Thomas, and R. H. Waterman. 1982. *In Search of Excellence.* New York: Harper and Row.

Ray, Carol Axtell. 1986. "Corporate Culture: The Last Frontier of Control?" *Journal of Management Studies* 23:3 (May):287–297.

Schacht, John. 1985. *The Making of Telephone Unionism 1920–1947*. New Brunswick, N.J.: Rutgers University Press.

Schlesinger, Leonard, and Janice Klein. 1987. "The first-line supervisor: past, present, and future." In *Handbook of Organizational Behavior*. Jay W. Lorsch, ed., 370–384. Englewood Cliffs, N.J.: Prentice-Hall.

Shuster, Jay, and Patricia Zingheim. 1992. *The New Pay: Linking Employee and Organizational Performance*. Toronto: Maxwell Macmillan Canada.

Tichy, N., C. Fombrun, and M. Devanna. 1982. "Strategic Human Resource Management," *Sloan Management Review* 2:47–61.

U.S. Department of Labor. 1990. *Outlook for Technology and Labor in Telephone Communications*. U.S. DOL, Bureau of Labor Statistics. Bulletin 2357.

Waldstein, Louise. 1988. *Service Sector Wages, Productivity, and Job Creation in the US and Other Countries*. Background Paper for Lester Thurow, *Toward a High-Wage, High-Productivity Service Sector*. Washington: Economic Policy Institute.

Walton, Richard. 1985. "From Control to Commitment in the Workplace," *Harvard Business Review*. March–April: 77–84.

Zachery, G. Pascal. 1993. "White-Collar Blues: Like Factory Workers, Professionals Face Loss of Jobs to Foreigners," *Wall Street Journal*, March 17, p. 1.

Automotive White-Collar | 4

The Changing Status and Roles of Salaried Employees in the North American Auto Industry

JOHN PAUL MACDUFFIE

The General Motors Corporation, acknowledging unrest among salaried employees over the erosion of pay and benefits, announced a pay package for them today that aims to match some gains made by hourly employees represented by the United Automobile Workers union. (*New York Times,* November 12, 1993)

An agreement between UAW Local 160 and GM sent 3,500 employees of GM's Technical Center back to the job following a five-day strike. The pact calls for limits on GM's use of outside contractors in designing parts. An eight-day strike by 850 employees at Chrysler's Technology Center, over similar issues, also ended. (*Automotive News,* June 13, 1994)

At Ford, salaried workers hired after November 1, 1988 must pay for part of their health care coverage, unlike UAW members or salaried workers with more seniority. To keep pace with the company's rising health care costs, those contributions will rise up to 7 percent in 1994. . . . About 25 percent of salaried workers fall into this category. (*New York Times,* November 13, 1993)

At Chrysler, there are now 50 workers to every manager. Ten years ago, that number was 20; soon, says the company, it will be 100. (*Financial Times,* May 11, 1994)

These headlines tell the story of unsettling change for the white-collar employees of the U.S. automotive industry.[1] The middle managers, corporate and divisional staff, engineers, clerical employees and firstline supervisors at General Motors, Ford, and Chrysler now find themselves affected by all of the woes commonly associated with blue-collar production workers—layoffs, outsourcing of work, concessions in pay and benefits, and redundancies due to the reorganization of work for greater efficiency. Indeed, in the early 1990s, some of these white-collar employees found themselves worse off than hourly employees represented by the

United Automobile Workers (UAW), with pay freezes, required co-payments for medical benefits, and less job security. Besides the erosion of status this implies, white-collar employees also face many new demands in their jobs, including more work, more decision-making responsibility, more cross-functional interaction, and more of a support role vis-à-vis blue-collar workers.

These developments are the consequences of two profound changes sweeping the North American auto industry that began in the 1980s: (1) the dramatic restructuring of the U.S. "Big Three" auto companies following major losses in market share to foreign competitors, and (2) the diffusion of "lean production" methods in North America, first in new Japanese-owned "transplants" and subsequently in new and existing plants of General Motors, Ford, and Chrysler. These changes are linked, since the competitive crisis of the Big Three revealed the limitations of the mass production model that had been dominant for most of this century, while the success of the Japanese transplants—operating with American managers, engineers, and workers—revealed that lean production was indeed transferable to very different cultural contexts. Thus, the painful restructuring in this industry has been driven as much by the transition to a new production paradigm that organizes work very differently as by the need for cost reduction and for smaller, more responsive corporate bureaucracies.

Much of the attention given to these changes has focused on the implications for blue-collar production workers, given the high number of plant closures and layoffs affecting this group, the labor-management dynamics involved in negotiating new policies to deal with such dramatic downsizing, and the societal implications of losing high-paying manufacturing jobs that once provided a ready path into the middle class. Furthermore, lean production makes production workers much more central to the production process than does traditional mass production.

This chapter will argue that the impact of these changes on white-collar employees has been just as profound. Restructuring in the auto industry has not only resulted in large-scale reductions in white-collar jobs, the removal of organizational layers, and the dissolution of the implicit lifetime employment contract—the litany familiar from many industries in recent years. The move toward a new production paradigm, still in process, has forced a redefinition of roles and responsibilities for white-collar employees and a rethinking of career paths and reward systems. These changes are important because U.S. auto companies—particularly General Motors under Alfred Sloan—provided the model for managerial employment and careers in large corporations in the postwar era, just as they shaped our ideas about blue-collar manufacturing employment.

The chapter is organized into six sections. The first section examines changes in employment levels at the Big Three over the past 15 years (1979–94), a period when each company experienced one or more serious competitive crises as well as the customary cyclicality of this industry. The section explains the patterns of employment reductions for hourly (blue-collar) and salaried (white-collar) employees at each company in relation to changes in vehicle sales and market share. Two kinds of restructuring are studied: one that results from shrinking a company to adjust to reduced sales and production volume, and one that results from rethinking more fundamentally how the core work tasks of the company should be organized and carried out. This sets the stage, in subsequent sections, for examining the various forces that lie behind these two types of restructuring and the consequences for white-collar employees.

The second section focuses on the innovative policies and practices implemented at General Motors by Alfred Sloan between 1920 and 1950, which established the dominant model for all the American auto companies and remained virtually unchanged at GM until the 1970s. The section will show that the evolution of white-collar employment practices was heavily influenced by policies developed for two other employee groups—top executives and blue-collar workers. The third section analyzes the unraveling of the GM model in the 1980s and 1990s, emphasizing both its internal problems and its inadequacy with respect to the changing competitive situation.

The fourth section explores how the shift from mass production to lean production promises to change the work of managers and engineers, drawing on both literature and field work observations from Japanese transplants in the United States to sketch out "ideal type" differences in managerial and engineering work between these two production paradigms. The fifth section considers the Big Three automakers separately and the extent to which, by the mid-1990s, managerial and engineering work at each company reflects the influence of lean production ideas. While there are some common trends across the Big Three, each company stands at a different point in the transition process from mass to lean production. The last section offers speculative thoughts on future developments for white-collar work in the U.S. auto industry, and whether this industry will continue to be a bellwether with a strong influence on other industries.

Restructuring at the Big Three, 1979–94

Employment reductions at the Big Three auto companies are amply documented in the business press but in piecemeal fashion. It is difficult to tell from these individual stories, often focused on announcements of planned cutbacks or particular short-term downsizing initiatives, what exactly the long-term trends have been or whether consistent definitions are being used. Data about hourly and salaried employees, as well as U.S. sales and market share, gathered from annual reports and other sources for the period 1979 to 1994,[2] provide a more accurate picture of white-collar and blue-collar reductions in relation to market conditions for the Big Three.

Three time periods within this 15-year span are examined: 1979–86; 1986–91; and 1991–94. In addition, the data are also aggregated into two longer periods: 1986–94 and 1979–94. The year 1979 marks the beginning of a severe recession in the U.S. industry and a serious competitive crisis for Chrysler and Ford that continued into the early 1980s, while 1986 represents the peak of the market cycle and the high point in Big Three sales during the 1980s. 1991 reflects the lowest point in the next major downturn in the U.S. market and a time of dramatic losses for GM and (to a lesser extent) Ford and Chrysler, while 1994 provides the most recently available data and chronicles the resurgence of the Big Three in sales and market share. Thus these subperiods serve to sketch out the recent history of the Big Three, including high and low points in the business cycle and ups and downs in their competitive success.

These data are presented in various ways. Figure 4-1 shows annual employment levels for hourly and salaried employees from 1979 to 1994 for each of the Big Three companies. These are plotted separately to reveal the changes over time more clearly for each company and because the data are not strictly comparable across companies (see note 2). Figure 4-2 shows U.S. sales data for cars and trucks over the same period, again plotted by company, while Figure 4-3 shows the trends in market share across the Big Three. Finally, Figure 4-4 examines reductions (in percentage terms) in all of these areas—hourly and salaried employment, U.S. sales, and market share—for the various time periods defined above. Bear in mind in the graphs in Figure 4-4 that positive quantities (e.g., bars extending above the x axis) show *percentage reductions,* while negative quantities (e.g., bars extending below the x axis) indicate *percentage growth* in employment, sales, or market share.

Reductions in Employment Levels, U.S. Sales and Market Share

It is worth noting, in Figure 4-1, the magnitude of the employment reductions shown here: ranging from 26% to 51% for hourly employees from 1979 to 1994 and from 31% to 49% for salaried employees. For General Motors, where the largest reductions took place, these percentages apply to employment levels in the base year of 1979 of 510,000 hourly workers and about 127,000 salaried employees, or an overall reduction from 637,000 U.S. employees to about 315,000. At Ford (where by 1994, hiring had begun an upswing), net employment dropped from roughly 245,000 to around 165,000, a reduction of 80,000 employees, while Chrysler (also hiring again by 1994) experienced a 15-year net reduction of around 30,000 employees, from nearly 110,000 employees to around 80,000. Figures 4-2 and 4-3 reveal the cyclicality of automotive sales in the United States and the major loss of sales and market share for GM (and gain for Ford and Chrysler) during this 15-year period.

Figure 4-4 shows the analysis of the various subperiods defined above. In the first period of 1979 to 1986, there are common patterns in the data across companies. For GM and Ford, employment cuts from 1979 to 1986 were heavily concentrated among hourly employees, with reductions for this group at both companies that were 30% to 50% higher than for salaried employees. The fact that these reductions were nearly twice as high, in percentage terms, for Ford than for GM (for both employee groups) is testimony to how much more severe Ford's competitiveness crisis was in the early 1980s. In contrast to GM and Ford, Chrysler's even more severe crisis of the early 1980s forced reductions in salaried ranks that were nearly as high as the 21% reduction in hourly ranks.

Note, however, that GM's modest reductions of 13–17% in this period occurred during a time when its market share dropped by nearly 17%. (GM's drop in sales is much less because 1986 was a peak year in the business cycle.) In contrast, Ford's much larger reductions accompanied a much smaller drop of 5% in market share. And Chrysler's net reductions over this period occurred despite a massive growth in both its sales and market share.[3]

This period reveals the extent to which the first reaction of auto industry managers to recession and competitive pressures during the early 1980s was cutting back on hourly (rather than salaried) employment levels. This was true despite the fact that 1986, the end point of this period, was a boom year, in terms of production and sales, which should have boosted direct labor employment (which is more volume-dependent) more than the overhead-related employment of managers, engineers, and staff.

In contrast, the next five-year period (1986 to 1991), from a market peak to a market valley, reveals a different pattern. At GM, hourly employment reductions still predominated (28%) but were more nearly matched by salaried employment reductions (25%). However, sales dropped by an even higher percentage (31%) during this time and GM lost another four percentage points in market share, a decline of 10%. In contrast, Ford turned its attention to salaried employment reductions (21%) that were more than twice as high as the amount of hourly reductions (11%). Ford's sales also decline during this period (16%), following the business cycle, but its market share gained two percentage points, a growth rate of nearly 10%. Finally, Chrysler resumed making reductions in both hourly and salaried employment (around 20% for each group) after its big upward surge in employment from 1983–86 (see note 3), in line with an abrupt drop (particularly from 1989–91) in both sales (29%) and market share (down one percentage point, for a 7% rate of decline).

During the final period of 1991–94, as the market began to move back up toward another cyclical peak in sales, Ford and Chrysler continued to experience gains in both sales and market share. In response to this achievement (and stretched thin by years of reductions), both companies began hiring again, with Ford boosting both hourly and salaried employment levels by about 7% and Chrysler primarily emphasizing increased hourly employment (up by 15%) while keeping the growth of salaried employment to about 7%. With massive demand for its popular new products and an inability to boost overtime any higher, Chrysler's need for production workers came as no surprise, but its restraint in increasing salaried employment revealed a commitment to avoiding the mistakes of the mid-1980s, when the recovery from near bankruptcy was celebrated with expansive hiring.

At GM in this period, with its market share still plummeting (and a boardroom coup that brought a new management team in 1992), the pace of employment reductions continued apace despite the general upswing in U.S. market demand. For the first time across these time periods, the rate of salaried reductions (21%) exceeded the rate of hourly reductions (18%) as new CEO Jack Smith took aim at GM's massive corporate staff. Also, in an effort to restore GM's traditional practice of conservative accounting practices (and its credibility in the financial community), Smith began including in the annual count of hourly employment those of GM's hourly workers that have been laid off but are still receiving close to full pay due to generous severance arrangements negotiated

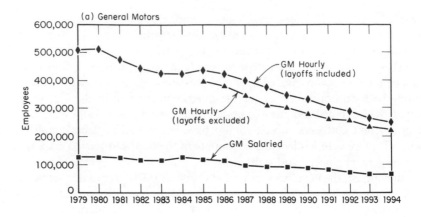

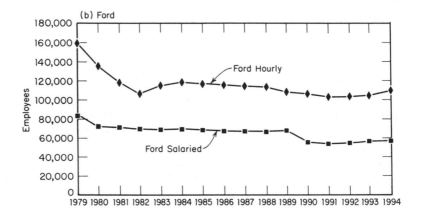

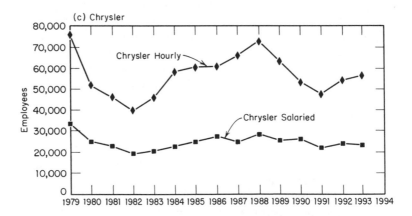

Figure 4-1. Big Three Hourly and Salaried employment, 1979–94.

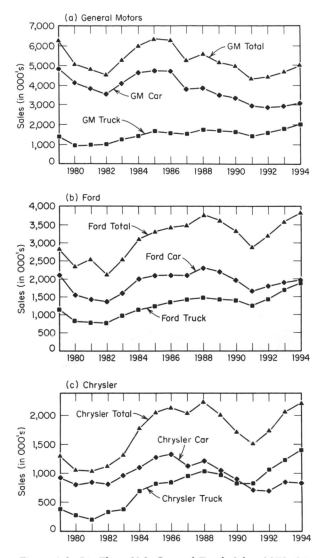

Figure 4-2. Big Three U.S. Car and Truck Sales, 1979–94.

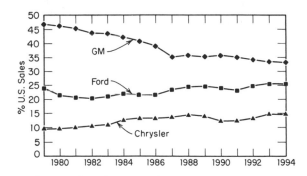

Figure 4-3. Big Three Market Share, Based on U.S. Car and Truck Sales, 1979–94.

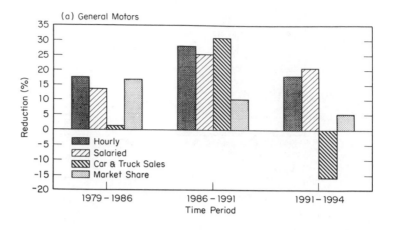

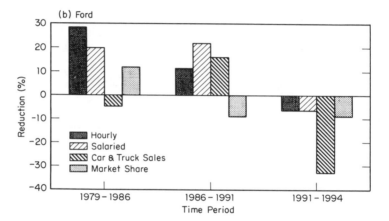

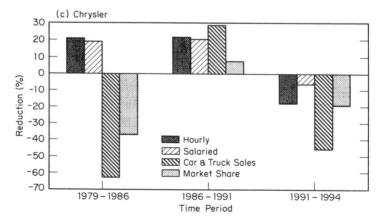

Figure 4-4. Reductions in Employment, Sales, and Market Share, 1979–94.

between the company and the UAW.[4] This broke away from former CEO Roger Smith's practice of excluding these laid-off employees from hourly employment figures from 1985–90, and thereby claiming more extensive and rapid reductions in GM's direct labor costs than were actually realized. This group of hourly employees on layoff is quite large from the mid-1980s on. Figure 4-1 (a) shows that the employment level for GM's hourly employees is 9% to 17% lower when laid-off employees are excluded from the count.

Two Kinds of Restructuring

It is important to recognize how common it has been, historically, in the U.S. automotive industry for hourly employment to rise and fall according to fluctuations in market demand and production levels, with salaried employment generally remaining relatively constant or rising. Prolonged downturns in the business cycle might bring a modest (and generally lagged) reduction in the level of "overhead" employees but this was typically accomplished through hiring freezes and attrition rather than layoffs, and often hiring resumed as soon as sales improved. This is the dominant pattern for the period 1979–86.

What is most *uncommon* is the simultaneous occurrence of major reductions in salaried employment during a time of increasing market share and/or sales. This is the behavior demonstrated by Ford and Chrysler as can be seen in Figure 4-5 (d) for the two aggregated time periods of 1986–94 and 1979–94. Both hourly and salaried employment are falling while sales and market share are rising. Examining the full 15-year period (1979–94) reveals similar percentage reductions for hourly and salaried employment overall, but clearly the past eight years (1986–94) are when the bulk of salaried employment reductions have occurred at these companies.

For General Motors, the pattern is different than for Ford and Chrysler. As shown above, the very large drop in hourly and salaried employment from 1979–91 primarily reflects the shrinkage of the company's sales and market share. Only in the most recent period of 1991–94 do we see any similarities to the Ford and Chrysler trend—reductions continuing strongly even as sales increase and market share, while still declining, does so at a less precipitous rate. Thus in both aggregated time periods (1986–94 and 1979–94), all indicators show reductions.

This analysis thereby reveals two kinds of employment reduction throughout this 15-year period. The first, *volume-reduction restructuring,* is focused primarily on reducing hourly employment and corresponding overhead as necessary due to declining sales and market share. Using this term, rather than the more common phrase "downsizing," acknowledges that a major volume-based decrease in a company's size inevitably results in substantial restructuring in how tasks are allocated and performed, and not simply fewer people in the preexisting organizational structure. The second kind of reduction, *work-redesign restructuring,* involves finding new ways to organize and carry out work tasks, in both hourly and salaried jobs, that are more efficient and require fewer employees. This latter kind of restructuring is different from "reengineering" because it encompasses a broader set of potential work redesign changes—not just the reorganization of

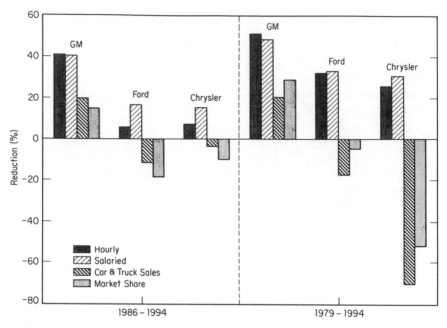

Figure 4-5. Big Three Reductions in Employment, Sales, and Market Share, 1986–94 and 1979–94.

functional responsibilities around business processes, to which the term "reengineering" most often refers. This distinction is similar to that made by Cameron et al. (1993), who differentiate between "workforce reduction" and "organization redesign" strategies for downsizing. These authors also identify a "systemic" strategy that "focuses on changing the organization's culture and the attitudes and values of employees" and "redefines downsizing as a way of life, an ongoing process rather than a program". While some changes in organizational culture have accompanied work redesign restructuring at the Big Three, particularly in recent years, it would be an exaggeration to say that any of these companies had, as of the mid-1990s, comprehensively pursued this "systemic" approach.

Using this terminology, we can see that all of the Big Three automotive companies engaged in volume-reduction restructuring during the 1979–86 period, although Chrysler was forced, by its brush with bankruptcy, to embark on some work-redesign restructuring as well. Chrysler gained relatively little advantage from this experience, however, because when its sales and market share swelled in the mid-1980s, it once again hired extensively. Furthermore, as various accounts suggest (Ingrassia and White, 1994; Keller, 1993), Chrysler managers mostly returned to their old ways during these boom years as senior management became preoccupied with making acquisitions and other peripheral projects. During the 1986–91 period, both Ford and Chrysler, under pressure from another industry downturn and foreign competitors, began more serious and lasting efforts at work-redesign restructuring. Although employment levels are now increasing at Ford and Chrysler, we see some evidence that this work-redesign restructuring is continuing, since increases in salaried employment are being kept low with respect to hourly employment levels, sales growth, and market share growth. At GM, in contrast, most of its substantial employment reductions from 1979–91 must be classified as volume-reduction restructuring. Only in recent years, with a new management team, is substantial work-redesign restructuring going on.[5]

While this characterization of two different kinds of restructuring helps make sense of the Big Three data presented here, it does not tell us what forces for change prompted these restructuring activities and what the consequences of these changes are for white-collar automotive employees. We turn to that task in subsequent sections.

General Motors Under Alfred Sloan: An Organizational Model of White-Collar Employment Practices

General Motors is the appropriate focus for discussing the postwar history of white-collar employees because of its dominance of the industry, not only in market share and profitability but also as an organizational model for other firms. Indeed, the fate of most automotive white-collar employees in the last 50 years has been determined, indirectly, by two important innovations established at GM that primarily affected other employee groups.

First, Alfred Sloan's masterful organizational structure for General Motors, put into place in the 1920s, not only established the multidivisional corporate form that swept American industry but also, by creating a central office of policy-making executives and staff, promoted differential treatment of this top group from other white-collar employees in terms of training, career paths and incentives. Second, the 1948 settlement between GM and the UAW established principles and mechanisms for determining wages and benefits that would not only set the pattern for collective bargaining through most of U.S. heavy industry but was also applied broadly and systematically to automotive white-collar employees.

Between the "bonus-eligible" executives and hourly blue-collar workers lie the bulk of automotive white-collar employees—the so-called "salaried" group that includes middle managers, engineers, technical staff, first-line supervisors, and clerical employees. While salaried employees traditionally enjoyed an implicit contract of employment security and a higher position in the status hierarchy than blue-collar workers, many employment policies for this group were more affected by the corporation's triannual negotiations with the UAW than by the policies devised for the executive group. Thus, the situation for most automotive white-collar employees can be likened to that of a moderately large country with poorly defined borders, whose citizens are heavily influenced by what is happening in two adjoining, powerful neighboring states—one small (top executives) and one large (hourly, unionized employees).

This section emphasizes four aspects of the GM model for white-collar employment practices: (1) organizational structure and staffing requirements; (2) pay and benefits; (3) promotion/career paths; and (4) employment security.

Organizational Structure and Staffing Requirements

Alfred Sloan's innovative move to establish a new organizational structure for General Motors in the 1920s was quickly recognized as a masterful way to manage the huge vertically integrated enterprises that the most successful of the early automotive companies were becoming.[6] Even Ford Motor Company, whose founder Henry Ford deplored Sloan's organizational charts and blend of decentralized operations with centralized control ("there is no bend of mind more dangerous than that described as 'a genius for organization'," Ford, 1926), adopted GM's multidivisional structure in 1946, at the insistence of Henry Ford II.

The most significant structural characteristic in Sloan's plan for GM, from the perspective of white-collar employment policies, was the establishment of a powerful central office with monitoring, control, and coordination responsibilities over decentralized operating divisions. The central office required a different kind of executive manager and new roles for specialized staff, along with different career paths and compensation plans for this elite group. This in turn affected the staffing requirements and responsibilities of white-collar employees in the divisions.

Ernest Dale (1956), an early academic observer of Sloan, argued that Sloan, even more than Frederick Taylor, was a pioneer of scientific management because he developed not just a "scientific methodology" for improving efficiency but also an "administrative ideology" that together constituted a "mental revolution" (p. 52–53). Fundamental to the ideology was the idea that decentralized operations with centralized controls would insure that "freedom and control are closely balanced" (p. 53). This would both inspire individuals with the promise of autonomy and opportunity, Dale argued, and provide an intellectually convincing way to overcome the "problems of diminishing returns from management as size grew" (p. 53).

The accompanying "scientific methodology"—the planning process and administrative framework—required that central management develop short-term and long-term plans for the corporation, assign a role for each division within this plan, and provide staff aid to help divisions meet their goals and to measure the results. The central office would also organize and facilitate cross-divisional "policy groups" to deal with coordination issues for key functions such as design, sales, labor relations, marketing. Division managers, in turn, were given authority to handle production and sales decisions within their divisions, appoint personnel except for top executives; determine factory methods, and handle most purchases.

While Sloan established the structure of decentralized operations and centralized controls, he managed it quite differently than his successors. Dale notes how crucial Sloan's own leadership style was to balancing the power of the new central office and achieving effective coordination.[7] "To devote at least half of his time to personal contact, he passed on detailed planning and coordinating work to his staff. . . . After the new organization was established, he devoted a large part of his time to dealer relationships. Traveling at night, interviewing during the day, he talked to . . . over one hundred dealers on each trip" (p. 47). At meetings of policy groups, "even though Sloan made the final decision, he employed group management in the sense that he relied on research and scientific findings, listened to recommendations, asked questions, might refuse to override the decision of a subordinate . . ." (p. 58).

Yet little of this approach survived beyond Sloan and his associates. Even by 1956, Dale notes that "the present chief executive makes an increasing number of decisions himself—his span of control is greater than that of his predecessors." Also:

> As fact-finding by central bodies tends to cover more and more phases of operations, the work of the division managers tends to become increasingly predetermined, one might almost say predestined. It will be hard to find justification for going contrary to "facts" centrally determined. (p. 58)

These comments foreshadow the difficult dynamics between the central office and the divisions that would plague GM in the 1980s.

Pay and Benefits

For pay and benefits, auto company policies are clearly dichotomized between the contingent compensation offered to the "bonus-eligible" group of top executives and senior professional staff and the pay offered to the remaining group of "salaried" employees. As mentioned above, important elements of the pay for the latter group were for many years determined by the terms of collective bargaining contracts with the UAW.

THE BONUS PLAN.   Both the bonus pay plan for executives and the key features of pay policies for blue-collar employees were first established at General Motors.[8] Sloan (1963) summarizes the key principle of the bonus plan as follows: "the interests of the corporation and its stockholders are best served by making key employees partners in the corporation's prosperity, and each individual should be rewarded in proportion to his contribution to the profit of his own division and of the corporation as a whole" (p. 407). Profits must exceed a certain threshold for bonuses to be paid. A certain percentage of earnings in excess of that threshold, after taxes, goes into the bonus reserve fund. This fund is allocated among three groups: (1) directors of the corporation who are also operating executives; (2) general managers of the divisions and the heads of staff groups; and (3) all remaining eligible employees.

Once the bonus and salary committee of the board of directors makes a recommendation for the first two groups, an allocation is made to the divisions for the third group, based on contribution to corporate performance. Individual bonuses within this third group are based on supervisor evaluation of individual performance. Initially, the criterion for bonus eligibility was an individual's salary, although this was later replaced by a "grade" system that covered all salaried employees; everyone above a certain grade level would be bonus-eligible. From 1923 on, executives were allowed to receive their bonuses in the form of GM stock; most bonuses are part cash and part stock.

The group of bonus-eligible employees expanded with great speed during the years of GM's greatest growth, from 550 in 1922 to 3,000 in 1929 and 9,500 in 1936, based primarily on lowering the salary threshold for eligibility. In 1942, the salary level was adjusted to cut the bonus-eligible group in half, to 4,200, but in 1950, the bonus and salary committee expanded eligibility to anyone earning at least $500 a month, which boosted participation to over 10,000 employees. By 1962, with a similar salary criterion (adjusted for inflation), 14,000 employees were bonus-eligible. The bonus plan remained relatively stable through much of the 1960s and 1970s—a time when most policies established by Sloan were maintained.

THE 1948 UAW WAGE FORMULA.   While the bonus plan solved one incentive problem for General Motors in its early years, the landmark 1948 collective bargaining agreement with the UAW solved another. The immediate postwar years were tumultuous ones for GM and the UAW. Sales surged due to pent-up demand and high economic growth, but labor relations were unsettled as the UAW pressed for large wage increases to make up for a decline in relative wages due to wage controls during the war (Katz, 1985). Long strikes at GM in 1945–46 and at GM and Chrysler in 1947 were fueled by political struggles within the UAW and the CIO and by federal government efforts to establish wage patterns across industries.

The financial cost and instability caused by these strikes prompted GM president Charles Wilson to propose a new labor contract in 1948 involving two innovations: (1) a multiyear duration (first two, then five, and eventually three years) for the contract, with a no-strike agreement during this period; (2) a wage formula, consisting of a cost-of-living allowance (COLA) to be applied each year to adjust for inflation and an annual improvement factor (AIF) to pass on a share of the benefits of technological progress and productivity gains to hourly workers.[9] The UAW accepted this proposal and, more important, the logic behind it.[10]

Inherent in this proposal was the idea that stable and predictable wage increases, even if generous, were preferable to the uncertainty of annual negotiations. In addition, GM managers argued that insuring a steady increase in the standard of living for production workers was one means of boosting purchasing power in the economy as a whole, and thus providing the mass consumption necessary for a mass production industry. These ideas were to prove appealing to companies and unions throughout the economy and formed the basis for subsequent pattern bargaining in the auto industry.

With the combination of COLA and AIF increases in each new contract, hourly pay of UAW members rose slightly more from 1948 to 1981 than what would have been predicted by inflation rate and growth of the U.S. economy. Beginning in the late 1960s and continuing into the early 1980s, this wage formula increased autoworkers' earnings relative to other blue-collar employees (Katz, 1985, p. 17–21).

By 1950, the UAW contract also included company payments of half the cost of health and life insurance benefits, in addition to pension contributions. Virtually every new contract contained further improvements in these benefits, as well as the expansion of employment security guarantees such as Supplemental

Unemployment Benefits (SUB), although the UAW gained more when contract negotiations occurred during peak production years (Katz, 1985).

While the primary motivation for the wage formula was stability in labor relations, GM soon began to grant the same pay increases, annual COLA and AIF adjustments, and fringe benefit improvements to salaried employees not covered by the bonus plan. There appear to be multiple reasons for this decision. First, the industrial relations (IR) department that negotiated with the UAW was combined with the personnel department, which had nominal responsibility for salaried employees, and IR staff far outweighed the personnel staff in both numbers and internal influence (Kanter, 1983). Thus the IR staff may have found that this arrangement perpetuated their control of employment policy. Second, there are obvious administrative efficiencies in providing the same benefits and annual pay increases to both groups of employees. Third, the UAW had some limited success in organizing groups of nonsupervisory technical employees during these years and GM management may have matched UAW contract terms in wages and benefits to eliminate these as possible organizing issues.

Career Paths

GM during the Sloan years was a prominent example of a classic internal labor market. Salaried employees were typically hired directly after completing their education, with many engineers and technical staff graduating from GM's own technical institute and most managers coming from a few Midwestern colleges and business schools. They could expect their career path to be one of steady upward movement through a hierarchy of positions, primarily within the same division. For a subset, this advancement would bring them into the bonus-eligible group, an achievement deliberately laden with great symbolic importance by the corporation.[11]

Two groups faced a somewhat different career path. Young employees being groomed for executive or senior staff positions in the general office were labeled as "high potential" (known around GM as the HI-POTS) and given a succession of short-term assignments (two years or less) throughout the corporation. Although very few young people were allowed into the bonus-eligible group (32 employees under 30 in 1960, dropping to 7–8 since the early 1970s, Keller, 1989), the HI-POTS typically received higher salaries than their peers in the divisions. The finance office in New York became the most prestigious training ground for HI-POTS.[12]

First-line supervisors or foremen represent the other extreme of the career distribution. For many years, this position provided a "port of entry" from blue-collar ranks into the salaried world, although (with rare exceptions) it was the end point of many career paths rather than the beginning. GM's treatment of foremen over the years revealed some mixed messages about their status within the white-collar group. Sloan emphasized GM's strong efforts to keep the morale of this frontline group high, including putting foremen on salary in 1934, adopting a wage rule in 1941 that their salary must be at least 25% higher than the highest-earning hourly workers under their supervision, and, also in the early

1940s, allowing them to receive overtime pay despite their exempt status under the Federal Wage and Hour Law (1963, p. 392).

But Drucker, in 1946, describes the status of foremen at GM as "marginal," heavily dependent on the extent of decentralization. "Wherever decentralization—at least in part—has been made to reach the foreman, he is a junior executive; wherever it has failed to integrate him into management, he is no better than a gang boss" (Drucker, 1972, p. 173). In fact, the reality for first-line supervisors was more complex—held accountable for results (mostly production volume) like other managers yet with negligible influence on managerial decisions, constrained in interactions with workers by the union contract and industrial relations staff, and yet subject to most of the tensions accompanying a culture of adversarial labor relations, as the most visible representative of management.

Employment Security

Employment security for white-collar employees in large U.S. corporations has almost always been implicit, and this is testimony to how fundamental the expectation of long-term employment, from both company and employee, has been. Jacoby points out (1985) that:

> Until the 1910s, American courts interpreted payment of a monthly or yearly salary as evidence that the employer had made an implicit employment commitment for the period of compensation, meaning that the salaried employee could not be dismissed at will. . . . Even low-level salaried employees enjoyed status privileges and had a degree of job security that manual workers lacked. (p. 279)

Although the pay and benefits for most salaried employees of the Big Three owed more to the wage formulas established in UAW contracts, employment security was one benefit that clearly differentiated white-collar from blue-collar positions. The clarity of this distinction was blurred over time, as the UAW made strenuous efforts to achieve more security for its members, first the form of income security (e.g., recall rights after layoffs, Supplemental Unemployment Benefits (SUB)) and eventually employment security based on restricting layoffs (e.g., those due to technological change). All the change lay on the blue-collar side, however. There was no challenge to white-collar employment security until the late 1970s (at Chrysler) and 1980s (at first Ford and then GM).

Furthermore, employment security was more than just another benefit of working for a large and prosperous corporation. As many observers of large U.S. corporations have observed (Whyte, 1956; Mills, 1951; Kanter, 1977), the expectation of a lifetime career provided the basis for strong corporate loyalty and a secure self-identity, influenced by

> mechanisms . . . that created a subtle "psychological" dimension of loyalty: cultural patterns that linked the personality to the company, so that one became an "IBM man" or a "General Motors" man. These mechanisms . . . include policies of frequent geographic transfers, which had the effect of weakening competing ties to other communities and friends; codes of presentation that defined the "right" kind of behavior; rituals of passage that reinforced the com-

pany image; an ideology of being a good "member of the team." (Heckscher, 1995, p. 24)

The tradition of white-collar employment security may have been the key factor in the development of powerful managerial loyalties to the corporate "family." Yet as Heckscher's recent study of middle managers at restructuring corporations reveals, white-collar loyalty can remain strong even when employment security is threatened or disappears altogether, as it did at GM, Ford, and Chrysler in the tumultuous 1980s. Below, we consider the implications of the resilience of corporate loyalty during a time of massive corporate restructuring.

The Unraveling of the GM Model at the Big Three Auto Companies

Since the time when the GM model was dominant, the most visible manifestation of the dramatic changes for white-collar employees at the Big Three is the huge magnitude of the cuts in salaried employment. One reason for these cuts, as noted above, is volume-reduction restructuring associated with the loss of sales and market share. While intensified foreign competition and changing market conditions are factors that help explain the Big Three's market losses, internal management problems and organizational inadequacies were responsible as well. Indeed, many aspects of the GM model for white-collar employment employees either ceased to be effective or diverged from their original intent, thereby contributing to the Big Three's woes—and the unraveling of the GM model—during the 1980s.

Organizational Structure and Staffing Requirements

The tremendous concentration of power in the central office that began under Sloan was accelerated by his successors and eventually became one of the most dysfunctional attributes of GM in the 1980s, as suggested by the following quote from a GM plant manager:

> Unless you're working on the Fourteenth Floor, you have about a zillion bosses. Every small thing requires approval up the line. They have thirteen thousand checkers in this company to make sure things are done right. Hell, they have checkers to check the checkers. It's madness. (Keller, 1993, p. 186)

Similarly, the policy groups or coordinating task forces that Sloan managed so expertly became, according to one GM executive, "the black hole" (Keller, 1993, p. 116) from which decisions never emerged. Former vice chairman Elmer Johnson described one typical example:

> The Product Policy Group (PPG) focuses on such issues as model changeovers, styling, and the capital investments that should be tied into it. There are deep divisions within PPG between the sales people, who fear they can't sell everything, and the financial planners, who are optimistic and want to spread our fixed cost by pushing volume on dealers. The Finance guys always prevail and drive us into an overproduction situation. These are not productive discussions. (Pascale, 1990, p. 240)

The ultimate consequence of Sloan's structure, according to various accounts of GM in the 1970s and 1980s (Wright, 1979; Kanter, 1983; Pascale, 1990; Keller, 1989, 1993), was the transfer of more and more power to the central office and staff over time, resulting in more dependence and defending of turf on the part of the divisions, less effective communication and coordination across divisions, more paralysis of decision making at the center, more evasive action to escape central controls in the decentralized operations, and the addition of more central staff to "check the checkers."

The dynamics of this process were somewhat different at GM than at other auto companies. Ford, with its long history of centralized control before switching to a multidivisional structure in 1946, struggled in the early 1980s with what it called "chimneys"—strong and relatively independent functional organizations (e.g., product design, manufacturing, sales) that struggled incessantly for resources and influence (Pascale, 1990). However, at both Ford and GM, the central office with responsibility for monitoring and control became the ideal location for the finance department to establish tremendous power over all aspects of the business (Halberstam, 1986; Keller, 1989). The privileged group of top executives at both companies, managing "by the numbers" from their offices, grew increasingly out of touch with their own operations, with dealers, with customers, and with the experience of buying, driving, and servicing their own products.

The inexorable buildup of corporate staff over the years at all three auto companies meant that headquarters would become a target of downsizing efforts both in terms of numbers and organizational levels. Corporate staff shrunk by 47% at Ford, nearly more than double the percentage reduction of all salaried employees, during their difficult years in the early 1980s. Jack Smith's most dramatic move at GM in 1992 was to move his office away from the famous "Fourteenth Floor" of the GM Building in Detroit to a modest location at the Technical Center in Warren, Michigan, in the process reducing staff at the central office from 13,500 to 2,500. This was not, in fact, an 80% reduction in the number of staff jobs but mostly a redistribution of responsibilities, since most of these salaried employees were reassigned to jobs in the divisions. Nevertheless, it sent a powerful message about Smith's resolve to eliminate the central office's "check the checkers" role.

Besides the downsizing of corporate staff, the Big Three in the 1980s and 1990s sought a reduction of vertical layers and an increase in horizontal, cross-functional activity. Ford took the first major initiative in this area in 1983 with a Blue Ribbon Committee of top executives that recommended a reduction from five to three layers in Ford's engineering hierarchy (Pascale, 1990). Ford also vastly expanded cross-functional activities at all levels, in an effort to break down the functional chimneys. The much publicized "Team Taurus" included full-time representatives from engineering, manufacturing, and finance and part-time representatives from components groups, purchasing, suppliers, dealers. At the manufacturing plants, subsystem groups brought together management and hourly employees from across departments to discuss all quality problems related to a particular part of the car.

But at GM, the dismal reputation of policy committees and task forces discredited such cross-group structures as a means for solving problems. Instead,

GM undertook a massive reorganization in 1984 to achieve more effective integration across functions, forming two groups of divisions—Buick-Oldsmobile-Cadillac (BOC) and Chevrolet-Pontiac-Canada (CPC), each of which was to oversee all aspects of producing a vehicle, from design through manufacturing through distribution. However, white-collar hiring actually increased immediately after this reorganization as each major group sought to become miniature versions of the old corporate structure. This reorganization is now seen as a failure that increased redundancy and inefficiency in GM's white-collar ranks just as its primary competitors, Ford and Chrysler, were taking the first painful steps towards work-redesign restructuring (Keller, 1989).

The more rapid pace of reduction in white-collar employment under Jack Smith has been accomplished more through the elimination of redundancy and the recentralization of key functions than through the elimination of layers of management. The BOC and CPC organizations have been replaced with one operational entity, North American Operations (NAO); one centralized purchasing group; a Vehicle Launch Center that combines engineering and marketing functions for all car lines; five car groups (large, medium, and small cars; trucks; and Saturn) to coordinate specific development projects; and one components group, Automotive Components Group Worldwide. The corporate staff—a central innovation in Sloan's original design for GM—has been virtually abolished and its functions absorbed in the various new entities.

Pay and Benefits

When the pattern of extending blue-collar bargaining gains automatically to salaried employees began to break down in the 1980s, the stage was set for an unexpected outcome—a decline in pay and benefits for salaried employees relative to both bonus-eligible and blue-collar employees. By 1994, with the Big Three reporting their best sales and profits in years, all three companies—but particularly General Motors—were scrambling to remedy a situation that has prompted serious discontent within white-collar ranks.

By the early 1980s, when GM began to experience financial difficulties, several changes were made to preserve high bonuses for directors and general managers. First, in 1982, the same year that GM sought (and achieved) major pay concessions from the UAW, the minimum threshold of profitability required to pay corporate bonuses was reduced (Kanter, 1983). Second, the number of bonus-eligible employees was reduced to 5,400 by 1982 and even further, to 4,000, by 1987. Third, during Roger Smith's tenure as CEO, accounting changes were regularly used to boost apparent profitability levels. Keller (1993) reports, "Before Smith became chairman in 1980, GM's financial strength was consistently underestimated by conservative accounting. By 1990, GM's liberal accounting policies were often the subject of ridicule in the financial community" (p. 35).

The bonus plan introduced further distortions during the 1980s because so much of GM's profits came from nonautomotive operations. Since these were reflected in corporate profits, directors and general managers continued to receive huge bonuses. Pascale (1990) quotes a GM manager on the situation in 1987, when Roger Smith received a bonus of $2.2 million and hourly and salaried automotive employees received nothing from the corporate profit-sharing plan (described below):

> [Automotive Operations] lost share that year and barely broke even. GM as a corporation reported profits based on: 1) accounting changes; and 2) profits from Electronic Data Systems (EDS) and GM Acceptance Corporation (GMAC) . . . EDS makes money because they charge Automotive Operations exorbitant fees . . . GMAC charges the Automotive Group at market rates to finance cars. Facing the enormous glut of unsold cars that year, the only way we could move them was through discount financing. Our incentives generated a windfall for GMAC. They lent at the full market rate and Automotive Operations made up the difference (since the customer was only paying interest rates of two and half percent). The problem is that these same top executives who were rewarded with bonuses were those responsible for overpricing and overproducing the product. (p. 241)

Thus the bonus plan, which Sloan viewed as critical to the company's success, became, over time, a significant source of inequities, ill will, and "gaming" by top corporate and divisional management seeking to boost their share of the pie. The situation at Ford and Chrysler, while less exaggerated, was similar, since all three companies follow similar bonus policies. While disparities between executive pay and blue-collar wage concessions got the most attention, similar disparities were being created with respect to the vast majority of salaried employees.

Because this system granted virtually automatic pay raises to nearly every GM employee, it came under severe challenge in the early 1980s, when GM was asking UAW workers to make major pay concessions. GM undertook the first of several attempts to replace the use of the blue-collar pattern with a system of merit pay, first by taking funds used for COLA payments for salaried employees and placing them in a merit fund.

Initially, this system shared certain attributes with the executive bonus plan. A fixed sum was allocated for merit rewards in each division each year, and lump-sum payments were made based on individual performance appraisals. Most salaried employees did receive yearly bonuses under this system as supervisors were reluctant to give employees a low rating. Indeed, one indicator of the paternalistic culture surrounding white-collar pay is that the appraisal process did not have a category for "unsatisfactory performance." However, since these lump-sum payments did not increase base pay and since the annual cap kept the size of bonuses small, salaried workers felt disgruntled by the new system.

The 1982 negotiations with the UAW did produce a new profit-sharing plan for hourly employees of the automotive divisions, and this was quickly extended to the non-bonus-eligible salaried employees. However, because only profits from North American automotive operations were included, there were several years when bonus-eligible executives got large bonuses while the profit-sharing plan paid out nothing. GM's profit-sharing plan was least generous of all the Big Three. From 1982 to 1989, the total profit-sharing payments at GM, Ford, and Chrysler were $1,754, $13,365, and $3,752 respectively (Katz and Meltz, 1991).

The next effort to change the pay of salaried employees came in 1987, when vice chairman Elmer Johnson implemented a new pay-for-performance scheme, in which performance appraisals would rank every employee in a given unit from top to bottom, with rankings to determine both layoffs and the size of bonuses. But salaried employees rebelled strongly against this system, challenging the criteria for the rankings, the subjectivity of supervisors, and the fact that only 10% of workers would be allowed to receive bonuses under this system. Within a few years, this system was dropped.

Since then, GM has established a midpoint pay level for categories of jobs, based on wage surveys of other large corporations, and then uses supervisor evaluations to place employees in quartiles above or below this midpoint. But there is no forced ranking system and most experienced employees who are performing well are placed at the midpoint level, so pay outcomes for salaried employees remain relatively undifferentiated.

In the 1992 crisis, one of Jack Smith's first actions was to freeze pay and suspend bonuses for all bonus-eligible and salaried employees. This was an obvious response to GM's staggering losses but was also assumed to have symbolic value in support of a hard-line bargaining position in the company's 1993 negotiations with the UAW. If salaried employees were making such sacrifices, surely GM's blue-collar employees should expect to do the same. While outside observers, including many Wall Street analysts, urged GM to take a hard-line stance with the UAW, Jack Smith was working to reverse the unhappy and adversarial union-management relationship.

When the 1993 negotiations with the UAW concluded, the contract included modest pay raises and the replenishment of funds to support "jobs bank" and SUB benefits. GM (and Ford) moved quickly to offer 5% raises to salaried employees in November, immediately following the approval of the contract by UAW members. The old pattern of replicating the terms of the UAW contract appears to have returned.

Despite the restoration of raises, a sizable number of white-collar employees at the Big Three continue to face co-payments for medical benefits. This marks one of the first times that white-collar benefits have been provided at a lower level than those offered blue-collar workers—primarily because of the UAW's adamant stance against any concessions on the co-payment issue. Big Three management were eager to achieve such concessions in the 1993 contract talks, and clearly recognized that they would have little bargaining room if white-collar employees were not also "sharing the pain" of co-payment. But GM, the initial target of the negotiations, decided to sign a contract that included no co-payment for hourly workers; instead, the UAW agreed to work with the company to establish a managed care plan to cut costs. Ford and Chrysler followed suit, and suddenly a new gap in benefits appeared between white-collar and blue-collar ranks.

The GM and Ford approaches to co-payment differ. Ford has established a two-tier system, with all employees hired since 1988 required to make co-payments. GM, starting in January 1994, established a new plan for white-collar employees that offers the option of either a co-payment of up to $25 a month or no co-payment but much higher deductibles ($2,500 to $5,000). To soothe discontented salaried employees, both GM and Ford restored two benefits established in 1990 that were cut back or eliminated in 1991–92: (1) an annual lump-sum payment of $1,600 for white-collar employees that can be taken either as cash, as investment in a company-run money market account, or as payment towards medical benefits, and (2) a 60-cent match per employee dollar contributed to a 401(k) fund.

Thus, by the mid-1990s, a variety of forces helped reestablish the tight interdependence between white-collar and blue-collar pay and benefits that had been the norm during the postwar years. The damage done by huge disparities in pay between top executives and the bulk of salaried and hourly employees gave rise to a suspension of executive bonuses in years when performance was poor. The failure to find a satisfactory pay-for-performance plan increased the appeal of following the UAW settlement closely, at least to establish the parameters for awarding individual raises. The fact that the dramatic downsizing eroded the economic benefits and status rewards for salaried employees much faster than for either top executives or hourly employees prompted discontent and efforts by the Big Three to close these gaps wherever possible. Just as in the affluent period from the 1950s through the 1970s, salaried employees at the Big Three have undoubtedly found themselves quietly rooting for the UAW to achieve certain gains at the bargaining table.

Career Paths

By the 1970s, changes were underway for the HI-POTS, first-line supervisors, and all other salaried employees. In 1971, GM established a new personnel administration and development department, split off from the industrial relations department in 1971. Stephen Fuller, a Harvard Business School professor, was hired by GM to head this department and implement a fully integrated human resources system. Because the corporate personnel staff had always been weak in comparison with the industrial relations staff, each division's personnel office had developed their own idiosyncratic approach. In many divisions, it was financial staff in the controller's office that oversaw P&S (progression and selection) reviews rather than personnel staff. Fuller had to coax the divisions into returning power over salaried personnel matters to the new department (Kanter, 1983). He also established HRM committees in each unit, headed by its chief executive; developed a corporate HR database to help fill internal positions more effectively; and introduced a consistent method of performance appraisal across the corporation.

By the end of Fuller's 10-year tenure, a "team audit," or shared appraisal system was applied to bonus-eligible managers and these managers were allowed to see their performance appraisals for the first time. Mandatory training for all new first-line supervisors began in 1979, with about 80% of the training oriented toward interpersonal skills. Recruitment efforts at colleges broadened beyond the small number of Michigan schools that had always provided most of the HI-POTS. However, soon after Fuller's departure, many of these policies began to be overturned. Supervisor training was eliminated because of GM's financial woes in 1982. A new policy of using performance appraisals rather than seniority to determine the order of layoffs was abandoned; Kanter (1983) alludes to concerns about white-collar unionization as a possible cause. Nevertheless, the more central role for the personnel department, particularly in matters of performance evaluation and promotions, persisted.

Despite a more systematic and open process for evaluating and promoting employees, the culture surrounding the HI-POTS continued to be a Faustian bargain of extreme loyalty in return for advancement and generous bonuses. Keller (1989) quotes one retired executive:

> The whole system stinks once you're in it. You continue to want to make vertical decisions: "What is it that I should decide that will be good for me. Never make a horizontal decision based on what is good for the company. I want to get promoted."

> So you get promoted because you're sponsored by someone; you get promoted before they catch up with you. I can go through a litany of those clowns. They go from this plant to that complex and then, all of a sudden, they've got plaques all over their walls that say how great they've done—but the plant's falling apart and the division's falling apart. (p. 34)

The rapid movement among jobs for the HI-POTS and the lack of accountability for anything but short-term results sent powerful messages about what was rewarded to all other salaried employees. Other ambitious salaried employees, either bonus-eligible or wanting to be, began to demand the same rapid promotion opportunities as the HI-POTS. In product development, the best young engineers worked for a couple of years on a new project and then moved quickly to the next project, with lower-status successors assigned to finish up the more mundane tasks. According to one young GM engineer:

> No one in a product development group solved all the problems that they knew of. You simply assumed that your replacements would tackle them when you were assigned to another task. It was the way things were done. And that's how cars got into production with so many problems. (Keller, 1993, p. 161)

Plant managers were also changed with great frequency, as the best ones were quickly moved to problem plants, then on to some special project, and finally into some corporate staff position. This rapid turnover was tremendously damaging to efforts to build stronger and less adversarial labor-management relationships at the plant level—not only because of the short-term focus of the plant manager but also because of the disruption of working relationships with union officials each time a change was made. (This problem was compounded by the relatively high turnover of UAW officials in many manufacturing plants, a common occurrence in a union where the norm of challenging incumbents is strongly established.)

For the bulk of salaried employees, the developments in GM's personnel department in the 1970s and 1980s to promote consistent performance appraisals, provide better information about internal job openings, and insure more careful decisions about recruitment and selection, evaluation, promotion, and bonus determination were welcome. But they were overshadowed by the sense of shrinking opportunities, as the bonus-eligible group continued to decrease in size and new merit pay systems allowed for smaller and less predictable pay increases.

For salaried employees at the top of the grade system but precluded from joining the bonus-eligible club, there was little sense that superior performance would (or could) be rewarded. For engineers, the two-track career path—a technical track and a managerial track—established at many corporations already imposed constraints (Bailyn, 1985). Originally developed to offer long-term career opportunities to engineers who did not want to cross over into management, the technical track was typically much shorter, less prestigious, and paid much less well than the managerial track; only those at the very top of the technical track were bonus-eligible. The managerial track, because it involved changing positions every two years, prevented engineers from overseeing technical projects from beginning to end. As fewer and fewer engineers on the managerial track had the opportunity to become bonus-eligible, they too felt the frustration of limited opportunities and inequitable rewards. Against this backdrop, the erosion of employment security—the most basic benefit of white-collar employment—was a strong shock.

Employment Security

As noted above, the implicit assurances of employment security at the Big Three were embedded in paternalistic company cultures that also provided virtually automatic annual pay increases (regardless of performance) and performance evaluations that could never be "unsatisfactory." Yet even after pay and performance appraisal policies began to change, employment security did not appear to be at risk. When Ford decided to eliminate two layers in the engineering hierarchy in 1983, it also identified about 200 middle management positions that could be cut—and then gave these managers four years of transition time to find another position in or out of the company. Otherwise, Ford's 23% cut in salaried head count from 1978 to 1986 was accomplished almost entirely by attrition (Pascale, 1990).

GM introduced its first major early retirement programs in 1986–87, soon after the massive corporate reorganization caused salaried head count to swell rather than to shrink. Management layers were preserved but large numbers of staff participated in voluntary retirement programs. Some former GM engineers were hired by independent consulting companies and then sold their services back to GM, which suddenly found itself short of engineering staff (Keller, 1989). Thus headcount was reduced but total costs for engineering probably increased, although in ways that weren't as visible in the accounting system.

Still, these initial programs did send a shock through a company known for "cradle-to-grave" security—even though GM's wealth allowed it to avoid having to take this step earlier, as Ford and Chrysler had. Since then the wave of cutbacks for salaried employees has come faster and faster, even as the pace of blue-collar cutbacks has slowed and as the UAW has gained further employment security provisions in its 1990 and 1993 contracts. During the cutback of 20,000 salaried jobs between late 1992 and early 1994, early retirement programs accepted employees as young as 51. While these programs were initially voluntary, the most recently announced plan offers "management-initiated" buyouts, meaning that the company selects buyout candidates from a group that meets age and service eligibility requirements. Volunteers who meet the current requirements may request a buyout but management can turn them down. Those who are selected may refuse the buyout but typically they are offered less generous severance arrangements in future programs (*Automotive News,* July 10, 1995).

In one recent situation, white-collar employees have borrowed blue-collar tactics to strengthen their employment security. Unionized technical employees at GM's Technical Center and Chrysler's Advanced Technology Center went on strike in the spring of 1994, following the UAWs new strategy for dealing with the outsourcing of work that can potentially be done by union members. A provision in the 1990 GM-UAW contract stipulated that before work could be outsourced from a Big Three plant, plant management and union officials would be able to prepare a bid to keep the work at the plant. In addition, the UAW has begun to use short, tactical strikes at certain key component and assembly plants to put pressure on Big Three management to bring back outsourced work.

For striking technical employees, the issue was the subcontracting of design work to suppliers and independent engineering firms. (In all likelihood, some of the design consultants are former GM employees, as noted above.) Both GM and Chrysler agreed to limit the use of outside contractors and to provide funding for additional training. GM also agreed to invest $5 million in new equipment and to hire 200 new apprentices, while Chrysler agreed that it would not hire any future outside contractors without the express consent of the UAW.

The long-term significance of this strike is unclear. The percentage of white-collar employees that are unionized at the Big Three is very small. The insecurity and frustration about pay freezes and benefit cuts faced by these employees in recent years—especially at GM—might appear to create conditions ripe for further unionization. Yet this seems unlikely, given the tendency of white-collar employees to identify with management and to view their problems as individual rather than collective, the long tradition of anti-union attitudes among Big Three managerial ranks, and, perhaps most important, the recent economic recovery of the Big Three and quick restoration of pay and benefits.

Underlying the premise that white-collar employees might be drawn toward unionization is the assumption that white-collar loyalty has been severely damaged in recent years. In contrast, Heckscher's study (1995) of middle managers at large U.S. companies undergoing major restructuring (his sample includes GM) finds that many managers have remained remarkably loyal despite the loss of employment security. However, he argues that the resilience of corporate loyalty has not helped, and may indeed have hurt, the ability of companies to respond effectively to a changing competitive environment and their own internal problems. With their internal networks of personal contacts—often crucial to getting things done in the old corporate bureaucracy—torn apart by restructuring, many middle managers cope by focusing ever more narrowly on the tasks most completely under their control. Furthermore, anxiety about possibly being the next to lose their job causes many managers to avoid decisions that appear risky or would make them vulnerable. The combined result, according to Heckscher, is white-collar employees who demonstrate *more* rather than less bureaucratic behavior—

in terms of narrow adherence to prescribed rules and procedures—than in the heyday of the "organization man."

The extent to which Heckscher's scenario applies to the Big Three auto companies is difficult to say. Yet GM, Ford, and Chrysler (along with many other American corporations) are clearly searching for new ways to stimulate the creativity and commitment—and not just the loyalty—of their white-collar employees.

The Changing Work of White-Collar Employees

While volume-reduction restructuring explains some of the dramatic changes in employment policies for automotive white-collar employees, there has been a corresponding major shift in the work performed by auto industry managers and engineers, consistent with the idea of work-redesign restructuring. This section explores those changes at various levels, from basic conceptions of managerial authority and expertise to the way that managers handle information, supervise their subordinates, and coordinate their efforts with managers in other functional groups. The section emphasizes those changes that arise directly from the diffusion of lean production ideas and practices throughout the industry.

Four paradoxical observations about lean production lie at the heart of changes in conceptions of managerial authority and responsibility: (1) Managers are much more exposed to market pressures and customer demands under lean production than under mass production, yet these contingencies are handled in a more systematic and flexible way that actually dampens the impact of market volatility on the production system; (2) Managers are no longer able to devote themselves exclusively to "conceptual" tasks, given the absence of protective buffers that shield them from dealing with "execution" tasks, yet as a result they develop a greater breadth of knowledge about the production system to guide their subordinates in integrative problem solving; (3) Managers are more concerned with the *process* of decision making undertaken by subordinates and are less likely to make substantive decisions by fiat under lean production, yet at the same time, procedures are highly standardized and decisions are much more frequently based on data drawn directly from daily operations; and (4) Managers are forced into much greater interdependence with managers from other functions and even at other companies (e.g., suppliers), yet are able to achieve lower coordination costs and speedier business processes (e.g., "time-to-market" for product development).

In each case, expectations conditioned by the mass production traditions are confounded. Exposing the firm more intensively to market volatility gives it more ability to maintain production stability rather than producing chaos. Shifting some of the "thinking" work from a manager to his or her subordinates increases the ability of managers to "integrate conception and execution" across entire business processes. Focusing more on the process of decision making allows for fact-based rather than imprecise or fuzzy decisions and for dynamic rather than static standardization. Greater interdependence and cross-boundary interaction with other functions ultimately reduces lead times and coordination costs rather than raising them.

"Market-In" and the Cultivation of Flexibility

One commonly observed characteristic of lean production is the deliberate reduction of buffers of all kinds to heighten interdependence within the production system and increase the vulnerability of the system to market fluctuations. While this approach is most notably obvious in the just-in-time inventory system, it reflects a more fundamental philosophy, sometimes called the "market-in" principle (Cole, 1993). Under market-in, the internal operations of an organization are deliberately exposed to the volatility of market demand and complex information provided by customers, in order to force the organization (and its employees) to recognize changes in environmental demands and to develop the flexible capabilities to cope with these changes. The contrast with the buffering approach of mass production—with its assumption that core business processes should be protected from environmental contingencies in order to achieve technical optimization and economies of scale—is striking.

Market-in has strong implications for managerial roles. Large quantities of information about market demand, customer needs and expectations, and other dynamic aspects of the firm's environment (e.g., suppliers, labor markets, regulations) are distributed throughout the organization on a regular basis—both to managers at middle-to-lower levels and to their subordinates. This shifts the managerial role away from being the guardian and steward of internal, functionally specific information. Instead, managers must work with subordinates to interpret and choose appropriate responses to customer (and other environmental) signals. Often these responses require a decentralization of decision-making and problem-solving responsibilities to lower level employees. Cole et al. (1993) note that:

> The heightening of uncertainty associated with this approach is linked directly to the motivational strategy of involving all employees in the change process. The amount of business information on performance and environment that [lean production firms] distribute to employees, including those at lower levels is staggeringly high compared to what occurs at most [mass production] firms. . . . Moreover, [lean production] firms provide the necessary training to insure that employees understand the information being provided . . . and empower employees to act on such information. By providing this framework in which employees are part of the improvement process, fear of changing existing routines is reduced. "Fearlessness" becomes an extraordinary asset as organizational environments become more uncertain in industry after industry. (p. 77)

Market-in also increases the utility for managers of employee involvement, because it helps focus participative activities on important organizational outcomes. Also, by emphasizing customer demands and competitor threats, market-in can reduce internal factionalism and help create a common language of customer needs that allows for better communication across organizational functions and levels. Overall, market-in makes managers dependent on employee involvement in a way they would never be in a buffered organization.

Furthermore, market-in provides incentives for managers to emphasize adaptability and learning as they plan organizational structures and policies,

rather than static optimization. Managers are best able to cope with the unexpected contingencies thrust into the organization through market-in by developing various kinds of flexibility: flexible people (through training for multiskilling
and lateral career paths that expose employees to all aspects of the business);
flexible technology (not only in the technical sense, that is, programmable, but
also in terms of the interface with the organization—the capability for quick
changeovers, rapid debugging of new equipment, and "giving wisdom to the
machine" through improvement activities); flexible scheduling (the ability to shift
either volume or product mix rapidly); and flexible supplier relations (the ability
to carry out effective problem solving related to quality issues across organizational boundaries).

It is often observed that organizational crises have the ability to "unfreeze"
people from their habitual routines and assumptions and permit transformational
change. A crisis resulting from competitive forces (as opposed to purely internal
sources such as a power struggle) can be viewed as an sudden influx of market-in
influences into an organization that has been able, for too long, to shield itself
from realistic appraisal of such information. While such a crisis offers the potential for change, it can just as easily prompt anxiety and rigidity in response to
feeling threatened, and resource constraints and self-protective behavior may
limit change (or make it dysfunctional) as well.

Thus, one way to think of market-in is that it regularly exposes the organization to "mini-crises" and thereby strengthens the capacity to respond to contingencies of all kinds. Market-in provides an organizational analogy to weight
training, which slowly builds up muscle in response to periodic, repetitive experiences of intense stress—or to inoculation with a vaccine that, by exposing the
body to a disease through a small dose, allows antibodies to develop that provide
protection against a full-scale infection.

Relinquishing Functional Expertise To Gain Integrative Expertise

The role of managerial expertise also changes under lean production. To understand this, it is critical to examine the relationship between lean production and
scientific management—particularly since it is scientific management, as a philosophy, that most underlies the mass production conception of what managers
should do. A critical element of scientific management is the separation of conception from execution—managers and engineers do the thinking work and
develop the standards and procedures with which workers are then expected to
comply. Under lean production, the reduction of buffers, the overall increase in
cross-functional and cross-company interdependence, and the emphasis on
shortening product life cycles all require managers to relinquish some "thinking"
work to their subordinates.

Yet this does not lessen the importance of managerial expertise. It means that
managers must develop more integrative expertise across entire business
processes—the ability to understand a business process conceptually but also to
understand the difficulties of execution. Only with such knowledge can managers

help guide the efforts of subordinates to carry out effective cross-boundary problem solving. Subordinates will develop the ability to handle problem-solving tasks that arise within the confines of one function or one part of a business process. But they will need managerial guidance to work effectively to resolve problems that arise from (or affect) other functional areas.

In traditional bureaucratic organizations, expertise has typically been linked to status, authority, rewards, and role clarity. When managers give up their monopoly on expertise and decision-making authority and devolve "thinking" work to employees at lower levels, all of these underpinnings of managerial identity shift (Kanter, 1989). With their specialized expertise either subsumed by subordinates or more open to challenge, managers must find ways to contribute that draw on their broad knowledge of the organization, its products, its suppliers, and its customers. With less ability to command based on positional authority, managers must instead persuade based on their skills in analyzing and interpreting what they learn from their subordinates and from their interactions across functional and company boundaries. Knowing how to guide subordinates as they develop expertise, how to pull together the appropriate people and resources to address various problems, and what balance to strike between autonomy and direction when allowing subordinates to take on "thinking" tasks become important skills for managers under lean production—skills typically learned through experience and observation of senior managers.

"Show-Me-Data" Decisions and the Improvement Cycle

Another set of changes in managerial roles from mass production arises from differences in decision-making and problem-solving processes within lean production companies. First, managerial responsibilities are less clearly delineated. While mass production companies typically attempt to provide clear boundaries separating the authority domains of individual managers, lean production companies prefer overlap and interdependence among managers and engineers, both within and across functional areas. This overlap provides some redundancy in the system that can compensate for the lack of slack in the form of buffers. Such redundancy is often seen as a sign of inefficiency, but it appears to be crucial to other aspects of managerial decision making and problem solving that are demonstrably very effective.

Second, managerial attention under lean production is more focused on the *process* of decision making, both because of overlap and interdependence in managerial responsibilities and the decentralization of responsibility to lower level employees associated with the market-in principle. When managers are not making decisions single-handedly but are dependent on their subordinates and peers to work through problems, their most important role is to monitor the problem-solving process.

Interviews with U.S. executives working for one of the Japanese transplant operations in the United States help clarify this point. One senior American executive told me that

American managers typically think that the authority of a position must be commensurate with its responsibility. Within your realm of responsibility, you have the authority to make decisions. Japanese managers seem to assume much less authority in connection with their responsibilities. What's more important than their authority to decide is who has been consulted during the decision process. When I review a possible decision with my boss, he doesn't seem as interested in the substance as in whom I've talked to. It's as if he assumes that if I've consulted the right people, those who are affected by the decision, that I'll have come up with the best solution to the problem.

Yet this emphasis on information sharing and consensus decision making may give a misleading impression that managers under lean production make decisions amid a "feel-good" climate of cooperation and unanimity. Instead, lean production companies place an extraordinary emphasis on the use of factual material as the basis for problem solving and decision making—as a corrective for the natural tendency of many managers to believe they can correctly identify the source of a problem (and even the best solution) on the basis of past experience. This tendency to rely on gut feelings and intuition is likely to prevail unless strong "show me data" norms exist.[13] Being required to gather data about a problem encourages the consideration of alternatives as to "root cause."[14]

Furthermore, when data are collected by the person closest to the problem, there is a far greater probability that the actual phenomenon underlying the data will be correctly recognized and understood. These data become part of the common language that allows for effective communication across functions and levels in resolving the problem. While data gathering can be mechanistic, the combination of data with a strong narrative about the process of problem solving can be a powerful learning tool. As Robert Cole reports about problem-solving presentations made by various cross-functional task forces in Japanese manufacturing firms:

> these include a history of the problem-solving activity, including a discussion of the blind alleys and failure modes that were pursued. Thus they document a process by which failure and errors are overcome to produce success. In so doing, we see that errors and failures are treated as positive learning experiences. Top management officials, who often attend such sessions, associate themselves with an event in which learning from failure is a key theme. (Cole, 1992, p. 12)

The role of standardization and organizational routines also differs under lean production in ways that affect managerial work. The *kaizen* or "continuous improvement" philosophy—what some (Adler and Clark, 1991) have called adaptive learning—is commonly observed to be central to lean production. Yet, this philosophy is often misunderstood as implying an uninterrupted process of constant change. Tyre and Orlikowski (1993) have usefully challenged this notion of continuous improvement, noting that most adaptive learning follows a "punctuated equilibrium" model—rapid learning immediately after the change is made, followed by a longer period of routinization during which minimal (or no) changes are made. They cite ample literature, and their own findings, to suggest that this is a normal pattern of human and organizational behavior.

Yet, under lean production, this learning cycle changes in one important way: the modification of organizational routines starts anew once standardization is achieved. Indeed, lean production deliberately utilizes organizational mechanisms that *limit* the period of stasis by jarring individuals out of their routines and motivating them to return to experimentation. This different role for standardization in adaptive learning represents another departure from scientific management assumptions (Imai, 1986; Adler and Borys, 1995). While the specification of organizational processes is extremely detailed and thorough, this work is done not by managers and engineers but by lower-level employees. This specification provides a crucial data baseline against which managers and engineers can evaluate the improvement efforts of these employees. It also codifies whatever gains have been made since prior improvement efforts.

Furthermore, the completion of the specification process, rather than fixing a policy or standard operating procedure in stone, becomes a signal that the search for problems or possible performance enhancements can (and should) begin again. Managers and engineers are responsible for reinforcing this approach, insuring that no business process remains static for too long—a difficult but necessary aspect of maintaining organizational flexibility.

The idea that standardization should be the beginning rather than the end of the adaptive learning process is analogous to the use of the term "commencement" to mark the graduation of students from high school or college. It orients employees and the overall organization toward the future rather than the past, and strives to overcome the inertia that can accompany the end of a long and difficult passage by providing a reason to look ahead to the next challenge. Under lean production, managers both promote this philosophy and oversee a concrete process for institutionalizing continual change in some part of the organization.

Tight Coupling and Delay = Coordination Efficiency and Speed

One of the most intriguing paradoxes of lean production is how much more interdependence, or tight coupling, exists between different stages of the production system than under traditional mass production, yet how different the consequences are from conventional wisdom. This paradox is explored here in the context of the product development process to investigate the implications for managers and engineers.

Considerable research on product development has distinguished between mass production's sequential approach and lean production's overlapping problem solving (or concurrent engineering) approach (Clark and Fujimoto, 1993; Nobeoka and Cusumano, 1994). Simply put, mass production product development proceeds in a sequence of discrete stages—product concept, product styling, product design, process development, preproduction, and production. The engineers responsible for each stage complete all of their tasks before handing their work over to the group responsible for the next stage. Generally, upstream decisions constrain the options available in downstream steps, but where a necessary change is discovered at a downstream stage, it may require repeating a substantial portion of the development sequence. In contrast, when utilizing overlapping or concurrent engineering, activities in adjacent stages are carried out simultaneously. Through extensive communication, those working on each stage exchange information about proposed design parameters with their colleagues on an adjoining stage. Both can make progress toward the most mutually beneficial solution without committing themselves irrevocably to one set of design characteristics, until very close to the time of production.

While Japanese companies (particularly Toyota) have pioneered the concurrent engineering approach, which is associated with shorter development times and fewer engineering hours, U.S. and European companies are experimenting with this approach as well. Engineers responsible for different stages of development are typically colocated for ease of communication and communication with suppliers (who are simultaneously developing parts for the new model) is intensive, utilizing many different forms. This approach is said to require managers who are comfortable with uncertainty, able to communicate effectively, and possessing a breadth of technical knowledge that spans product and process development.

While much of the interest in concurrent engineering emphasizes the structure of cross-functional teams, the logistics of colocation, and the authority given to project managers, there are other important differences in the design process that have important implications for managers and engineers. Ward et al. (1995) claim that a set-based design process for product development is "Toyota's second paradox" (just-in-time being the first). For our purposes, the key feature of this process is the effort to develop and continually refine a "map" of the set of feasible design possibilities, while consciously delaying choosing one specific design until as late as possible.

The set of possibilities is defined in part by past experience with the design of certain components or subsystems of the vehicle. At Toyota, engineers put this information in "lessons learned" books that serve as the institutional memory for the product development organization. These books contain technical knowledge derived from previous development projects about individual components as well as the feasible relationships among components from a design and manufacturing point of view. Designers add to these books through their experiments with design prototypes. The process of physically manufacturing the prototypes (many are made) is seen as crucial to what is learned about the "design space"—learning that computer-based simulations of different designs cannot provide.

The "set" is also influenced by the design activities of suppliers. Toyota gathers information and data from suppliers early in the process, uses this to assess what design advances might be possible, then gives suppliers a set of design parameters to explore. As suppliers discover what design alternatives are feasible for their components, they feed this information back to Toyota. Only when the total design space is well understood and key tradeoffs are thoroughly investigated are the defining design decisions (e.g., the "body hard points," which determine the key dimensions of the vehicle shape) made. By overseeing the consultation process, managers can try to insure that the entire "solution space" of possible remedies to a problem is mapped out before deciding which remedy makes most sense in a given situation.

This set-based approach (which can be applied to other decision processes as well) requires patience, trust, and the ability to endure considerable uncertainty. According to one Toyota manager, "the manager's job is to prevent people from making decisions too quickly" (Ward et al., 1995, p. 48). Yet the ultimate goal of this design process is a very short product cycle. So managers must have the ability to move smoothly from the "mapping" stage, when key decisions are delayed, to the implementation stage, which moves very quickly and during which very, very few changes are allowed. The communication necessary for both parts of this process is facilitated by the way in which mapping out the design space provides a common language. Furthermore, exploring sets of design alternatives both requires and builds trust by discouraging the gaming that often occurs in sequential design when upstream and downstream processes both try to limit the flow of information that might constrain their design options.

Changes in Managerial Work at the Big Three
Auto Companies

As the above observations suggest, managers and engineers working under lean production must learn to deal with different approaches to information, authority, expertise, and time. This section considers the extent to which the work of managers and engineers at each of the U.S. Big Three auto companies has actually changed as a result of the influence of the lean production paradigm.

The section begins with overall observations about changes in white-collar work in the U.S. auto industry and then moves to company-specific assessments. First of all, with respect to changes in the division of labor, it is important to recognize how extremely specialized the auto industry has been historically. Piore (1989) writes of the importance of Adam Smith's insight that "the division of labor is limited by the extent of the market." In an industry that has achieved (and been preoccupied with) massive economies of scale, the scope for specialization by the Big Three companies has been very high indeed. Furthermore, while the threshold for minimum economies of scale has dropped, it will always be higher in this industry than in many others where the complexity of the product or process is less. Thus, even where there is a strong impetus to make the division of labor less specialized, the sheer size of most auto companies will make the move away from a highly specialized division of labor for white-collar work extremely slow.

Second, change opportunities have a cyclical quality in the auto industry. The greatest opportunity for change comes when a new product is being designed or introduced into a manufacturing plant. The traditional goal in the auto industry has been to move quickly down the learning curve following such a change and then to maintain stable conditions during the remainder of the life of that product, apart from minor model changes annually. Thus even in a period where there have been considerable pressures for change, change efforts are likely to be concentrated every few years, thus creating a lag between the impetus for change and the implementation opportunity.

Third, generational dynamics within the Big Three may be having an impact on changes in managerial roles. Blue-collar workers at the Big Three have a high average age and seniority, particularly given the reverse seniority rules governing layoffs during the plant closings of recent years. But many are reaching retirement age and given the surge of new car buying in the last few years, the Big Three are hiring for the first time in years. Some observers expect that as many as half of all production workers working for the Big Three in the year 2000 will be new faces. Early evidence from recent hiring suggests that companies are screening carefully and selecting highly educated employees, often college graduates, for these jobs. For example, 25% of the 600 workers hired by Chrysler in 1994 for a new third shift at its Windsor minivan plant have university degrees. Only 2% didn't graduate from high school (*Chicago Tribune,* May 29, 1994).

Senior managers at the Big Three companies clearly see this as a major opportunity for boosting the responsibilities given to production workers, thus increasing span of control and reducing various white-collar staff positions. This is certain to change the roles and responsibilities of the fewer managers who remain. Given that there will be little new hiring of supervisors and middle managers, the new blue-collar workers may have higher education levels than many of their bosses. Presumably, more highly educated production workers will not only be more capable of taking on tasks once done by managers, engineers, and white-collar staff, but they will demand greater responsibility and challenges commensurate with their education. This trend may help boost the influence of lean production ideas in the Big Three companies, but it may also lead to power struggles between "old-time" managers and the new workforce that would slow the implementation of lean production.

Fourth, and perhaps most significantly, there is clear variance in the extent to which lean production ideas have been adopted at each of the Big Three companies. For one thing, each company experienced a competitiveness crisis at different times. For Chrysler and Ford, the initial crisis came in the late 1970s and early 1980s, when both faced massive financial difficulties.[15] Because the crisis came so early in the period of intensified international competition and was so severe, both companies got a jump on the restructuring process. In comparison, GM's crisis was drawn out and many of the danger signs were kept well hidden from the board of directors, senior management, and many outside observers. Size and extensive financial resources carried GM through the recession of 1980–82 without much trauma, but in the 1990–92 recession, which created new problems for all of the Big Three companies, GM faced the most dismal prospects and was much less prepared to respond to the crisis than its more nimble competitors.

Furthermore, each company had different perceptions of what were the underlying reasons for its competitive crisis (or crises). For example, while Chrysler and Ford both experienced crises in the early 1980s, Ford defined its problem in terms of an internal organizational culture plagued by turf battles between overly rigid functional groups, while Chrysler focused more on cost cutting. Thus, Ford was quicker to embark on internal change efforts, compared to Chrysler, which, as noted above, did make dramatic cuts in both hourly and salaried employment in the early 1980s but then returned to "business as usual" once the improvement in its competitive position allowed the refilling of many positions. It was only during Chrysler's second crisis, in the late 1980s and early

1990s, that the company began to emphasize the need to redesign its internal processes, particularly product development.

At General Motors, despite difficult years in the 1980s, full acknowledgment of its competitive crisis only came in the early 1990s. As noted above, GM's major restructuring initiative in the 1980s—creating two major groups of product divisions—actually increased managerial layers and redundancies in white-collar positions, as well as slowing decision-making processes. It took a new management team to acknowledge these and other internal problems and to redirect attention toward fundamental work redesign. These differences in the timing and interpretation of crises (and the framing of appropriate solutions) are critical for understanding where each of the Big Three companies is today.

Ford

As noted above, Ford was the first among the Big Three to experiment with cross-functional teams and the elimination of organizational layers. Emboldened by the successes of the Blue Ribbon Committee, Team Taurus, and middle management "theme" groups in the early 1980s, Ford CEO Don Petersen announced plans in 1985 to eliminate, through attrition, 20% of white-collar positions by the beginning of the 1990s (Ingrassia and White, 1994).

However, Ford was not able to sustain the gains that accompanied its dramatic recovery in the 1980s. After three years of recordbreaking profits from 1986–88, top management became preoccupied with studying potential diversification moves and possible purchases. The next set of Ford products to come to market after the successful Taurus—the Ford Thunderbird and Mercury Cougar—exceeded both price and weight targets and did not sell well. White-collar employment, rather than shrinking as promised, was only 1.5% lower at the end of 1989 than in 1985. After a change in CEO, an ill-fated attempt to acquire Lockheed, and a bidding war with GM to acquire Jaguar, many of Ford's initiatives of the 1980s to change corporate structure, managerial culture, and business processes were sidetracked or stalled.

In product development, the unimpressive Thunderbird/Cougar project was followed by a massive effort to develop a "world car" for both European (Mondeo) and U.S. (Contour/Mystique) markets that ultimately consumed six years and over $6 billion. By 1990, it became clear that the cost-effective and speedy Taurus effort was the exception rather than the rule and that Ford's product development had not been fundamentally changed in the direction of lean production.

In 1994, with new CEO Alex Trotman, Ford embarked on its most significant organizational restructuring project, a global effort known as Ford 2000. This ambitious effort extends beyond past "world car" projects to try to achieve durable, global economies of scale in product development, purchasing, and manufacturing. Ford's intent is to establish five "vehicle centers," each focused on a different vehicle category that will develop all products for that category for Ford worldwide. For example, the vehicle center for front-wheel-drive small and medium cars will be in Europe and the vehicle center for rear-wheel drive large cars will be in Dearborn, Michigan. This means that all future generations of the Ford Escort will be developed outside the United States, while future products under the Jaguar badge may increasingly be developed in the United States. Common engines and drive trains will be developed for vehicles sold in different countries, and a small set of long-term suppliers will be chosen who can provide parts (and design assistance) on the necessary global scale.

While this massive change will take years to fully implement, it is already clear that Ford anticipates major changes in the nature of managerial work. A 15-member committee of senior managers from Ford Automotive Operations is assessing the "managerial characteristics" of 300 senior executives and 1,800 senior and middle managers. Managers are expected to have "the skills and personality to work within a team, interact with many departments, and listen to several bosses." The traditional functional organization has been eliminated, replaced with a matrix organization in which departments interact horizontally with the five vehicle centers. Finally, no more than seven management layers are permitted between a first-line supervisor and the CEO.

Quotes from Ford senior managers reveal expectations for the "new-style" managers that are consistent with the lean production ideas described above. Bob Transou, head of the Ford 2000 transition team, says: "People will make or break Ford 2000. You've got to have tremendous tolerance for this global approach. Often, you have two, three or four bosses to satisfy. It is non-autocratic. And you have to clearly understand your authority and responsibility" (*Automotive News,* October 31, 1994). Richard Ogren, also from the transition team, speaking about the reduction in organizational levels, says, "If you've got 10 or 15 people reporting to you, you have to be more process-oriented. You insist upon better people because you are relying upon them more" (*Automotive News,* October 31, 1994). To help Ford managers prepare for these changes, Ford's training center is having them take personality tests. Older managers who decide they aren't able or willing to make the change are being offered early retirement. By early 1995, 400 of the top 2000 managers in Ford worldwide had accepted this offer.

It is too early to tell whether Ford's massive organizational change will be successful. The strategic assumption that "world cars" and global economies of scale is the most effective way to be a global automotive company is open to question. Customers seem to like choosing among large numbers of products, often produced in relatively low volumes, that are customized to different market niches. Furthermore, organizational changes conceived on such a grand scale often falter before being fully implemented. Nevertheless, the scope of this effort and the degree to which it is focused on changing all aspects of managerial work—structure, process, and leadership style—indicate how serious Ford is about moving away from traditional mass production.

Chrysler

For Chrysler, the major move towards lean production has come primarily in product development, in response to the company's second crisis of the 1980s. While minivan and Jeep sales kept Chrysler going through the mid-1980s (and provided the profits to fund a series of ill-fated acquisitions), its passenger car lines were almost entirely based on a platform design (the K car) from the late

1970s. When sales of these cars plummeted and the overall industry headed towards recession, Chrysler was again in severe financial difficulty.

Three separate developments supported Chrysler's sweeping reform of its product development process. A senior engineer, Glenn Gardner, who was assigned to Chrysler's joint venture with Mitsubishi (Diamond-Star Motors), spent the mid-1980s observing the concurrent engineering approach used by Mitsubishi. A product development manager, Francois Castaing, who came to Chrysler in 1987 with prior experience at Renault and American Motors, was appointed vice president of engineering in 1988 and soon made Gardner head of the development team for the LH car. Finally, a group of junior managers had been carrying out their own study of Honda's product development process beginning in 1988.

In 1989, Gardner won approval for setting up a "platform team" organization for the LH car that would implement the "lean production" ideas drawn from Mitsubishi and Honda. The LH team consisted of product planners, product and process engineers, manufacturing people, and finance staff, all located in one place and working simultaneously on decisions across different stages of the development process, that is, the overlapping or concurrent engineering approach.

At first, Gardner and Castaing had trouble recruiting engineers to the LH team. According to Scott (1993),

> Many Chrysler employees targeted for the program considered it career-limiting, for its staffing pulled members away from the company's centralized engineering organization. [Senior management] had to compel recalcitrant managers to submit lists of engineers to fill the openings. The startup took several months. The 850 members of the team (compared to 1400 on a typical project) were a mix of "old-timers" and less senior employees looking for a chance to "show their stuff."

The LH would prove to be a huge success, praised for its innovative design and bold appearance and selling extremely well. Yet it was only a partial test of the platform team concept, since it had been started under a traditional development process. In 1990, Chrysler took the significant step of reorganizing its entire product development organization around platform teams. To gain support for this change from top management, the vice presidents running major departments were asked to oversee each platform team (Ingrassia and White, 1994).

The first project to be fully undertaken under this structure was the Neon subcompact. The Neon platform team was further bolstered by support from Chrysler's new vice president of manufacturing, Dennis Pawley, who had learned lean production at Mazda's U.S. plant. Pawley oversaw the extensive involvement of production workers (from the Belvedere, Illinois, plant that would build the Neon) in the design process, contributing ideas about design-for-manufacturability. Accounts of the Neon team's efforts (e.g., *Business Week,* May 3, 1993; Ingrassia and White, 1994) reveal a communications-intensive and focused effort marked by numerous creative compromises on issues that would traditionally have resulted in function-based feuds. The Neon was completed in 39 months (check), faster than most Japanese development efforts. Like the LH, it was a success, both in the perception of industry observers and in sales.

By 1995, Chrysler was able to add several other products to its list of innovative designs created through the "platform team" process—mostly notably the Ram truck, Cirrus/Stratus midsize passenger car, and Jeep Grand Cherokee. It appears that Chrysler has successfully institutionalized a new approach to product development that draws on lean production ideas to achieve both efficient and innovative product designs. To do so, it has convinced product development engineers that the best path to career success lies in moving beyond their narrow technical specialties and embracing the broader set of responsibilities and the intensified interaction associated with platform teams.

Chrysler is also the Big Three company that has most successfully reformed its supplier relations and reoriented its financial and accounting systems toward "activity-based costing," an innovation aimed at allocating overhead more precisely to specific manufacturing activities. While the crisis of the early 1990s may have provided the impetus for these changes, other factors have also had an effect. Chrysler is the smallest of the Big Three and the least vertically integrated, which has helped it be more nimble in responding to environmental changes than Ford or GM. Chrysler has been far more open to bringing in executives from outside the company, including the majority of the current top executive team. With the oldest blue-collar workforce of the Big Three now reaching retirement age and white-collar ranks kept relatively thin by the double financial crises of the 1980s, Chrysler has had less downsizing to do and more opportunity to bring in a new generation of production workers and young managers.

Finally, Chrysler seems, in recent years, to be the Big Three company most able to learn from other companies, both inside and outside of the industry. While the move to lean production has been slower in Chrysler's manufacturing plants than in its other functions, the company has recently embarked on a relationship with Freudenberg NOK, a German supplier that has plants in the United States, to learn more about lean production in manufacturing. Chrysler believes that Freudenberg is a better learning partner for them than Japanese companies, given the systematic way Freudenberg has transformed its manufacturing methods during the past decade.

On balance, then, Chrysler's challenge is less daunting than Ford's. It needs to continue on its current path of change, but it is not facing the potential chaos and disorientation associated with the massive restructuring of Ford 2000. Furthermore, the company has a management team that understands how to implement changes in white-collar work and has been able to attract new employees at all levels who are likely to adapt readily to these changes.

General Motors

Over the past 15 years, more ink has been spilled trying to unravel the mysteries posed by the decline of General Motors than any other U.S. company. It seems impossible that so much could have gone wrong at a company with such a proud history, so many resources, such a domineering position in the industry, and so many genuinely talented employees, capable of achieving amazing innovations— at least in isolated pockets of the company, for brief periods. The lengthy analysis of GM in the 1980s provided above is a discouraging and cautionary tale. And despite the promising changes made by the new top management team, headed by Jack Smith, since the 1992 boardroom coup, GM's troubles seem so deep and the difficulties in turning around such a big company so large that it is hard to sustain any optimistic scenario.

As noted above, many of Jack Smith's early efforts have focused on undoing the damage done to GM during the Roger Smith years. This has meant abolishing the two groups of divisions and recentralizing many key processes and decisions. It has meant dismantling a dysfunctional system of managerial incentives and working to restore the external credibility of the company's financial reports and market forecasts. It has meant a "shock treatment" approach to renegotiating supplier contracts that has saved the company millions of dollars but has done untold damage to GM's relationship with many suppliers. It has meant adding hours of overtime work in some plants while closing other plants (because of GM's inability to build multiple products in one plant), both developments (along with the outsourcing of component work) which are straining relations with the UAW.

Finally, it has meant a period of confusion, cynicism, fear, and chaos for most white-collar employees. Yet there is some reason to believe that this state of mind is paradoxically combined, for many GM employees, with continued company loyalty and a strong inclination to believe (to the point of self-deception) that a return to the old dominance and prosperity is just around the corner. According to GM vice president Harry Pearce, a member of the new top-management team, "I constantly worry that we will slip back into the complacency that got us into trouble in the past. We work every day at disabusing people of the notion that we have this thing fixed" (Smith, 1995).

With so much undoing to do, it will take time before GM can achieve the new product development processes that Chrysler already has in place or the manufacturing efficiencies that Ford has long mastered. In the meantime, it may well continue to lose market share, thus putting additional strain on the organization. For both Ford and Chrysler, it seems to have taken two crises (or near crises) to reach the point of fundamental change in the direction of lean production and new approaches to managerial work. For GM, this is the first crisis that is leading to substantial change, but it follows a period in the late 1980s and early 1990s of nearly constant smaller crises and an equally constant string of new programs (each with its own acronym) as potential remedies. Achieving the changes in managerial and engineering work associated with lean production on a lasting basis may require a relatively healthy organization. GM cannot yet be described as healthy.

Still, it is too soon to count GM out. If GM can judiciously add "new blood" in its white-collar and blue-collar ranks and restore damaged relationships with suppliers, the union, and white-collar employees who have lost ground in the past decade, perhaps it can achieve organizational innovations like those that made Alfred Sloan's GM the marvel of the industrial world.

Conclusion

The preceding discussion of the progress by the Big Three auto companies toward lean production suggests some speculative thoughts about future developments for white-collar work in this influential industry. By 1995, despite fitful progress during the 1980s, lean production ideas had gained a strong foothold at all of the Big Three companies. This learning process has not been self-sustaining but has been spurred on by periodic crises. While there has been retrenchment after the advances associated with each crisis, this has allowed companies to identify the next set of changes that need to be made.

With respect to the relative effects of volume-reduction versus work-redesign restructuring, an oversimplified story would say that the first competitive crisis for Ford and Chrysler in the early 1980s was primarily oriented toward volume-reduction restructuring, with some tentative movement toward work-redesign structuring that was mostly reversed (particularly at Chrysler) during the mid-1980s boom years. Subsequently, the second competitive crisis for both companies (a near crisis for Ford) in the early 1990s was primarily oriented toward work-redesign restructuring, influenced by lean production ideas. From this perspective, GM's current problems arise from both the fact that it is trying to carry out the two kinds of restructuring simultaneously, as well as the paradigm-shift changes that were distributed over a decade for Ford and Chrysler.

Most available evidence suggests that changes in organizational structures and business processes at Chrysler and, prospectively, at Ford have outpaced the rethinking of employment practices—pay systems, career paths, employment security—for white-collar employees. Thus, the next step for these companies may be figuring out how to achieve some consistency between the changes in managerial and engineering work associated with their new strategic direction and their human resources (HR) systems.

Here the U.S. companies have the potential to gain some ground on their Japanese rivals, particularly global companies such as Ford. The top Japanese automakers, which have had considerable success in transferring their HR practices for blue-collar workers to the United States and Europe, have had much more difficulty achieving the same success with white-collar employees—particularly managers. Perhaps Ford is in a better position than Toyota or Honda to handle the demands of a global HR system that must produce managers (and managerial skills) able to work effectively in many different cultural contexts. Yet Ford still has much to learn about lean production and this will constrain its ability to achieve the right fit between production/business strategy and the HR system.

There is every reason to believe that the auto industry will continue to be a bellwether industry with respect to white-collar work. The international reach of the industry and its importance to many national economies will keep it an influential actor in the process of globalization. The complexity of the managerial tasks, particularly with respect to coordination and communication, and the competitive pressures for simultaneous progress on productivity, quality, and product variety will continue to pose significant challenges of both conception and execution that will continue to attract the attention of other industries. Finally, the auto industry is characterized by a strong production paradigm—lean production—that has significant economic advantages in the current competitive environment and is beginning to diffuse internationally. As this paradigm diffuses into different cultural contexts and adapts to different institutional arrangements, it is possible that stable hybrid models combining elements of mass and lean production will emerge. The consequences of this diffusion process for automotive white-collar employees—from the executive suite to the shop floor and in all the offices in between—will continue to hold considerable fascination for scholars and practitioners alike.

Notes

1. There are five categories of white-collar employees at the "Big Three" auto companies (General Motors, Ford, and Chrysler): (a) executives who fill the top management ranks, both at headquarters and at the head of various divisions; (b) middle management at divisional and plant levels; (c) professional staff, including technical professionals (i.e., engineers), who work at headquarters, in the product development organization, and in the manufacturing plants; (d) nonprofessional staff, such as clerical employees; and (e) first-line supervisors at the plant level. Of these groups, top executives and the highest-ranking among middle management and professional staff are typically eligible for performance-based pay (cash bonuses and stock options tied to annual financial results), while the bulk of middle management, professional and nonprofessional staff, and first-line supervisors are included in a "salaried" category (i.e., paid a salary rather than hourly pay and potentially receiving annual raises based on individual performance evaluation). All five categories are "exempt" employees, in terms of the National Labor Relations Act, and are thus not subject to the requirement that overtime be paid for work beyond 40 hours. A small percentage of the salaried group at each of the Big Three are unionized, typically lower-level technical employees who support product and process design engineering work. While all of these groups will be covered in this chapter, "salaried" employees, the largest and least understood, will receive the most attention.

2. The employment data are for the United States only and are drawn from annual reports from 1979–94 or from company sources. (Sales and market share data are also for the United States only and include both car and truck sales. The source is *Automotive News Market Data Books*, 1979–94.) Only employment data that are defined consistently over time for each company have been used. But these data are not completely comparable across companies because of four differences in the measures of employment levels:

(a) Since annual report data for General Motors combine U.S. and Canadian employees, it is estimated (using other sources) that GM's U.S. employment was 90% of the combined total.

(b) Hourly employment figures for General Motors *include* employees that are on temporary or indefinite layoff status or are in the Jobs Bank program, while hourly figures from Ford and Chrysler *exclude* such employees. This means that hourly employment levels at Ford and Chrysler show more volatility year-to-year than at GM since they reflect the movement of employees back and forth between layoff and active status.

(c) Each company follows different conventions in terms of including or excluding employees from subsidiaries from these figures. GM's figures exclude GMAC (General Motors Acceptance Corporation), Hughes Aircraft, EDS (Electronic Data Systems), and GMHE (General Motors Hughes Electronics). Ford's figures *include* Ford Credit, Ford Electronics, and Ford Microelectronics in addition to its automotive operations, although car rental operations (Hertz) are excluded. Chrysler's figures include all U.S. subsidiaries making automotive components but exclude Chrysler Financial Corporation and car rental operations.

(d) The degree of vertical integration at these companies differs dramatically throughout this period, so that the fact that GM's employment levels are so much higher than Ford and Chrysler is not only a function of its higher sales and market share but also of the higher number of fully owned component suppliers included in its numbers.

3. Trends during this time were examined by comparing two periods that reveal the huge cyclicality of the U.S. industry: 1979 to 1982, which was the worst year of the recession in terms of sales and employment levels, and 1982 to 1986, which captures the buildup to the next market peak. GM reduced its hourly and salaried employment in both periods (12% for hourly and 9% for salaried from 1979–82 and about half that percentage reduction from 1982–86). (Recall that the GM numbers, unlike those for Ford and Chrysler, include laid-off workers still on the company payroll, so this probably understates the extent of reductions in working hourly employees during this period.) Ford followed a different pattern— a massive reduction from 1978–82 in both hourly employment (34%) and salaried employment (16%) followed by a modest increase from 1982–86 in hourly employment (8%, based on recalling workers from layoff status) and a modest decrease in salaried employment (4%). Chrysler also reduced hourly employment massively from 1979–82 (by 48%) but also made huge cuts in salaried employment (43%) during this same period. Then, from 1982–86, Chrysler reversed course and boosted their hourly and salaried employment (from the 1982 low) by 53% and 42% respectively.

What must be remembered is the difference in company fortunes during this time. All three companies experienced a drop in sales from 1979–82, but they differed dramatically in their gains during the market upswing. Chrysler and Ford's increases in employment from 1982–86 can be attributed to their phenomenal rise in sales, by over 90% for Chrysler (based on high demand for the new minivan) and over 60% for Ford (based on high demand for the Taurus). GM's gain in sales during this period was much more modest, at 38%, and as a result, its market share dropped by over 4 percentage points (from 43.5% to 38.9%), a reduction of nearly 11%.

4. As noted above, these more conservative hourly employment numbers are used here. Because GM only began using this definition of hourly employment levels in the 1992 annual report (covering the years 1990–92), I rely on data that GM provided to the *Los Angeles Times* (September 25, 1993) that give a time series of hourly employment from 1979 to 1992 using this new definition. The 1993 and 1994 figures are then drawn from GM's annual reports.

5. The 1992 GM Annual Report, issued shortly after Jack Smith became CEO, says "GM is hard-pressed to ask for loyalty and commitment from its employees. Here in the U.S., we've had to reduce the number of our hourly employees by over 125,000 in the last eight years, and our salaried employees by about 50,000, mainly by early retirement programs. And it's not their fault we're not competitive. It's our fault for not responding quickly enough to competitive pressures. . . . We know that we have had organizational structures and business practices that have required a noncompetitive number of people." (p. 4–5)

6. The innovations of Sloan and his group of top executives also had a formative impact on the academic study of management. Chandler (1977) notes, "Because the executives at General Motors described their achievements in the new management journals, theirs became the standard model on which other enterprises later shaped their organizational structures." (p. 459) Beginning in 1924, a journal titled *Management and Administration* carried many articles by GM executives about their reorganization of the massive company. Peter Drucker's 1946 book, *The Concept of the Corporation,* focused on GM as the exemplar of the well-managed industrial enterprise. Later, the first issue of *Administrative Sciences Quarterly* carried an article entitled "Contributions to Administra-

tion by Alfred P. Sloan, Jr. and GM" (Dale, 1956). Sloan's own memoir, *My Years with General Motors,* written when he was 90, is often included on academic reading lists. In turn, GM has continued to be a source of fascination for many management scholars (e.g., Kanter, 1983; Pascale, 1990) as well as industry observers (e.g., Keller, 1989, 1993).

7. Sloan himself downplayed the importance of his relationship-building with dealers and among divisional managers to emphasize the "scientific" aspect of his contributions. His book *My Years with General Motors* (1963) is criticized by Drucker, in a 1972 epilogue to a new edition of his *Concept of the Corporation,* as "focusing exclusively on politics, business decisions, and structure, even though Sloan himself was a master at working with and managing people, and was personally exceedingly 'people-focused.' Yet there are no people in Sloan's book, no mention of Sloan's own great strength, the leadership of people, no discussion of relations with people, no mention of the time and attention he himself gave to placing people in the right jobs and to making their strengths effective. It is probably the most impersonal book of memoirs ever written—and this was clearly intentional. It is what Sloan meant by 'professional management'." (p. 307)

8. Dale (1956) mentions the bonus plan as one of Sloan's great administrative contributions at GM. In addition, Sloan devotes a chapter of his memoirs to "Incentive Compensation" and asserts that GM's "Bonus Plan," established in 1918 and essentially unaltered until the 1980s, was a major factor in the success of the company.

9. Sloan (1963) points out that the AIF was never intended to be linked to productivity increases at GM. He argues that productivity increases, at the corporate level, are very difficult to measure and that, in any case, such a policy would reward technologically advanced operations (and companies) disproportionately. Thus the AIF was intended to be matched to the long-term productivity increase in the U.S. economy as a whole. However, GM's commitment to the AIF would hold throughout the contract, regardless of actual productivity performance in any given year. Thus, Sloan writes: I prefer to think of it [the AIF] as a group merit raise of sorts and I suspect many GM employees see it in that light. . . . In the end, increased efficiency flows not so much from the increased effectiveness of the worker, but primarily from more efficient management and from the investment of additional capital in labor-saving devices. . . . I think the fact that our workers benefit on a definite and prescribed basis, resulting in an increased standard of living, gives us a more sympathetic cooperation in the introduction of labor-saving devices and other improvements that flow from technological progress." (pp. 399, 402)

10. The initial COLA "escalator," in 1948, provided a one-cent per hour wage increase for every 1.14 point increase in the consumer price index and the initial AIF was set at three cents per hour per year, or roughly 2% of the average production worker's hourly wage. The AIF was boosted to four cents an hour in 1950, five cents an hour in 1955, and varied between 2.5% and 3% of average hourly earnings from 1955 to 1979 (Katz, 1985, p. 16).

11. Sloan quotes a letter from one of his top executives: "I well remember the thrill that came with the time when I was first awarded a bonus—the feeling of having made the team and the determination to continue to advance in the organization. . . . The potential rewards of the Bonus Plan to ego satisfaction generate a tremendous driving force within the Corporation." (Sloan, 1963, p. 426)

12. GM has had a steady succession of finance-trained executives to the top executive positions—Frederick Donner in the late 1950s and early 1960s, Thomas Murphy in the 1970s, Roger Smith in the 1980s, and in the 1990s Jack Smith and several of his top executives (Louis Hughes, Rick Wagoner).

13. Two examples of such a norm at Honda include a manufacturing philosophy known as *genba kanri,* which means "go to the shop floor, which is the source of all

knowledge" and a more general exhortation to understand the detailed context of a problem (known as the "three A's"—actual part, actual place, actual situation) before trying to develop a solution (Helper and MacDuffie, 1995).

14. Here a commonly used technique is called the "five why's," in which one searches for the true underlying cause of a problem by repeatedly asking "why."

15. Although Chrysler's woes are better known because of the government-funded loan guarantee package needed to rescue the automaker from bankruptcy, Ford's North American automotive operations were not in much better shape than Chrysler's during that time. But strong profits from Ford Europe concealed the extent of the domestic operation's problems from many outside observers.

References

Adler, Paul S. and Kim B. Clark. 1991. "Behind the Learning Curve: A Sketch of the Learning Process," *Management Science,* 37, no. 3.

Adler, Paul S. and Brian Borys. 1995. "Two Types of Bureaucracy: Enabling and Coercive," forthcoming in *Administrative Sciences Quarterly.*

Automotive News. 1994. "UAW gains outsourcing concessions," June 13.

Automotive News. 1995. "New wave of execs taking GM buyout," July 10.

Bailey, Lotte. 1985. *Living With Technology: Issues at Midcareer.* Cambridge: MIT Press.

Business Week. 1991. "GM slices but flab survives," December 23.

Business Week. 1993. "Chrysler's Neon," May 3.

Cameron, Kim, Sarah J. Freeman, and Aneil K. Mishra. 1993. "Downsizing and Redesigning Organizations," in Huber, George P. and William H. Glick (eds.), *Organizational Change and Redesign.* New York: Oxford University Press.

Chandler, Alfred D., Jr. 1977. *The Visible Hand: The Managerial Revolution in American Business.* Cambridge: Harvard University Press.

Chicago Tribune. 1994. "Assembling a new auto worker," May 29.

Clark, Kim B., and Fujimoto, Takahiro, *Product Development Performance: Strategy, Organization and Management in the World Auto Industry,* Harvard Business School Press, Boston, 1991.

Cole, Robert E., Paul Bacdayan, B. Joseph White. 1993. "Quality, Participation, and Competitiveness," *California Management Review,* vol. 35, no. 3.

Cole, Robert E. 1992. "Issues in Skill Formation and Training in Japanese Approaches to Automation." In Paul S. Adler, ed., *Technology and the Future of Work,* pp. 187–209. New York: Oxford University Press.

Dale, Ernest. 1956. "Contributions to Administration by Alfred P. Sloan, Jr. and GM", *Administrative Sciences Quarterly* 1, no. 1: 30–62.

Drucker, Peter. 1972. *Concept of the Corporation,* rev. ed. New York: John Day Company.

Financial Times. 1994. "Blue-collar team, white-collar wise How a Better-Educated Workforce Is Helping the U.S. Car Industry to Raise Productivity," May 11.

Ford, Henry (in collaboration with Samuel Cr. ʰher). 1923. *My Life and Work.* Garden City, N.Y.: Doubleday, Page, and Company.

Guest, Robert H. 1979. "Quality of Work Life: Learning from Tarrytown," *Harvard Business Review,* 57 (July–August): 76–87.

Halberstam, David. 1986. *The Reckoning.* New York: William Morrow.

Heckscher, Charles. 1995. *White-Collar Blues: Management Loyalty in an Age of Corporate Restructuring.* New York: Basic Books.

Helper, Susan, and John Paul MacDuffie. 1995. "Creating Lean Suppliers: Diffusing Lean

Production Through the Supply Chain," working paper, International Motor Vehicle Program, M.I.T.

Imai, Kenichi. 1986. *Kaizen*. New York: Free Press.

Ingrassia, Paul and Joseph B. White. 1994. *Comeback: The Fall and Rise of the American Automobile Industry*. New York: Simon and Schuster.

Jacoby, Sanford. 1985. *Employing Bureaucracy: Managers, Unions, and the Transformation of Work in American Industry, 1900–1945*. New York: Columbia University Press.

Kanter, Rosabeth. 1977. *Men and Women of the Corporation*. New York: Basic Books.

Kanter, Rosabeth Moss. 1983. *The Change Masters: Innovation and Entrepreneurship in the American Corporation*. New York: Simon and Schuster.

Kanter, Rosabeth. 1989. "The New Managerial Work," *Harvard Business Review* (November–December).

Katz, Harry. 1985. *Shifting Gears: Changing Labor Relations in the U.S. Automobile Industry*. Cambridge: MIT Press.

Katz, Harry, and Noah Meltz. 1991. "Profit-Sharing and Auto Workers' Earnings: The United States vs. Canada," *Relations Industrielles*, 42, no. 3: 513–530.

Keller, Maryann. 1988. *Rude Awakening: The Rise, Fall, and Struggle for Recovery of General Motors*. New York: Harper Perennial.

Keller, Maryann. 1993. *Collision: GM, Toyota, Volkswagen and the Race to Own the 21st Century*. New York: Doubleday.

Los Angeles Times. 1993. "Shrinking Auto Maker," September 25.

Los Angeles Times. 1994. February 11.

Mills, C. Wright. 1951. *White Collar: The American Middle Classes*. London: Oxford University Press.

New York Times. 1993a. "GM gives salaried staff pay raises," November 12.

New York Times. 1993b. "Ford salaried workers get raise," November 13.

Nobeoka, Kentaro, and Cusumano, Michael. 1994. "Multi-Project Strategy, Design Transfer, and Project Performance," working paper, International Motor Vehicle Program, M.I.T.

Pascale, Richard Tanner. 1990. *Managing on the Edge: How the Smartest Companies Use Conflict to Stay Ahead*. New York: Simon and Schuster.

Piore, Michael. 1994. "Corporate Reform in American Manufacturing and the Challenge to Economic Theory," in Allen, Thomas J., and Michael Scott Morton (eds.), *Information Technology and the Corporation of the 1990s*. New York: Oxford University Press.

Scott, Greg. 1993. "New Product Development Series: Chrysler Corporation," working paper, International Motor Vehicle Program, M.I.T.

Sloan, Alfred P., Jr. 1963. *My Years with General Motors*. New York: Doubleday.

Smith, Hedrick. 1995. *Rethinking America*. New York: Random House.

Tyre, Marcie and Wanda Orlikowski. 1993. "Exploiting Opportunities for Technological Improvement in Organizations." *Sloan Management Review* 35: 13–26.

Ward, Allen, Jeffrey K. Liker, John J. Cristiono, and Durward K. Sobek II, et al. 1995. "The Second Toyota Paradox: How Delaying Decisions Can Make Better Cars Faster," *Sloan Management Review*, Spring: 43–61.

Whyte, William H., Jr. 1956. *The Organization Man*. New York: Simon and Schuster.

Wright, J. Patrick. 1979. *On a Clear Day You Can See General Motors*. Grosse Pointe, MI: Wright Enterprises.

Management Jobs in the Insurance Industry

5

Organizational Deskilling and Rising Pay Inequity

ELIZABETH D. SCOTT,
K. C. O'SHAUGHNESSY, & PETER CAPPELLI

The attention of both the research community and the popular press has begun to shift from a traditional focus on production jobs and toward management positions in part because of a perception that fundamental change is underway in the management ranks. Perhaps the most examined issue has been the reduction in job security experienced by managers (Cappelli, 1992). Unlike the temporary layoffs of production workers that were historically driven by business cycles, the changes in management job security seem to be permanent and, in large measure, driven by developments inside the firm (see Pfeffer and Baron, 1988). The most important of these forces appears to be changes in the structure of management and in the organization of work processes.

A unique set of data is used to examine the structure of management jobs among a sample of companies and observe how those jobs have changed over time. In particular, this chapter examines changes in the skill requirements of jobs by functional area and by level in the organization, changes in the "shape" of the organizational chart (the distribution of employees across management job titles), and changes in compensation for these jobs. That is, are managers becoming more or less skilled, are hierarchies becoming steeper or flatter, and is compensation becoming more or less equal within companies? The results present one of the first systematic attempts to examine how management job structures are changing in the U.S. economy. They suggest growing inequality in skills and compensation and widening spans of control in the management ranks. A final question addressed is whether these changes have an effect on overall company performance.

The Insurance Industry

Studies of the structure of jobs in the United States have tended to focus on manufacturing, perhaps because manufacturing, especially its effects on business cycles, has historically been seen as central to the economy, and because of the volatility of employment in it. The financial services industry represents the other end of the spectrum with respect to volatility, though it is also an important part of the U.S. economy.[1] One of the most important aspects of financial services for the purposes of this study, however, is that a disproportionate number of its jobs are white-collar. Nationally, 18.9% of all workers in the private sector held supervisory jobs while 27.5% of workers in the financial services sector fell in this category (U.S. Department of Labor, 1992). Employees in financial services, therefore, were more typically managers, were higher-paid, and had greater job security, typically in organizations with extensive management hierarchies and elaborate systems of progression.

Within financial services, we are focusing on the life insurance industry, which has been a very stable segment of financial services and has a higher proportion of supervisory employees. The percentage of employees in supervisory positions in the life insurance industry is extraordinarily high and has declined only gradually since 1966 (from 42% to 40% over a 15-year period) (U.S. Department of Labor, 1992). This is slightly different from the financial industry as a whole, which experienced an *increase* in percentage of supervisory employees over the same period, but the financial industry as a whole started out with a much smaller percentage of supervisory employees (20% in 1966) and ended 12 percentage points less than the life insurance segment of the industry (28% in 1989) (U.S. Department of Labor, 1990). What this suggests is that managers in the insurance industry have always had a smaller span of control than their counterparts in other areas of financial services such as banking. One reason why life insurance companies are an interesting industry in which to examine management jobs is because such an exceptionally large proportion of all its jobs are in management.

Another fact that makes the insurance industry interesting is that, unlike the savings and loan industry and, to a lesser extent, banking and investments, the life insurance industry has not been rocked by changes in regulation or by developments in foreign markets; nor has it experienced the boom and bust cycles that real estate has experienced. One reason to look at insurance for a study of management jobs, then, is because it has experienced relatively few unique shocks from the outside environment. The changes in management jobs here have therefore been driven largely by changes within the companies themselves. These developments are likely to translate well to other industries regardless of their market circumstances.

Managers in the insurance industry have been concerned with developments that also concern managers in other industries. Aging populations, increases in divorce rates, increases in dual-income families, and other similar national phenomena have affected both the products and the employment practices of life insurance companies (*National Underwriter,* 1987). Changes in technology and its acceptance have seen an increase in Local Area Networks (LANs), voice mail, imaging systems, and electronic data transfer in the insurance industry just as it has happened in other industries (Doyle, 1993; Jones, 1993). New theories about management have swept the insurance industry as broadly as they have other industries, with advice on Total Quality Management and reengineering being abundant in the industry publications (Knowles, 1990; Bucker, 1992; Hall, 1992; Helldorfer and Daly, 1993; Rohm, 1993; Scites, 1993).

As in the rest of the economy, managers in the insurance industry are facing an increase in competition, customers who are more sensitive to price and quality issues, shorter time horizons for investors, and market segmentation (Brooks, 1987; *National Underwriter,* 1987; McClure, 1992). As a result, managers who once had only a few products aimed at a mass market now have multiple products and multiple markets. Competition has increased to include banks and brokerages as people have come to view life insurance as just one of a broad spectrum of financial instruments. This change affects not only the job of the marketing or sales manager but every aspect of the organization. Underwriting managers must develop expertise in the new products and new markets; data processing managers must develop new systems to provide comparisons of different packages; accounting managers must devise new billing and payment procedures, and so on.

The Changing Nature of Management Jobs

In the 1980s, the job of a life insurance manager was very much like that of a manager in any manufacturing organization with a production line, except that the production staff consisted of clerical workers processing reams of paper and producing insurance policies. Managers had to be sure that each functional unit completed its tasks effectively and efficiently and passed on the work to the next unit in a timely fashion. Managers could evaluate individual performance in terms of relatively equivalent inputs and outputs. Career ladders were defined hierarchically, and steep hierarchies were needed to ensure coordination among the various functional areas. As a manager in one of the companies reported, "There was a lot of fat back in those days—it was easy to make money then."[2] The skills needed from managers were planning, delegation, motivation, evaluation, coordination, and control.

Now, insurance management jobs are more like those in lean-production manufacturing organizations, where teams of workers are responsible for production and the manager is responsible for leadership. One human resources manager told us, "We reengineered the way we did the work. There is more accountability, consolidation. Instead of doing only one piece, you do the whole thing. For example, we used to have four people in accounts payable—accounting, operations, accounts payable, and bookkeeping. Now it's broken out by client area. We have billing and accounting teams—western, northern, southern—to respond to agencies. This gives each person a career path as their levels of experience increase." Different skill sets are needed for managers to coordinate these independent teams. "We replaced our traditional supervisor with a team leader. This person does not do hiring or firing but coordinates workflow and motivates members. They may sit in on interviews and advise the manager of discipline problems as well." One manager said "managers' jobs are not as well defined as they were." Managers are having to demonstrate more "soft" skills. The skills required to <u>motivate a team</u> are different than those needed to motivate individuals in an authoritarian environment. In one company, for example, the managers are responsible for a program to teach the agents the values of the home office and ethical sales conduct.

One manager near retirement said, "If I were starting again as a manager, I would have a more intense, focused attitude toward the business—more responsibility for trying to accomplish goals. I'm working harder now and sleeping less than ever in my life." In particular, our interviews suggest that managers who were comfortable with only a few direct subordinates are now having <u>to juggle the concerns of multiple staff members</u>. In an era of downsizing and rightsizing, one manager who was responsible for cutting staff reported "managers are having to deal with the emotional stuff that goes with laying off people." Managers who used time at work or number of applications coded to evaluate individual performance are finding that teams do not break work down into easily measurable jobs. One manager who had expected regular promotions reported that her career progression had slowed, saying, "there isn't a whole lot of movement in managerial careers these days—people move between product lines, these are the fast trackers they want to give exposure to, but people don't move up so fast." Another observed that "more people are making lateral moves, broadening experience, preparing themselves for the next step." At least at the first level of supervision, managers are finding that the rules of the game with respect to compensation are changing. According to one of the compensation managers, "now technical people can be rated as high or higher than a manager, and receive the same or more pay."

As in the rest of the economy, changes in technology affect how managers manage. One manager reported, "We are leveraging with systems. We use expert systems, electronic claims . . . Human Resources has everything on systems now. We just put in an on-line salary increase system. It has a lot of built-in edits telling the manager what actions are outside of policy, cutting down on paperwork for the compensation staff."

Managers all over the country are having to face these demographic, organizational, and technological changes in their workplaces. Data allow us to see how the changes have played out in the insurance industry, and, because the insurance industry is so much more protected than the rest of the economy, the results likely provide a conservative assessment of how change is taking place elsewhere.

One characteristic of the insurance industry which differentiates it from other industries is its use of independent agents for its retail sales.[3] The number of employees reported in SIC code 64, "Insurance agents, brokers, and service"[4] is frequently greater than the reported employment of life insurance companies as a whole (U.S. Department of Commerce, 1992) which suggests that agents make up a large segment of the industry. The supervisory ratios reported above from the Bureau of Labor Statistics (BLS) data do not include independent agents or the work they perform. And because independent agents often sell more than one product, it is not possible to break down the numbers in these categories to determine the full-time equivalents of the number of subordinates for life insurance managers. When the agents, brokers, and so on are included along with the employees of insurance companies, however, 20.3% of all workers held jobs in the category of executives, administrators, and managers in 1990 (U.S. Department of Labor, 1990). The trend is toward fewer independent agents (a 14% decrease from 1987–92) and more career agents, further changing the jobs of managers from that of negotiating with independent contractors to developing long-term loyalty from employees (Dauer, 1992).

BLS data suggest that over 50% of all insurance workers are in administrative support positions, 20% are in executive, administrative, and managerial positions, 16% are in marketing and sales, and 7.5% hold professional or technical positions (Bureau of Labor Statistics, 1990). The BLS projects a change in the distribution of employees among these classes over the next 15 years with sharp increases in the professional (+46.3%) and technical (+44.6%) areas and decreases in the areas of typing (−18%), filing (−3.9%), and bookkeeping (−5%). Executive, administrative, and managerial jobs are projected to increase by 28.2% between 1990 and 2005, including a 26% increase in general managers and top executives, slightly greater than the 21.8% increase projected for overall industry employment (U.S. Department of Labor, 1990a). As the data in Appendix A suggest, there has been a general trend in the 1990s toward a smaller number of insurance companies with more employees per company.

These general trends in industry employment suggest a picture of reasonable stability: slow but steady growth in overall employment and only modest changes in the management ranks. These projections are based on extrapolating industry employment trends, however, and will not foresee any radical change in the structure of employment. More detailed information about changes in the internal organization of companies is needed in order to understand how management jobs may be evolving in the future.

The Hay Data

Detailed data obtained from Hay Associates on the internal organization of management jobs for 11 life insurance companies are used in the analyses that follow. Hay Associates is well known for its system of job analysis and evaluation, which begins with detailed and consistent measures of job requirements and skills. The measure of skill used by Hay is similar to that used in the *Dictionary of Occupational Titles* and captures the autonomy and complexity of jobs that are issues central to academics. The submeasures of the Hay scale are grouped into three classifications: Know How, which measures the capabilities, knowledge, and techniques needed to do the job ranked according to their complexity; Problem-Solving, which measures how well defined and predictable job tasks are; and Accountability, which measures autonomy in decision making. These measures get at the autonomy-complexity dimension of skill that concerns fields such as psychology and sociology.[5]

There is considerable debate about the validity of any measure of skill (see Levin, Rumberger, and Finnan, 1990 for a summary) but the Hay measure appears to be at least as valid a measure as any others proposed.[6] Further, the Hay measures have widespread influence on how jobs are structured and evaluated in the economy as a whole and, in that sense, have good external validity. During the 1980s, for example, Hay claimed that two million employees were in jobs evaluated by its system, including those in most of the country's largest corporations, and comparisons by non-Hay firms with these establishments extend the influence of the Hay system even further. The fact that much of Hay's original work in developing the system was in financial services may make it especially appropriate for a study of the insurance industry (Henderson, 1985).

The most important point about the Hay measures for the purposes of this discussion is that they are reliable and consistent over time. They have been constant at Hay for decades and, more important, are applied consistently across establishments. Hay staff receive considerable training in applying the measures, they visit the clients, conduct the job analysis on the jobs being examined, and the results are then checked for reliability by a central office. Indeed, the product that Hay ultimately sells its clients is the assurance that its information is comparable over time and across organizations.[7] The various skill measures are then combined into a single measure, the job evaluation score, which represents an aggregate assessment of the demands associated with the job.[8] Comparison of these scores over time make it possible to estimate changes in skill. In addition to the skill measures, data on employment across job levels (i.e., position in the management hierarchy) and on compensation for each position are also examined.

Data on all of the Hay-classified positions for each company in the sample (see Appendix A describing sample) are considered for three points in time: 1986, 1989, and 1992. These positions include all but the lowest-level nonexempt jobs, which are excluded from our calculations.[9] Jobs are grouped according to four levels with respect to the organizational chart or hierarchy: The first level is for top executives who manage policy (e.g., group vice presidents); the second level is for general managers who direct other managers or supervisors (e.g., heads of a division within a conglomerate); the third level is for supervisors who directly manage individual workers (e.g., head of a department like accounts receivable): the fourth level is for exempt, nonsupervisory positions (e.g., accountant jobs). Again, nonexempt jobs are excluded from the data. The Hay points and the total employment for each job in the sample is known as well as the base and total compensation and functional skill (e.g., underwriting, data processing, accounting, sales) used in that job. These data paint a rich picture of the internal labor market in these organizations. Since the identities of these companies are known, this picture is supplemented with additional data about each firm's performance.

Analyses with the Hay Data

Structure   Perhaps the most important use of these data is to see whether and how the size and shape of the organizational chart is changing. Are we in fact seeing a "flattening" of the organizational structure in companies like these—is the proportion of lower level employees rising as responsibility is pushed from higher to lower levels of the organization? Further, is there a change in the distribution of employment by functional area that reflects new developments in the power and importance of different fields?

The practitioner journals report some changes in organizational structure in insurance companies such as centralization of field activities to central or regional offices (Dauer, 1991, on adjustment activities; King, 1991, on sales expertise; Hoyt, 1992, on customer service). They also suggest a stronger emphasis on certain functional areas, such as customer service (McGrath, 1992). There is similar evidence of change for the banking industry's line workers, suggesting that changes in management levels and functional areas are important in both segments of the financial services industry (see, e.g., Bird, 1991, on flatter organizational structures; Violano, 1990, and Klein, 1992, on reduction of tellers; and Lunt, 1992, on increased customer service). A study of insurance industry adjusters shows that changes in the span of control associated with the decision to delegate work were driven solely by the work load of the manager. (The decision to delegate, however, was associated with improved job performance [Leana, 1986]). The picture for the 1980s is one of geographically dispersed staff, with much of the responsibility for sales, claims adjustment, and customer service performed by agents of the company at remote locations. We see a steep hierarchy, with experts in various specialties assigned to each of the geographic locations. The picture for the 1990s is very different. Hierarchy is flattening. More of the functions have been brought in-house and centralized. Technology (800-numbers, laptops, modems) is being used to bring expertise close to the customer without having to move the experts.

Skill A second and closely related issue is how skill requirements might be changing for jobs. Whether jobs are being upskilled or deskilled is a central issue both for academic research and for policy. The Hay data are uniquely suited for addressing whether skill requirements are changing and have been used for this purpose with other jobs (Cappelli, 1993). The deskilling of one job, for example, may come about because of a transfer of requirements to other jobs, so it is important to examine the entire job structure within firms in order to identify such transfers.

Most analyses of changing skill requirements in companies and in the economy as a whole rely simply on changes in the distribution of employees across jobs. With these data, in contrast, we can examine how skill requirements are changing for individual jobs and then add data on changes in employment across occupations to see how they are changing for the organization as a whole. It is also possible, for example, that each job may see a rise in requirements and yet changes in the distribution of employment across jobs—for example, reducing the proportion of high-skill jobs—may help produce an overall reduction in skill levels. It is important to include measures of skill changes for jobs along with changes in the distribution of employees across jobs in order to make that analysis.

The studies of skill in financial service industries have centered on the introduction of new technologies. The results suggest that new technologies do not necessarily deskill jobs (Adler, 1986; Attewell, 1987), although examples in the practitioner press do find examples of deskilling operations at local offices

(Dauer, 1991; King, 1991).[10] This suggests the importance of disaggregating the analysis to functional levels where specific technologies might be examined.

There are many different ways to assess changes in the distribution of skill requirements across jobs. Perhaps the simplest comparison is whether the means are different—in this case, whether the average job in a job family or level has a higher or lower evaluation score than in the past.

Compensation   Finally, changes in compensation across jobs are examined in order to see first how the income distribution is changing within internal labor markets and second to see how compensation changes relate to changes in employment and in skills. There is a general interest in whether income inequality is changing in the United States (Levy and Murnane, 1992), and those changes are driven at least in part by developments in compensation within firms.

There is a certain amount of determinism in the relationships with pay that are built into the data. One reason firms have Hay consultants construct these skill measurements for each job is to relate pay to job requirements. Changes in points should, within the system, lead to changes in pay. On the other hand, skill requirements and pay should be related in any rational organization, other things equal, and the Hay system in fact allows the relationship between skill requirements and pay to vary by company and by job. So examining changes in compensation with these data will not be identical to examining changes in skill, as the data below will reveal.

Results   Table 5-1 presents changes in employment, skills, and compensation for each of the four organizational levels in the sample of firms in 1986 and 1992. With respect to employment, we see a sharp expansion in the proportion of line workers, absolute declines in the number of top management positions, and only modest growth in the number of middle managers and supervisors. As a result, the shape of the organizational chart in these companies has changed dramatically, becoming considerably flatter. While this result clearly corresponds to descriptions in the popular press, there have been few analyses before that have documented it. The span of control has increased for every level of the organization and especially for the first level of management (supervisors). When asked how the span of control had changed, people in these companies said, "Before, a manager might have 60 subordinates under her, with two layers of supervision. Now, the manager manages 30 to 40 people directly." Having two additional layers of supervision would have reduced the manager's span of control to three or four direct reports—a drastic difference from 30–40 direct reports. This is certainly what the numbers show.

The results for skill changes are somewhat different than descriptions in the popular press would suggest. If the widening of the supervisory span of control resulted from taking decision making and responsibility from supervisors and pushing it down to line workers, it does not seem to have increased the average skill requirements of the exempt line workers. It could be, for example, that the skill requirements of individual job titles within the "Line" level were rising as a result of empowerment efforts but that the huge number of new jobs added to the

Table 5-1. Employment, Skills, and Compensation by Management Level

| | Number | | | | Skill Points | | | Compensation | | |
	1986	% of Total	1992	% of Total	% Change	1986	1992	% Change	1986	1992	% Change
Top manager	138	0.90	137	0.89	−0.72	721	755	4.72	122,891	157,908	28.49***
Middle manager	570	3.70	591	3.84	3.68	360	359	−0.28	60,056	66,155	10.16***
Line supervisor	1,288	8.36	1,716	11.14	33.23	225	228	1.33	39,338	39,023	−0.80
Exempt, nonsupervisory	2,726	17.69	4,755	30.86	74.43	172	170	−1.16	29,596	29,972	1.27*

*significant at the .1 level.
***significant at the .001 level.

line category over this period had lower than average skill levels, depressing the average. This dataset enables us to examine this question more closely, as we can look at the numbers of jobs added in each functional area and at the average skill levels in those areas. This is discussed in more detail below when we look at changes by functional area. It could also be that the skill requirements that are rising from empowerment efforts are for nonexempt workers who are not included in the sample. Applebaum (cited in Hartmann et al., 1986), for example, found a change in one company's customer service function in the 1980s that indicated upskilling of nonexempt workers:

> By 1983, a new, highly skilled clerical position had been designed. Customer service representatives handle sales, have access to the computer program that assesses risks and to the rating program, explain rating procedures to customers, answer customer questions, and respond to complaints by telephone or mail.

Skill requirements for the other levels rose over this period, especially for top management positions. Overall, however, the average level of skill in this sample of firms *fell* substantially between 1986 and 1992—even though skills were rising in two of the four levels—because of a sharp shift in the distribution of employment away from management and toward line positions. Overall, the average skill requirements for the average job dropped by 17 Hay points from 1986 to 1992. A decline of this size is of practical significance. It is the equivalent, for example, of moving from the top of the range of clerical jobs by skill to the midpoint of that range. When breaking down the overall change, the change in the distribution of jobs across levels accounted for a 19 point *reduction* in average skills, but upskilling of jobs within levels accounted for a two point *increase* in skill.

It may be reasonable to wonder how to characterize a situation where the skills of most job levels are rising even though the average level of skill in the organization is falling; is this an example of deskilling or upskilling? Perhaps the best description is that it represents upskilling of individual jobs and deskilling of organizations.

The changes in compensation do not map neatly onto changes in points. None of the levels experienced increases in skill that were statistically significant, but top managers received a huge (28%) increase in pay, middle managers received a modest (10%) increase, and the lower two levels received virtually no increases. One conclusion from these data is that earnings inequality is increasing substantially inside these firms in a manner that is not attributable to any increases in skill, and the dividing line for that growth in inequality is no longer exempt/nonexempt but supervisor/manager.[11]

One possible explanation for the rising inequality in compensation is that it helps offset changes in the probability of promotion. Both simple expectancy and tournament models suggest that the possibility of a promotion to a position with considerably higher pay is an important source of motivation to employees inside an internal labor market. The fact that the span of control is increasing and the organizational chart flattening means that the probability of the average worker being promoted is declining. Other things equal, the decline in the probability of promotion might reduce the incentives to work hard. Increases in the compensation of top jobs, in contrast, increase the return to securing a promotion and may offset some of the effect produced by the decline in the probability of promotion.

There is another explanation: top managers are in "better positions to legislate their own pay increases."[12] If true, this sample of companies may actually underrepresent the true extent of income inequality in the economy, because it consists of companies using an external consultant to help set compensation where internal consistency is an important characteristic of the pay system. Presumably, these companies have a greater interest in the fairness of their compensation system than do those that do not seek independent advice.

Conversations with these companies suggest that they may be adapting their compensation practices to the reduced promotion opportunities associated with flatter organizational structures. Pay levels may now be somewhat more removed from organizational level. One company gave the example of two employees who were being considered for promotion, one who had good people skills and good technical skills, and the other who had good technical skills only. The one with both sets of skills was promoted to a supervisory position; the other was kept in the nonsupervisor level but given supervisory-level pay and more technical responsibilities. Developments like these may explain some of the decrease in the gap between the pay of nonsupervisory and supervisory employees.

Changes by Functional Area   Table 5-2 outlines the change in the distribution of employment across functional areas. We see a relative shift away from some of the "core" insurance functions, especially underwriting and actuarial work, in part because of the rise of expert systems in these areas (see below). We also see some decline in functional areas that are not part of the "core competence" of insurance operations, such as marketing and accounting. The biggest gainer is insurance operations, which handle the day-to-day work of processing insurance premiums, and then investment and portfolio management, reflecting the increased importance of investment opportunities to insurance operations during the late 1980s. The deregulation of parts of the investment industry during the 1980s and the increasing complexity associated with investments made this function much more important to the organization.

Table 5-3 presents the changes in employment, skill and pay across those functional areas that represented at least 1% of the jobs in the dataset. In general, the same pattern is seen with respect to hierarchy within functions as with the sample as a whole: there are proportionately fewer managers in each area, they have higher skills, and they are receiving more pay. Average skill levels for the function as a whole are down in all but one area while the overall pattern for pay is mixed.

In general, the organizational chart represented by the distribution of employment across levels is remarkably similar across functional areas in 1992 (see Figure 5-1). This was not the case in 1986 when some areas, like underwriting, were quite flat in structure while others, like insurance operations, were very steep. Much of the variance in the experience across functional areas in the six-year period, therefore, appears to be driven by the convergence toward a common organizational structure in 1992.

Table 5-2. Employment in Functional Areas

	1986	1992	Change (%)
Underwriters	503	537	6.76
Customer Service	632	854	35.13
Data Processing	922	1580	71.37
Benefits Administration	347	666	91.93
Actuarial	249	377	51.41
Portfolio Management	144	279	93.75
Investment Management	51	107	109.80
Insurance Operations	95	277	191.58
Finance/Accounting	310	430	38.71
Marketing	697	905	29.84
Human Resources	147	274	86.39

The functions that are gaining the most jobs turn out to also be the functions that, on average, show the greatest amount of deskilling. This is because the growing functions are seeing most of the expansion in lower-skilled jobs. Similarly, the functions with the greatest pay increases overall are those with the slowest growth in employment because average skill is rising the most in those areas. The one exception is portfolio management, which sees a sharp overall increase both in jobs and in pay. Pay in this area may have been responding to the sharp expansion of the investment management industry outside of insurance during this period.

The relationship between supervisors and nonsupervisory employees (levels three and four) has received the most attention in the popular press because of new practices like employee empowerment and team work that are aimed at that level. Changes in the span of control at level three account for most of the flattening in the overall organizational structure across functions. Skill levels were up for all the supervisory functions except marketing—no doubt related to the more extensive responsibilities associated with supervising more workers. Skill levels declined in six of the 11 areas for nonsupervisory workers, suggesting again that any transferring of responsibility from supervisors to exempt nonsupervisory workers was not sufficient to raise skills measurably. As noted previously, however, this does not address the question of whether the skills were transferred down yet another level to the nonexempt, nonsupervisory workers.

Interviews with the companies in this sample suggest that new technology—specifically, the use of expert systems—accounts for some of the variance across functional areas. Expert systems are computer decision trees that apply the decision rules used by experienced staff (experts) to complex decision-making processes such as the underwriting decision (Forester and Morrison, 1994). The system takes all the information on the insurance application and evaluates it in terms of risk factors, generating decisions about coverage and price. Underwriting and benefit administration in particular are using expert systems extensively. They have seen modest increases in the skills of nonsupervisory workers (level

Table 5-3. Employment, Skills, and Compensation by Function and Level

	Number			Skill			Pay		
	1986	1992	Change (%)	1986	1992	Change (%)	1986	1992	Change (%)
Data Processing									
Top manager	11	9	−18.18	549	599	9.11	96.2	123.6	28.48
Middle manager	69	69	0	340	336	−1.18	55.3	60	8.50
Line supervisor	172	248	44.19	229	240	4.80	40.1	42.4	5.74
Exempt, nonsupervisory	670	1254	87.16	163	167	2.45	29.2	29.8	2.05
Total	922	1580	71.37 Average	193	188	−2.59	34	33.6	−1.18
Underwriters									
Top manager	2	2	0	543	634	16.76	84.2	119.7	42.16
Middle manager	43	28	−34.88	354	359	1.41	57.2	65.9	15.21**
Line supervisor	87	98	12.64	246	255	3.66***	40.3	42.9	6.45****
Exempt, nonsupervisory	371	409	10.24	174	181	4.02	28.6	30.1	5.24****
Total	503	537	6.76 Average	203	205	0.99	33.3	34.7	4.20
Customer Service									
Top manager	1	5	400.00	470	568	20.85	65	113.5	74.62
Middle manager	58	62	6.90	310	311	0.32	49	55.8	13.88*
Line supervisor	248	263	6.05	184	197	7.07****	30.2	33	9.27****
Exempt, nonsupervisory	325	524	61.23	154	151	−1.95****	27.9	27.4	−1.79****
Total	632	854	35.13 Average	181	179	−1.10	30.8	31.7	2.92
Benefits Administration									
Top manager	1	1	0	650	632	−2.77	103	119.9	16.41
Middle manager	30	14	−53.33	307	343	11.73*	46.9	57.8	23.24*
Line supervisor	148	269	81.76	192	202	5.21****	31.7	31.8	0.32
Exempt, nonsupervisory	168	382	127.38	141	145	2.84	24.1	25.1	4.15
Total	347	666	91.93 Average	179	173	−3.35	29.5	28.6	−3.05
Actuarial									
Top manager	8	8	0	574	580	1.05	84.7	108.7	28.34

Middle manager	55	57	3.64	419	422	0.72	68.5	80.9	18.10
Line supervisor	46	68	47.83	237	291	22.78**	40.7	52	27.76**
Exempt, nonsupervisory	140	244	74.29	183	178	-2.73***	31.1	33.3	7.07
Total	249	377	51.41 Average	258	244	-5.43	42.9	45.4	5.83
Portfolio Management									
Top manager	9	11	22.22	642	691	7.63	116.8	151.7	29.88
Middle manager	30	58	93.33	407	377	-7.37	67	80.6	20.30*
Line supervisor	28	38	35.71	313	376	20.13	51.7	52	0.58
Exempt, nonsupervisory	77	172	123.38	200	212	6.00	33	39.5	19.70
Total	144	279	93.75 Average	291	275	-5.50	48.6	54.3	11.73
Investment Management									
Top manager	6	9	50.00	958	847	-11.59	168.6	179	6.17
Middle manager	7	11	57.14	316	356	12.66	54.1	61.7	14.05
Line supervisor	9	17	88.89	217	245	12.90****	33.1	43.1	30.21****
Exempt, nonsupervisory	29	70	141.38	179	168	-6.15	30.9	30.7	-0.65
Total	51	107	109.80 Average	307	257	-16.29	52.8	48.3	-8.52
Insurance Operations									
Top manager	19	18	-5.26	795	830	4.40	138.5	185.4	33.86
Middle manager	18	32	77.78	452	363	-19.69	84.5	62	-26.63****
Line supervisor	21	56	166.67	208	219	5.29****	31.5	36.6	16.19****
Exempt, nonsupervisory	37	171	362.16	183	148	-19.13****	29.3	26.6	-9.22****
Total	95	277	191.58 Average	361	231	-36.01	62.1	42.8	-31.08
Finance/Accounting									
Top manager	6	10	66.67	592	721	21.79	94	136.5	45.21
Middle manager	51	44	-13.73	339	335	-1.18	54.2	60.1	10.89
Line supervisor	87	110	26.44	194	222	14.43*	31.4	36.7	16.88
Exempt, nonsupervisory	166	266	60.24	167	160	-4.19	27.6	27.4	-0.72
Total	310	430	38.71 Average	211	207	-1.90	34.4	35.6	3.49

(continued)

Table 5-3. (Continued)

	1986	1992	Change (%)	1986	1992	Change (%)	1986	1992	Change (%)
Marketing									
Top manager	11	15	36.36	668	684	2.40	107.7	141.8	31.66*
Middle manager	104	91	−12.50	369	383	3.79*	64.7	70	8.19*
Line supervisor	241	255	5.81	292	254	−13.01****	57.9	45.8	−20.90****
Exempt, nonsupervisory	341	544	59.53	185	193	4.32*	32	33.9	5.94***
Total	697	905	29.84 Average	257	238	−7.39	47.1	42.7	−9.34
Human Resources									
Top manager	4	4	0	531	654	23.16	92.8	137.5	48.17
Middle manager	19	28	47.37	324	330	1.85	51.5	60.2	16.89
Line supervisor	26	52	100.00	192	214	11.46*	33	35.8	8.48*
Exempt, nonsupervisory	98	190	93.88	176	161	−8.52	28.5	28.3	−0.70
Total	147	274	86.39 Average	208	196	−5.77	34	34.6	1.76

*significant at the .1 level
**significant at the .01 level
***significant at the .001 level
****significant at the .0001 level

four) and the smallest increases in the span of control for supervisors. Level-four employees are not necessarily the targets of expert systems. Some of the skill and decision making of level-four jobs is built into the expert systems that are then used by lower level, often nonexempt, employees. Level four workers are then left with the more complicated tasks that raise their average skill levels.

Overall, level three (supervisors) had an increase in skill but did not have a correspondingly significant increase in pay (see Table 5-1). This can be attributed to changes in the distribution of jobs across functions: Every area except marketing experienced increased skill for its supervisors, but the two areas adding the most supervisors (data processing and benefits administration) were also among the lowest paid, and they helped depress the average increase.

Understanding the Variance Across Firms

A central question raised by the analyses by function is whether there are policies and practices that might influence the pattern of changes. These factors should be most noticeable across firms. As Table 5-4 shows, there is considerable variance across firms in the various outcomes considered above. Perhaps that variance is related to policies and practices that are within the control of the organization. For example, the companies with more health insurance business have larger benefits administration staffs. (There are more health insurance claims per policy to be processed than there are life insurance claims per policy.) We found larger marketing staffs in the companies that used the branch model of marketing, but we also found larger customer service staffs in these companies. This suggests that companies that employ their own agents have a stronger involvement in servicing the policies sold by those agents, while the companies that use the agency model expect the agents to perform the customer service function as well. We found flatter hierarchies in the stock companies, suggesting that market pressure is operating to make these firms more efficient. See Appendix B for additional details on the firms.

With a sample of only 11 firms, we are limited in the types of analyses that we can perform to examine the factors that drive changes in the employment distribution, skill, and pay. One of the most important to examine, however, is the relationship with overall firm performance. This relationship is complicated because the causation can potentially go in either direction. We use as a measure of performance the change in the ratio of net gain from operations after FIT and dividends to book equity. This is basically a return on equity measure. While there are better measures of overall efficiency (see, e.g., Cummins and Zi, 1993), this is the only one that was available for all three types of companies for both 1986 and 1992.

The sample of firms is divided into those where performance was improving during this period and those where it was declining. There was a clear break between the five firms that had improved their performance and the six that had declined in performance, with the closest values to zero being .53 and −.009. The companies are also divided into better performing and worse performing companies in each year. As noted earlier, all of the companies in the sample were

Table 5-4. Employment, Skills, and Pay by Level and Company

	Top manager			Middle manager			Supervisor			Exempt, nonsupervisory		
	1986	1992	% Change	1986	1992	% Change	1986	1992	% Change	1986	1992	% Change
						SKILL						
Company 1	752	759	0.93	353	338	-4.25	189	193	2.12	161	151	-6.21
2	801	701	-12.48	322	303	-5.90	166	173	4.22	166	155	-6.63
3	839	1118	33.25	469	615	31.13	272	256	-5.88	165	186	12.73
4	895	846	-5.47	383	467	21.93	193	297	53.89	199	190	-4.52
5	729	814	11.66	325	375	15.38	190	195	2.63	161	159	-1.24
6	629	614	-2.38	305	324	6.23	210	209	-0.48	184	179	-2.72
7	658	778	18.24	325	398	22.46	252	249	-1.19	187	182	-2.67
8	703	837	19.06	373	408	9.38	202	221	9.41	209	196	-6.22
9	473	535	13.11	282	302	7.09	198	195	-1.67	157	154	-1.60
10	716	660	-7.82	393	353	-10.18	177	197	11.30	198	143	-27.78
11				406	370	-8.87	177	194	9.60	152	148	-2.63
						COMPENSATION						
Company 1	122,781	168,864	37.53	54,622	62,069	13.63	31,204	33,853	8.49	28,457	27,890	-1.99
2	148,572	139,697	-5.97	60,083	59,777	-0.51	28,071	33,038	17.69	30,126	30,206	0.27
3	158,909	264,488	66.44	84,741	100,683	18.81	51,226	42,374	-17.28	29,049	30,665	5.56
4	161,214	188,783	17.10	68,852	89,415	29.87	32,870	56,843	72.93	34,250	33,687	-1.64
5	118,288	147,867	25.01	54,013	64,448	19.32	33,416	35,056	4.91	28,079	27,569	-1.82

6	103,422	117,319	13.44	46,617	56,290	20.75	34,295	37,866	10.41	30,533	32,692	7.07
7	114,045	167,328	46.72	51,157	87,966	71.95	40,270	43,123	7.08	31,518	33,569	6.51
8	110,963	199,040	79.38	55,985	85,425	52.59	28,249	35,191	24.57	30,146	32,248	6.97
9	68,566	89,119	29.98	45,300	48,973	8.11	33,670	36,635	8.81	29,133	28,799	−1.15
10	109,628	98,276	−10.36	54,760	50,214	−8.30	26,577	29,725	11.84	29,309	25,657	−12.46
11				62,265	64,877	4.19	32,660	34,898	6.85	26,278	27,266	3.76

EMPLOYEES

Company 1	27	39	44.44	118	265	124.58	204	341	67.16	633	1758	177.73
2	11	7	−36.36	102	84	−17.65	108	75	−30.56	231	170	−26.41
3	21	14	−33.33	56	23	−58.93	507	705	39.05	902	1405	55.76
4	7	7	0.00	80	20	−75.00	61	74	21.31	212	383	80.66
5	9	6	−33.33	45	43	−4.44	43	33	−23.26	161	122	−24.22
6	27	34	25.93	39	39	0.00	145	189	30.34	246	396	60.98
7	11	8	−27.27	42	29	−30.95	44	70	59.09	83	161	93.98
8	11	7	−36.36	42	33	−21.43	79	57	−27.85	159	193	21.38
9	6	4	−33.33	1	1	0.00	10	10	0.00	12	15	25.00
10	7	11	57.14	25	25	0.00	49	97	97.96	55	92	67.27
11				20	29	45.00	38	65	71.05	32	60	87.50
stock	20	20	1.69	72	107	48.61	263	368	39.62	565	1119	98.11
mutual/fraternal	11	11	−1.28	47	41	−11.29	68	71	4.81	130	156	20.25

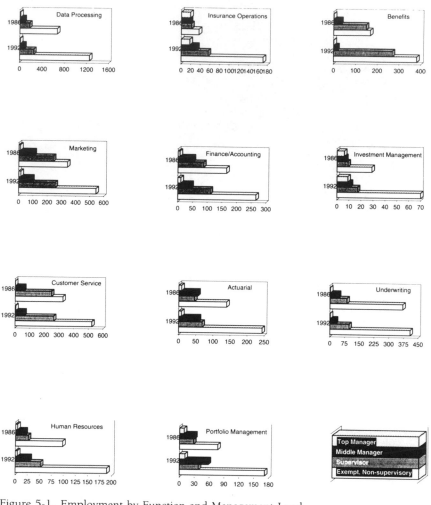

Figure 5-1. Employment by Function and Management Level.

better than average in performance, so even the "worse" performers are not representative of the bad firms in the industry.[13] Table 5-5 presents data on changes in the distribution of employment, in skills, and in pay for these two groups of firms. The declining group cut 20% of its top management jobs, greatly increasing the span of control of middle managers and supervisors, increased the skill requirements of top jobs by 18% (but not of middle management jobs), and increased the pay of top jobs by 39% (but not middle management or supervisors). In other words, the declining firms concentrated their change efforts on the top management positions. And as their performance declined, they increased their emphasis on the top jobs.

What cannot be told from this simple analysis is which way the causation is running. As the performance of firms declined, did they shift emphasis toward

Table 5-5. Improving and Declining Firms

	Number					Skill			Compensation		
	1986	% of Total	1992	% of Total	Change (%)	1986	1992	Change (%)	1986	1992	Change (%)
Improving firms											
Top managers	65	3.58	61	3.09	−6.15	713	697	−2.24	120,621	140,470	16.46
Middle managers	308	16.94	219	11.11	−28.90	343	352	2.62	59,198	66,652	12.59
Supervisors	436	23.98	428	21.70	−1.83	193	218	12.95	31,372	39,728	26.64
Exempt, nonsupervisory	1,009	55.50	1,264	64.10	25.27	183	180	−1.64	30,768	32,097	4.32
Total	1,818		1,972								
Declining firms											
Top managers	46	2.39	37	1.31	−19.57	715	845	18.18	126,163	175,107	38.79
Middle managers	144	7.49	107	3.79	−25.69	404	426	5.45	66,345	75,257	13.43
Supervisors	648	33.71	947	33.53	46.14	257	244	−5.06	47,258	40,567	−14.16
Exempt, nonsupervisory	1,084	56.40	1,733	61.37	59.87	168	182	8.33	29,170	30,535	4.68
Total	1,922		2,824								

top management in an effort to turn things around, or did their performance decline because of that shift in emphasis?

Kendall rank correlations suggest that changes in the administrative ratio—level two and three managers to level four employees—are positively and significantly related to increases in organizational performance between 1986 and 1992, as well as to performance in 1992. The Kendall's tau for the correlation between change in administrative ratio and change in performance was $-.6$ ($Z=-2.415$), while the same statistic for the correlation between change in administrative ratio and performance in 1992 was $-.511$ ($Z=-2.057$). This is a potentially important finding that suggests that reducing the proportion of middle management overhead in an organization is associated with improved performance. Changes in skill and salary did not reveal any significant effects on performance or on change in performance.

Conclusions

The most important results from this study are the overall findings suggesting that insurance companies have moved toward a flatter organizational hierarchy, that skill levels are rising for individual jobs but falling for the organization as a whole (because of shifting employment toward lower-skilled jobs), and that income inequality within the companies is rising. Managers have fewer promotional opportunities, but those who succeed receive a larger payoff. This suggests that management as a career will remain attractive, albeit less certain in terms of promotion prospects. Shifts to team-based approaches and the elimination of functional designations would suggest a greater need for generalists than specialists. As technology such as expert systems reduces the need for large units of experts, the manager's skill will be in recognizing when an expert needs to be called. Leadership skills, and the ability to adapt to a changing environment are two qualities that will be sought in the future. Fortunately, these skills will also be useful to team members who are not selected for promotion to manager. Increasing income inequality may lead to distrust within the organization, though this may be offset by the creation of technical tracks that allow highly skilled non-managers to earn equivalent levels of pay. The fact that insurance companies are relatively unique in facing no major industry-specific shocks from the outside environment suggests that these results should translate well to organizations in other industries.

Appendix A

The Sample of Companies

The 11 firms used here cannot be identified for reasons of confidentiality, but it is clearly a sample of convenience. Like all longitudinal samples, this one is censored in the technical sense in that companies that began business during the time period were excluded. (None of the companies originally in the database failed during this period.) In practical terms, this censoring may not be much of an issue for external validity given that start-up insurance companies are virtually nonexistent.

Three types of life insurance organizations are represented in the sample: mutual, stock, and fraternal. In 1991, mutual insurance companies represented only 5.6% of the companies in the life insurance industry, while they composed 55% of the sample. However, the mutuals, which are usually older and larger than stock companies, had 46.1% of the assets of all life insurance companies. The companies in the sample are therefore representative of the insurance industry, although not necessarily of the average company in that industry.

The companies in our sample are also disproportionately larger and older than the norm. The average life insurance company has around 250 employees (American Council of Life Insurance, 1993), while the average size of companies in our sample is around 2,000. Again, the larger companies have a disproportionate share of the market, which again makes the sample more representative of the industry than of companies in that industry. Because the sample concentrates on mutual companies, it is also older than the industry average: Only four of the companies in this sample were founded in this century, and all of them before 1920. Forty-three percent of all mutuals were founded before 1926, as opposed to 6% of all insurance companies. Population ecology research has found insurance companies to experience competition as exhibiting an inverted-U-shaped relationship between density and founding rates (Ranger-Moore et al., 1991), perhaps explaining the age of companies in the sample. Haveman (1993) also finds that larger savings and loans are more capable of taking advantage of opportunities to enter new markets, a result that may well translate to the larger insurance companies in the sample.

Regionally, this sample also resembles the distribution of mutuals, having 45% in the Midwest, 18% in the Northeast, and 27% in the South, as compared to 51% in the Midwest, 30% in the Northeast, and 13% in the South for the entire population of mutuals. Stock companies are more common in the West (40%) and South (36%), with some representation in the Midwest (16%) and Northeast (8%). (Lederer, 1971; American Council of Life Insurance, 1993)

Life insurance is the predominant product for these firms, although some also have health or long-term care product lines, and all market annuities. They are mostly in Best's financial size categories VII, VIII, or IX. (A. M. Best Co., 1992) Most follow the general agency model for sales, while a few use the branch model for at least some of their business. (Details of the firm characteristics are presented in Appendix B.) As discussed earlier, our data relate only to the *employees* of these firms and do not include sales agents who are not employees of the companies. All but three firms increased their numbers of employees over the six-year period on average at about the same rate as the industry as a whole. One that did not was acquired by another firm in 1993. Data on their performance show that they are slightly more efficient than the average life insurance company, no doubt because no "failed" firms are in the sample. Appendix B provides additional details about the sample.

The 11 companies chosen here are all clients of Hay Associates, and it is worth considering whether there is anything about being a Hay client that would select in firms with particular characteristics. For example, there has recently been a move in many companies away from using detailed job descriptions in some firms. These descriptions and structures are a strength of the Hay system.

Possibly firms that have these broader jobs might have other distinctive charac-teristics as well—such as other innovations in work organization—and would be less likely to use Hay's services. The movement toward broader jobs was not underway in 1986, however, and no firms left the sample since then. The fact noted above that they are slightly more efficient than the industry average sug-gests that this may not be a sample of firms that are lagging new developments.

Appendix B

In 1986, there were 2,254 life insurance companies in the United States. By 1988, there were 2,343. The next few years showed decreases in the number of compa-nies (2,270 in 1989, 2,195 in 1990, 2,065 in 1991, and 2,005 in 1992), but the numbers of establishments and employees and the dollar value of the payrolls did not begin to drop as sharply or as soon. Sales, income, and assets of these companies maintained a steady rise over the same period.

Mutuals have no stockholders and no capital stock. The policyholders own these companies, elect the boards of directors, and may receive profits as divi-dends. Stockholders own stock companies, sharing in the profits and losses and electing the boards of directors. Fraternals have no capital stock, and the activities of these organizations are carried out for the mutual benefit of the members of the organization. They have representative forms of government. Stock companies are by far the most common, while fraternals are becoming so uncommon that they are not included in reports of numbers of life insurance companies. In 1971, there were 150 fraternals providing life insurance, out of 1950 companies. The data below pertain to stock companies and holding companies:

	1988	1989	1990
Establishments	14,400	14,300	14,100
Employees	538,300	568,800	571,800
Payroll (billions)	$ 13.7	$ 14.8	$ 16.3
Sales (billions)	$1,716	$1,788	$2,024
Income (billions)	$ 338.1	$ 367.3	$ 402.2
Assets (billions)	$1,167	$1,300	$1,408

Source: U.S. Department of Commerce, 1992

Company size has changed as follows over the years:

	1985	1988	1991
Employees	565,000	538,300	561,200
Companies	2,261	2,343	2,065
Employees/Company	250	230	267

Source: U.S. Department of Commerce, 1992

Appendix C

Company	Human resources practices	Product line	Efficiency/financial condition
1	Uses general agency model for individual life insurance, branch model for group lines, accident, and health insurance Reorganized corporate structure in 1987, sold its property/casualty company in the same year	life, health, annuities, disability	.726 A+ Experienced significant loss in 1987, but has good performance generally
2	Holding company, uses different practices in different subsidiaries		.69
3	Uses general agency model Merged with an affiliated company in 1987	life, annuities, disability, health Markets life and annuities through banking institutions	A+ profits reduced in 1988 due to losses in other lines
Mutuals, fraternals			
1	Uses agency model Formed two subsidiaries in 1981	Life, annuity, disability, no group life or health	.725 A+
2	Uses branch model, accepts brokerage Purchased two subsidiaries, one in 1981, one in 1985	Life, annuity, health	.454 A+
3	Uses agency model in United States, branch model in overseas operations	life, annuity, disability	.644 A+
4	Uses agency model	life, annuity, disability	.625 A+ A court judgment against this company is pending appeal
5	Uses agency model New president, CEO 1987	life, annuity, disability, long-term care	.666 A++

(*continued*)

Appendix C (*continued*)

Company	Human resources practices	Product line	Efficiency/financial condition
6	Uses agency model	life, annuity, disability, health	.462 A
7	Uses agency model for individual business, branch model for group and corporate business	life, annuity	.508 A++
8	Uses agency model	life, annuity dropped several lines from 1986–92	.681 A+

1992 Staffing Patterns (Average by Type of Firm)

Firm type	Product lines		Governance		Human resources	
	Health and life (%)	Life only (%)	Stock (%)	Mutual and fraternal (%)	Branch (%)	Agency (%)
Finance/accounting	10.09	8.83	5.62	9.64	8.49	9.14
Data processing	29.70	25.26	18.47	29.26	24.57	28.26
Human resources	3.74	4.18	3.26	3.84	3.28	3.68
Marketing	13.32	12.80	15.33	12.56	16.58	12.64
Investment	0.91	1.54	1.24	1.78	2.09	1.16
Portfolio	1.83	2.77	3.43	2.08	1.68	2.13
Operations	4.31	1.87	6.23	2.25	2.27	3.38
Accounting	4.80	5.71	5.62	5.49	3.53	6.83
Underwriting	7.16	9.01	7.41	7.76	8.13	7.71
Customer service	8.17	8.88	11.23	7.96	9.05	7.26
Benefits administration	2.93	2.63	10.33	2.12	6.62	2.16

Notes

This research is supported by a grant from the Alfred P. Sloan Foundation to the Financial Institutions Center at the Wharton School for a study of the financial services industry. Thanks to Steve Gross and Hay Associates for the use of the data analyzed in this study. Thanks also to Frank Levy and Richard J. Murnane for their comments on an earlier draft of this paper.

1. It has traditionally been the highest-paid industry in the United States (current fourth highest [U.S. Department of Labor, 1992]) and has seemed to be virtually recession-proof with respect to job security, at least when compared to other industries. For exam-

ple, when national unemployment rates were 7.2% in 1985 and 7.4% in 1992, they were 3.5% and 4.5%, respectively, for the financial services industry, and 2.6% and 3.8%, respectively, for financial services managers. (U.S. Department of Commerce, 1993) Employment has grown steadily over the past decades with only a slight drop between 1990 and 1992 (from 6,729,000 employees back to 6,672,000). About 7% of the U.S. workforce is in financial services, which includes finance, insurance, and real estate. Together these services account for about 17% of the gross national product in the United States (U.S. Department of Labor, 1992; U.S. Department of Commerce, 1993).

2. Uncited quotations are from managers in the industry.

3. An important characteristic of the insurance industry is that it has always made extensive use of contract sales managers—general agents—who are not employees of the company. This is known as the *agency* model of insurance human resource management where independent insurance agents handle many of the marketing and retail functions of the business. One reason why the supervisory ratio or span of control noted above is so small in this industry is because the retailing operation, which in most industries accounts for many low-level employees who need supervision, is handled outside of the company. Sales managers in insurance companies that use the agency model are not company employees, and neither are their sales agents. Under this model, the agents are under contract to the general agent, not the insurance carrier. The *branch* model, in contrast, uses company employees as sales managers. Under this model, the salespeople are under contract to the company, and in some companies, they are company employees. Some companies use both models, selling individual policies through agents and group policies through employees. See Lederer (1971) for a more detailed explanation of these arrangements. For an interesting sociological account of the evolution of these models, see Zelizer (1978), who posits that the use of person-to-person contact was necessary to overcome the early view of life insurance as tempting fate or putting a price on human life. The current shift to more branch models may well be attributable to seeing life insurance as another investment.

4. Agents contract to sell insurance and provide service on policies. Brokers negotiate with carriers to write policies for specific organizations or individuals. Service organizations provide such services as data gathering, education, and consulting specifically for the insurance industry or a part thereof.

5. This description of the Hay system is based on materials provided by Hay and interviews with Hay consultants. Bellak (1984) provides a good summary of the Hay system.

6. Other proxies for skill, such as education, suffer from lack of consistency and from contamination by other sociological factors. Measures that examine the characteristics of workers are in general a poor proxy for skill requirements as they may vary—depending on labor market circumstances—independent of any changes in actual demand for skill. The Hay measures, by evaluating the job and not the person, avoid this problem. Hay analysts, carefully trained to ensure consistency, further enhance this measure.

7. The reliability tests appear to be qualitative—questioning outliers, for example, or unusual patterns in the data. The incentives are clearly for Hay to be consistent over time in its methods. Long-term clients (the bulk of their business) know which of their jobs have remained constant, and it would be painfully obvious if Hay generated different job evaluations for those positions over time.

8. The separate measures are combined through use of a constant algorithm that weights the various measures and creates an index from them. Unfortunately, only the final job evaluation total is available (measures of the separate components were not retained), and it is impossible to recreate the separate component scores from the aggregate score.

While some might argue that this algorithm neglects shifts in importance of various skills over time, we maintain that this is still the best measure available to address this question.

9. As with most organizations, the nonexempt staff represent more than 50% of the employees of these companies, so conclusions about the whole companies cannot be based on these data. However, since the focus here is on management jobs, the lack of data on nonexempt employees is not critical.

10. For additional studies of the effects of technological change on specific jobs in this industry, see Hartmann, et al., 1986; Chamot, 1987; Kraut, 1987 (pages 81–94); and U.S. Department of Labor, 1990a.

11. One must be careful in making attributions of income inequality based simply on differences in group means. The dispersion in salary about the mean must also be considered to complete the picture. We calculated gini and thiel coefficients for the dispersion of salaries over the six year period and found that the distributions did not change substantially. (1986 Gini: 0.255, Thiel: 0.058, 1992 Gini: 0.243, Thiel: 0.055) Within the management levels, the story was much the same.

12. The authors thank Frank Levy and Dick Murnane for this observation.

13. There seemed to be a break in the sample between ratios of .28 and .52 in 1982, so we divided our "better" and "worse" firms at this point. Five firms were in the "better" category and six were in the "worse" category. In 1992, there was not such a clear break. There were two possible breaks: between .51 and .36 and between .36 and .28. We selected the first break, deciding that a rate of .50 as the dividing line for both years would be the most interpretable.

References

Adler, Paul. 1986. "New Technologies, New Skills," *California Management Review* 29(1):9–28.

A. M. Best Co. 1986–92. *Best's Insurance Reports—Life/Health*. Morristown, N.J.: A. M. Best Co.

American Council of Life Insurance. 1993. *1993 Life Insurance Fact Book*. Washington: American Council of Life Insurance.

Attewell, Paul. 1987. "The Deskilling Controversy," *Work and Occupations* 14(3):323–346.

———. 1990. "What is Skill," *Work and Occupations* 17(4):422–448.

Bird, Anat. 1991. "Organizational Flattening Within the US Banking Industry," *Bankers Magazine* 174, no. 4:67–70.

Brooks, N. A. 1987. "Strategic Issues for Financial Services Marketing," *Journal of Services Marketing* 1:57–66.

Bureau of Labor Statistics. 1990. *Insurance Employment Outlook*. Washington: U.S. Government Printing Office.

Cappelli, Peter. 1992. "Examining Managerial Displacement," *Academy of Management Journal* 35(1):203–217.

———. 1993. "Are Skill Requirements Rising? Evidence from Production and Clerical Jobs," *Industrial and Labor Relations Review,* 46(3):515–530.

Chamot, Dennis. 1987. "Electronic Work and the White Collar Employee." In *Technology and the Transformation of White Collar Work*. Robert E. Kraut ed. Hillsdale, N.J.: Lawrence Erlbaum Associates.

Cummins, J. David, and Hongmin Zi. 1993. "A Comparison of Econometric and Mathematical Programming Cost Efficiency Estimates for the U.S. Life Insurance Industry." Working Paper, Philadelphia: Wharton School, Financial Institutions Center.

Dauer, Christopher. 1991. "Industry is Moving Away from Field Adjusters," *National Underwriter* 95(18):17, 46.

———. 1992. "Industry Officials Consider Future of Insurance Distribution," *National Underwriter* 96(40):15.

Doyle, Walter F. 1993. "Agents need technology to customize their service." *National Underwriter* 97(32):15, 17.

Feuer, Dale. 1985. "Where the Dollars Go," *Training* 22, no. 10 (October):45–53.

Forester, Tom, and Perry Morrison. 1994. *Computer Ethics*. Cambridge: MIT Press.

Hall, P. 1992. "Living With TQM," *Risk Management* 39(3):20–22.

Hartmann, Heidi I., Robert E. Kraut, and Louise A. Tilly. 1986. *Computer Chips and Paper Clips*. Washington: National Academy Press.

Haveman, Heather. 1993. "Organizational Size and Change: Diversification in the Savings and Loan Industry after Deregulation," *Administrative Science Quarterly* 38:20–50.

Helldorfer, Sharon, and Michael Daly. 1993. "Reengineering Brings Together Units." *Best's Review (Prop/Casualty)* 94(6):82–85.

Henderson, Richard I. 1985. *Compensation Management: Rewarding Performance*. Reston, Va.: Reston Publishing Company.

Hoyt, B. 1992. "Striving for Efficiency in Personal Lines," *Agent & Broker* 64(2):26, 28.

Jones, David C. 1993. "Agents are warming up slowly to high-tech tools." *National Underwriter* (97)46:9, 13.

King, Carole. 1991. "Sales Help When Agents Need It," *National Underwriter* 95(9):23–24, 34.

Klein, Elizabeth. 1992. "Thinking Machines Add New Expertise to Banking Functions," *Savings Institutions* 113(2):37–38.

Knowles, Robert G. 1990. "Answers Challenged to Revamp Systems." *National Underwriter* (Property/Casualty/Employee Benefits). 94(16):363.

Kraut, Robert E. 1987. *Technology and the Transformation of White-Collar Work*. Hillsdale, N.J.: Lawrence Erlbaum Associates.

Leana, Carrie. 1986. "Predictors and Consequences of Delegation," *Academy of Management Journal* 29, no. 4 (December):754–774.

Lederer, R. Werner. 1971. *Home Office and Field Agency Organization—Life*. Homewood, Ill.: Richard D. Irwin.

Levin, Henry M., Russell Rumberger, and Christina Finnan. 1990. *Escalating Skill Requirements or Different Skill Requirements?* Brown University: Conference on Changing Skill Requirements: Gathering and Assessing the Evidence.

Levine, David I. 1993. "What Do Wages Buy?" *Administrative Science Quarterly* 38:462–483.

Levy, Frank, and Richard Murnane. 1992. "U.S. Earnings Levels and Earning Inequality: A Review of Recent Trends and Proposed Explanations," *Journal of Economic Literature* 30(3):1333–1381.

Lunt, Penny. 1992. "Children's Savings Stir New Interest," *ABA Banking Journal* 84(1):73–74.

McClure, K. A. 1992. "Telephone Service Sells," *Best's Review (Life/Health)* 93(5):65–66.

McGrath, Richard A. 1992. "It Pays to Provide Good Service," *American Agent & Broker* 64(2):20–21, 43–45.

National Underwriter. 1987. "Companies Upgrading Product Development," *National Underwriter* 91(29a):23–25.

Nelson, Warren A. 1992. "Boost Retention," *Managers Magazine* 67(7):23–26.

Pfeffer, Jeffrey, and James N. Baron. 1988. "Taking the Workers Back Out: Recent Trends in the Structuring of Employment," *Research in Organizational Behavior* 10:257–303.

Ranger-Moore, James, Jane Banaszak-Holl, and Michael T. Hannan. 1991. "Density-Dependent Dynamics in Regulated Industries: Founding Rates of Banks and Life Insurance Companies," *Administrative Science Quarterly* 36, no. 1 (March):36–65.

Rickard, Henry C. 1972. "The Hay Compensation Comparison." In *Handbook of Wage and Salary Administration: 3–60—3–66.* Milton L. Rock, ed., New York: McGraw-Hill.

Scites, Janice L. 1993. "Transforming the Dinosaur." *Best's Review (Life/Health).* 94(7):76–78.

U.S. Department of Commerce. 1985–93. *Statistical Abstract of the United States.* Washington: U.S. Government Printing Office.

U.S. Department of Labor. 1990. *Technology and Its Impact on Employment in the Life and Health Insurance Industries.* Washington: U.S. Government Printing Office.

———. 1990. *Occupational Outlook—Life Insurance.* Washington: U.S. Government Printing Office.

———. 1992. *Employment and Earnings.* Washington: U.S. Government Printing Office.

Van Horn, Charles W. G. 1972. "The Hay Guide Chart-Profile Method." In *Handbook of Wage and Salary Administration: 2–86—2–97.* Milton L. Rock, ed. New York: McGraw-Hill.

Violano, Michael. 1990. "Bankers Tickled with Teller Automation Toys," *Bankers Monthly* 107(7):42–46.

Zelizer, Viviana A. 1978. "Human Values and the Market: The Case of Life Insurance and Death in 19th-Century America," *American Journal of Sociology* 84:591–610.

Evolution of Management Roles in a Networked Organization

6

An Insider's View of the Hewlett-Packard Company

SARA L. BECKMAN

A new organizational form is capturing the attention of practitioners and academics alike. This form, described in the management literature as the "virtual corporation" (Davidow and Malone, 1992), by economists as a "Möbius strip" organizational form (Sabel, 1991) residing somewhere between the hierarchical and market forms, and by organizational behaviorists, (e.g., Miles and Snow, 1986), as a highly evolved form of the "organic" organization, originally defined by Burns and Stalker in 1961, applies to organizations operating in highly fluid environments for which managing numerous internal and external relationships in a dynamic, real-time fashion is critically important.

Baker (1992) provides a useful definition:

> A network organization can flexibly construct a unique set of internal and external linkages for each unique project. Unlike a bureaucracy, which is a fixed set of relationships for processing all problems, the network organization molds itself to each problem. Moreover, it adapts itself not by top-management fiat but by the interactions of problems, people, and resources; within the broad confines of corporate strategy, organizational members autonomously work out relationships. (p. 398)

Fluid management of relationships external to the firm (with suppliers, customers, technology partners) as well as relationships internal to the firm (across functional and divisional boundaries) characterizes the networked firm.

A broad-based literature addresses various aspects of the networked organization ranging from microorganizational perspectives on how to measure the existence of a network (e.g., Baker, 1992), to the use of information systems to facilitate network interactions (Rockart and Short, 1991), through strategic and policy implications of networked organizational forms employed by other, particularly Asian (e.g., Biggart and Hamilton, 1992) and Italian (e.g., Piore and Sabel, 1984) cultures. Also addressed are the implications, some known and some projected, of the networked form on how white-collar and managerial work is planned and executed. Kanter (1983) suggests ways in which career paths must be altered to accommodate less linear paths to the top. Snow, Miles, and Coleman (1992) define the roles—architect, lead operator, and caretaker—that managers play in creating and maintaining networked organizations. Miles (1989) forecasts the industrial relations policy changes that will be required by the networked organization, and various popular articles (e.g., O'Reilly, 1994 and Stewart, 1992) paint graphic pictures of the life of the white-collar worker in these organizations.

This vast literature does not, however, address the unplanned and organic way in which organizations come to be networked—at least more networked— or the role managers play in that transition and in the resulting organization. Empirical work on networked organizations tends to focus either on a snapshot in time of a networked organization (e.g., Nohria, 1992) or on a broad set of industry relationships (e.g., Saxenian, 1990). Little longitudinal work has been done at the firm level that provides insight into how firms develop their networks over time.

This chapter provides an insider's view of the evolution of the networked organizational form at the Hewlett-Packard Company over the past 10 years. Hewlett-Packard (HP), a prosperous company by any financial measure and a company widely renowned for its human resources management practices, pro- vides a rich case study.[1] The company's networked structure has emerged slowly over the past 10 or more years through a series of incremental changes in its organization, reflected most dramatically by changes in the structure of its manu- facturing function. Choice of the networked organizational form was not an explicit one at HP; rather the form is the result of gradual adaptation to a changing external environment.

In great contrast with much of the literature on the subject, managers and white-collar workers at HP today do not seem to have a sense that there has been a major reorientation in their roles and responsibilities relative to 10 years ago. Rather, they feel that their jobs have evolved in a well-reasoned and understood, albeit not necessarily predicted, way. Development of the internal and external networks has seemingly been a natural part of the progression of their work rather than a radical or explicit departure from the status quo. To these workers, change and adaptation have always been required by the markets in which they operate and the technologies with which they work. Nevertheless, human re- sources management practices at the company have changed, doing so again in a gradual response to the needs of the business environment at the time rather than in response to an explicit plan to become more networked.

This chapter provides a comprehensive picture of the transition HP has made over the past 10 years to being a more networked organization. The stage is set by describing the industry in which HP plays and major changes that have occurred in that industry making it more networked. Within this context, this chapter then describes the transformations HP has undergone during the past 10 years to accommodate industry forces and the roles that managers have played in those changes. Finally, with this rich tapestry as background, the chapter focuses di- rectly on managers and white-collar workers, describing the changes they have experienced in their work and the evolution of their evaluation and reward structures. The chapter takes a broad view, as it is important for those researching the networked organization and the roles of managers in organizational transition to appreciate the multitude of forces that have caused change and the organic fashion in which that change has occurred.

The chapter draws on eight years (1984–93) of personal experience at Hewlett-Packard,[2] spent primarily in a strategic planning role at corporate headquarters which provided a companywide perspective and access to the reasoning behind many of the organizational changes that were made. Recent interviews with HP managers at various levels and locations throughout the organization yielded knowledge of changes that happened subsequent to 1993 and impressions of what the changes have meant to people working there.

The Industry Context

The evolution of the networked organizational form has been particularly rapid in the computer industry[3] over the past 10 years, affecting structures at both industry and firm levels. The list of factors causing this change is well rehearsed (see, for example, Nohria and Eccles, 1992): Globalization pressures drove establishment of operations in developing countries such as China and India and expansion of operations elsewhere to better access growing markets. Competition from smaller, niche players (e.g., Silicon Graphics, Apollo, and Sun Microsystems in the workstation business) created pressure for their larger counterparts to be nimble and responsive. Competition from larger foreign competitors, mostly Asian, boasting new technologies and highly effective manufacturing capabilities, intensified. Customers, ever more savvy, increased their demands for cost, quality, and timeliness, as well as for fully integrated, often customized, solutions to their problems. Fast, unpredictable changes in technology led to more rapid new product development cycles, less internal technology development and formation of numerous technology access alliances.

Industry participants responded at multiple levels, improving operations within their own factories, integrating functional areas across their organizations, and forming partnerships outside the bounds of their own organizations, all of which increased the degree of networking in the industry. By 1984, most companies had implemented some version of total quality management (TQM) and were attempting to move to just-in-time (JIT).[4] Focused on the shop floor, these programs increased networking within companies as well as with critical suppliers. Quality improvement teams, an important part of many TQM programs, caused cross-departmental groups to meet around resolution of specific problems.[5] JIT reduced inventory buffers between adjacent operations in the manufacturing plant, facilitating increased communications among workers. Often suppliers were engaged as well, in recent years through electronic data interchange (EDI) that reduces need for human interface and speeds communication. In Galbraith's (1973) terms, increased horizontal and vertical communications were substituted for decreases in slack resources. Networking, particularly at the plant level, increased.

Horizontal process management followed. Early forms focused on design for manufacturability and concurrent engineering, pairing manufacturing and R&D functions to reduce cost and improve time-to-market. As marketing became involved, a broader view of the product generation process was developed to monitor the product from "concept to customer." Recently, many computer companies (including DEC, HP, IBM, and Apple) have adopted supply chain management programs to optimize the performance of their order fulfillment processes (Davis, 1993). Integrating players from procurement through distribution, these programs simultaneously improve customer satisfaction, as measured by number of orders shipped correctly and on time, and reduce total inventory. Networking across the functions in the organization thus increases as well.[6]

Finally, the form of the industry changed radically as the larger U.S.[7] companies (e.g., HP, DEC, IBM) vertically disintegrated, shedding upstream operations such as machining, sheet metal bending, plastic injection molding and transformer winding. At the same time, they formed tighter partnerships with original equipment manufacturers (OEM's) and other types of value-added partners for delivery of complete systems solutions to customers. The smaller and younger companies (e.g., Apple Computer, Sun Microsystems, Apollo) opted not to backward integrate from their beginnings, choosing instead to purchase raw materials such as sheet metal computer housings, and form strategic alliances and partnerships for acquisition of technologies like disk drives and display monitors. Like their larger counterparts, they also developed partnerships for delivery of their products to the marketplace. Recent popular literature (Prahalad and Hamel, 1990) suggests that this is a process of focusing on core competencies.

This collection of changes created an intricate web of relationships that continues to grow ever more complex, with continued vertical disintegration on the back end and regular addition of new—sometimes surprising (e.g., the Taligent partnership between Apple and IBM)—technology and marketing partnerships. Competitors now buy products from one another, share the same value-added dealer and OEM channels, jointly develop new technologies, and yet compete fiercely for market share, pushing one another rapidly down the price/performance curve. (See Saxenian, 1990, for a rich description of the networks within Silicon Valley.) It is within this complex and changing industry environment that Hewlett-Packard competes and its managers have learned to work.

The Hewlett-Packard Company

HP is a *Fortune* 25 company, with 1995 revenues of about $32 billion and 102,300 employees worldwide.[8] Its product lines range from computers (e.g., the HP9000 workstation and HP3000 minicomputer) and computer peripherals (e.g., the widely popular LaserJet) to both low-end (e.g., portable voltmeters) and high-end (e.g., network spectrum analyzers) instrumentation. It participates in businesses that serve the mass market (e.g., printers and personal computers) as well as more specialized businesses (e.g., ultrasound imaging and monitoring devices for critically ill patients), creating a wide range of strategies and process requirements. These diverse activities are integrated under a single purpose statement: To create information products that accelerate the advancement of knowledge and fundamentally improve the effectiveness of people and organizations.

HP is a very successful company whose revenues grew steadily from $7 billion in 1985 to about $32 billion in 1995, and net earnings, while not showing stable growth through this period, were always positive (Figure 6–1) unlike those of some of its primary competitors. The company is credited with being highly innovative, gaining much of its annual revenue growth from products introduced within the prior two years (Figure 6–2). A recent article praised HP's innovativeness and ability to "eat its own," regularly introducing new products that cannibalize the old (Deutschman, 1994).

HP is renowned for its strong company culture, often referred to as the "HP Way." This culture, established by Hewlett and Packard when they founded the company 55 years ago, emphasizes creativity by individuals in the interest of making profit for the company (Packard, 1995). Reward systems in the company emphasize this balanced culture, as companywide profit sharing motivates individuals to "put on their HP hats" when making critical decisions while generous recognition programs (e.g., stock options) reward individual achievement. Until the mid-1980s HP also offered job security to anyone meeting minimal performance standards. At that time, voluntary severance incentive (VSI) and early retirement packages were offered and job security was modified to employment security.[9]

In recent years, HP sharpened its competitive responses by finding a new balance between its consensus-oriented management style and top-down, authoritative direction. Several planning tools and processes were introduced to assist businesses in clarifying and integrating their business goals. Hoshin planning, borrowed from the Yokagawa-Hewlett Packard (YHP) division in Japan, entailed a top-down discipline of setting breakthrough, or change, objectives. Ten-step planning provided a process for thoroughly thinking through market segmentation, product positioning, and technology focus for competitive advantage. A stronger set of management committees (e.g., the operations, marketing, and planning and quality committees) brought senior managers together to make critical policy decisions for the company. Collectively, these changes better integrated strategic decision making in the company and reduced the "terminal niceness" for which Pascale (1990) soundly criticizes HP, as consensus is now sought around business, rather than personal, objectives.[10]

A cornerstone of HP's success was its "integrated multidivisional firm" structure (Perrow 1992) of autonomous, product-oriented divisions. Begun by Hewlett and Packard, the divisionalized form allowed the company to grow rapidly, spinning off new divisions as product lines achieved self-sufficiency or when an existing division got too large (over about 2,000 people or $200 million in annual revenues). Each division was a stand-alone entity containing all of the resources—manufacturing, marketing, R&D, human resources, and finance—it needed to support its profit-making endeavors. General managers (GMs) of divisions were expected to make profit and grow. Those who succeeded in this pursuit were rarely questioned; those who did not received "help" from Hewlett

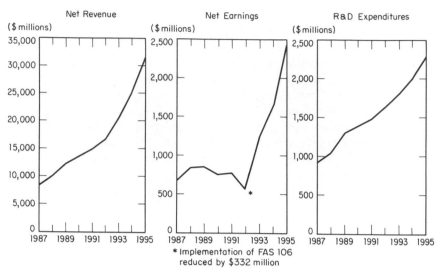

Figure 6-1. Hewlett-Packard Worldwide Growth, Fiscal Year 1995.

or, more often, Packard. The primary objective of a new hire to the company was to become a division manager, running his or her own autonomous business. By 1984, there were roughly 50–60 product-oriented divisions and numerous sales divisions scattered about the world.

As the company grew, the number of divisions to be managed became too large, so groups of divisions, and ultimately sectors to contain the groups, were formed.[11] These were at best loose confederations; the divisions within them behaved quite autonomously, rarely seeking support, input, advice, or any form of partnership with other divisions within or outside the group or sector. Some groups, such as the Medical Products Group, were coherent, logical collections of divisions (e.g., Waltham Division responsible for monitoring devices for critically ill patients, Andover Division making ultrasound imaging devices). Others, like the Manufacturing Systems Group, housed divisions as diverse as the Loveland Instrument Division making low-end instruments such as voltmeters, the Data Systems Division making HP1000 real-time computers, and the Manufacturing Productivity Division making manufacturing systems software.

Although divisions autonomously formulated and executed product development, manufacturing, and marketing strategies, control of financial and human resources policy was retained at the corporate level. HP senior management, concerned about being fair, imposed common personnel policies across the company for hiring, reward, evaluation, and termination. The human resources and finance and accounting functions developed strong corporate organizations and maintained tight control over divisional practices.[12]

In the mid-1980s, three major forces jeopardized the divisional structure that had been so important to HP's growth: (1) Customer need for fully integrated computer systems solutions meant that disk drive, operating system, mainframe,

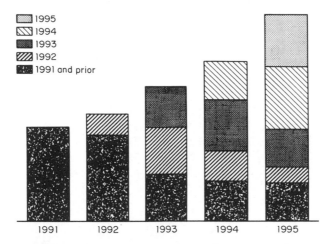

Figure 6-2. Hewlett-Packard Product Orders by Year of Introduction.

and integrated circuit divisions could no longer make fully independent decisions about their product designs. (2) Independent resources, affordable in the days of 80–90% market share and rapid growth, were too expensive for the competitive computer and peripherals markets.[13] (3) It became clear that divisions in radically different businesses (e.g., peripherals products divisions in the highly price sensitive consumer market and minicomputer divisions in the business solutions market) required different organizational structures to compete.

Three strong sectors emerged in the company, each choosing the organizational form that fit it best: The Computer Products Operation (CPO), housing products primarily delivered through dealer channels (e.g., printers, disk drives, and personal computers), chose a very lean, vertically disintegrated structure that was still highly divisionalized, but controlled by well-developed group- or strategic-business-unit-level strategies; the Computer Systems Operation (CSO), containing the minicomputer, workstation, and systems integration businesses, chose a centralized, functionally organized structure to develop and deliver fully integrated and customized systems solutions cost effectively; and the Measurement Systems Operation (MSO),[14] home to HP's traditional instrumentation product lines, remained more conventionally organized with little integration among the divisions (Figure 6–3). After painful reflection, the executive committee increased each sector's freedom to set its own human resources management policies.

Thus, HP has evolved from an integrated, multidivisional organizational form comprising autonomous divisional operations to a more complex and highly networked structure in which organizations are expected not only to manage more external relationships as part of their everyday operations, but to integrate more fully with other internal operations as well. This evolution, a response to critical competitive needs, never took the form of a "grand plan" to become more

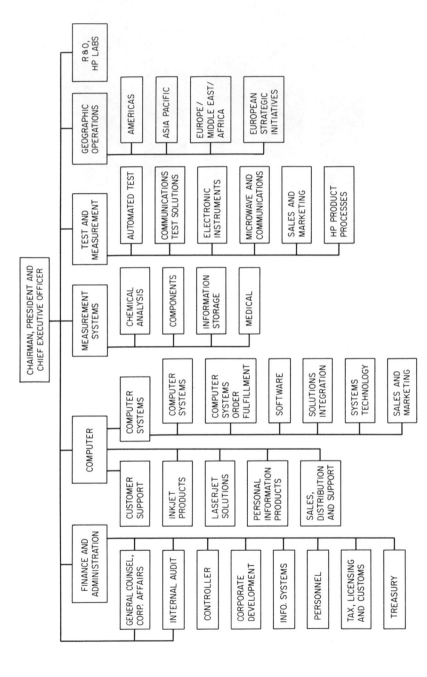

Figure 6-3. Hewlett-Packard Corporate Organization, December 1995.

networked, but rather occurred as a series of small adjustments over time. The manufacturing function provides a particularly good lens through which to view this evolution and its effect on managerial work, as it often led the way in making change. Not as sacred as R&D, and better understood than marketing, the manufacturing function was frequently the forcing function for change in the other areas.[15]

Evolution of the Manufacturing Organization: 1984–94

In 1984, the manufacturing function at HP was highly decentralized, with each division in the company containing its own manufacturing activity. Some divisions, such as the Santa Rosa Division making network measurement devices, invested in a full range of manufacturing processes from precision machining through microcircuit assembly to final product assembly and test. Other divisions, such as the Computer Systems Division making HP3000 minicomputers, limited its investments to printed circuit board assembly and final product assembly and test. Many chose a position in between, investing only in the processes they deemed critical to business success. Although manufacturing managers made decisions in concert with their R&D and marketing counterparts, the three functions were not highly integrated.

The mid-1980s marked the beginning of a radical transformation of the manufacturing function at HP, moving it to a more internally and externally networked organization. Three critical and interrelated changes occurred: First, the company recognized that it was duplicating expensive and underutilized manufacturing resources; it chose to downsize and consolidate them. Second, divisions began vertically disintegrating, eliminating capabilities for sheet metal, machining, plastic injection molding, transformer winding, and the like. At the same time, a few critical processes became more centrally managed. Third, in the late 1980s, there was a strong push to recognize and improve performance in "horizontal" processes—specifically product generation and order fulfillment—that cut across functional silos.

These changes, drastic in hindsight, developed slowly throughout the 1980s and early 1990s. In the process, manufacturing managers and white-collar professionals learned new skills and adopted new roles commensurate with a more networked environment. A brief description of each change and the process used to make it explains the means by which managers and white-collar workers developed their abilities to accommodate change and foster relationships.

Consolidation

Development of the "Spectrum" product line of RISC-based[16] computers motivated the first serious consideration of manufacturing consolidation. The new product line replaced much of the existing HP1000, HP9000, and HP3000 product lines, thus requiring fewer manufacturing resources. Immediate targets were two divisions located 200 yards apart in Cupertino, California. The Data Systems Division (DSD), parent to all other computer divisions in the company, produced the old HP1000 real-time minicomputer and the Computer Systems Division, a younger spin-off of DSD, produced the high-end HP3000 minicomputer. Both performed basic board assembly and test as well as final assembly and test operations, but DSD's operations were more complex due to its myriad old products.

Cursory analysis of the two divisions' manufacturing cost structures, carried out by a small group of DSD and corporate managers, suggested potential savings of nearly 20% with consolidated operations. Highly emotionally charged discussions, conducted at senior levels in the company, ensued. Despite the projected savings, the two division managers saw no reason to relinquish their autonomy, allowing their manufacturing capability to be subsumed by the other. Ultimately, the decision to consolidate was made by the chief operating officer and, unlike most decisions made at HP, imposed on the two divisions.

As the first consolidation transpired, a massive data collection effort by the corporate manufacturing organization established, for the first time, a central repository of information on HP's manufacturing capability. With these data, the duplication of effort became clear: Most manufacturing processes were used 50% of the time or less (very few were used on more than one shift) as they built product for their division alone; there were nearly 200 engineers companywide working on the printed circuit board assembly process alone, about 3–4 to a division;[17] replicated procurement specialists purchased the same components causing vendors to increase their overhead in response;[18] some capital-intensive processes, such as printed circuit board fabrication, were housed in divisions that were unable to invest adequately to keep the processes up to date. These data were used to get senior management and divisional personnel alike to recognize the problem and buy into the possibility of change.

The precedent was thus set for further consolidation and a less autocratic means of deciding which divisions would be consolidated. Target groups of divisions—usually business groups or geographically proximate groups—were chosen based on the extent of duplication that existed and strength of business need for improvement.[19] Mid-level personnel (e.g., manufacturing engineering managers, procurement managers) were drawn from the set of divisions being examined, and asked to work as a team, facilitated by members of the corporate Change Management Team, to develop detailed cost models of various consolidation scenarios.[20] When recommendations were made to senior management, they were made by the divisional representatives; when implementation started it was faster and more effective due to early planning and buy-in on the part of the team and a sense on the part of division personnel that they had been represented in the process.

Over the course of the following five to seven years, consolidation became an accepted behavior as 30–40% of the manufacturing organizations in the company were participants in a consolidation effort, and close to 90% participated in conversations or studies of consolidation opportunities. The side benefits of the consolidation studies were increased communications among the divisions, sharing of best practices, and awareness of strategic manufacturing issues. In many cases, rather than consolidate, groups chose to place more emphasis on standardizing information systems, components, and processes to achieve benefits of consolidation without physical moves. Significantly increased networking among divisions resulted.

Vertical Disintegration and Core Process Management

When HP started manufacturing, it was difficult to find qualified vendors: Sheet metal vendors did not have "class A" paint and finish capability; machine shops, focused primarily on the automotive market and long product runs, were not interested in the high-mix, low-volume work HP had to offer; and printed circuit board fabricators were not sufficiently technologically advanced. To invest in a new manufacturing process, HP manufacturing managers had simply to show that a new product required it; little, if any, financial justification was required. Thus, a tradition of backward integration began that carried over into the early days of computer manufacturing, and HP as a whole became highly vertically integrated.[21]

In the early 1980s, when maintaining the investment required to stay technologically current in multiple processes at multiple sites became onerous, HP began to question its levels of backward integration. A desire to forward integrate and form partnerships with value-added resellers caused many division general managers, particularly in the highly competitive low-end businesses, to put pressure on their manufacturing managers to reduce costs and free up cash for other investments.[22] Growth of a strong and capable external vendor pool facilitated change. Vertical disintegration began with the least critical activities (e.g., sheet metal and machining) and moved rapidly downstream towards product final assembly and test.

Early decisions to vertically disintegrate were extremely painful and highly contested. Some predicted the inevitable "hollowing" of the corporation[23] and subsequent loss of competitive advantage. Others proclaimed the need to concentrate on those areas from which competitive advantage was truly derived (before Prahalad and Hamel, 1990, popularized the notion). As the debate raged, several experiments began. Consolidation, already socially acceptable, was an early choice of process for vertical disintegration that often failed when participating divisions, no longer feeling ownership for the capability, determined to do better with a vendor outside the company and pulled their work from the internal shop.[24] Volume in the shops dropped, performance followed, and the shops entered the slowly winding death spiral familiar to many internal manufacturing organizations at HP and elsewhere. This slow death approach to vertical disintegration was extremely painful for those managers trying to make the internal fabrication shops work.[25]

Over time, decisions to vertically disintegrate became more strategic and explicit. Rather than allow their fabrication functions to die as the result of a drawn out process of reacting to individual make/buy decisions, manufacturing managers chose more direct paths to disintegration: (1) Finding another internal HP site to perform the work. The Loveland Instrument Division, for example, chose to improve its utilization ratios by selling its excess capacity to other HP divisions. (2) Locating one or two external vendors and turning all work over to them. The Andover Division found good local vendors for its sheet metal parts and, after cleaning up its documentation, quickly transferred the work. (3) Selling off the fabrication shop to employees or to an external fabrication company. The Avondale Division sold its very successful machining operation to the fabrication shop managers who have continued its excellent performance as a stand-alone company. The Lake Stevens Instrument Division sold its through-hole printed circuit board assembly operation to Solectron, a major Silicon Valley-based operation dedicated to the board assembly business.[26]

As vertical disintegration occurred with less critical processes, capabilities considered core (Prahalad and Hamel, 1990) to the company became more centrally managed. Integrated circuit and printed circuit board fabrication were consolidated at the corporate level, facilitating control over both investment levels and use. Lengthy debates over pricing policies (whether they should be cost- or market-based), investment levels, and strategic direction (high mix to meet the needs of the instrument sector or high volume to meet those of the peripherals organizations) resulted. Surface mount board assembly processes, in contrast, were only partly centralized, with strong emphasis given to consolidated efforts at the group level. A centralized Surface Mount Development Center, charged with defining a companywide standard SMT process, was established and an attempt made to limit the number of SMT centers put in place for production work.

Vertical disintegration continues today. Printed circuit board fabrication, although consolidated as a critical corporate-managed function, lost its relevance and the remaining few shops are targeted for imminent closure or sale.[27] Surface mount printed circuit board assembly is being widely subcontracted, and internal shops consolidated. Even integrated circuit fabrication, seen by some as a critical technological cornerstone, is on tenuous turf, particularly in light of the formation of a new partnership with Intel. Many managers see this trend continuing as divisions subcontract the entire design, development, and production process for given products.[28] Examples of $200–300 million businesses in the company being run by four or five people whose jobs primarily entail managing the logistics of a set of outsourced activities are provided as evidence of the possibilities.

Horizontal Process Management

While consolidation and vertical disintegration happened largely in response to cost pressures, horizontal process management answered a need for faster time-to-market and customer response times. Functionally based responses, such as manufacturing consolidation, and small-scale programs in concurrent engineering and design for manufacturability, early precursors of horizontal process management, were no longer sufficient. Instead, the product generation and order fulfillment processes became management focal points.

The change to horizontal process management was foreshadowed by shifts in strategic thinking, management metrics, and language. In several sessions of the manufacturing council (described later), senior manufacturing managers defined the critical three processes to be managed: strategic investment, product generation, and order fulfillment. The strategic investment process, least well-defined of the three, comprised the activities whereby resources were acquired and allocated to the product generation and order fulfillment processes. Work to define these activities in ongoing.

Product generation was defined as the process commencing with a product concept and concluding with achievement of break-even performance in the marketplace. John Young, CEO at the time, issued a breakthrough objective of cutting break-even time or BET (described in House and Price, 1991) in half. This metric, while never fully implemented throughout the organization, provided strong incentive to think across functional boundaries: R&D and marketing developed closer associations to ensure products were correctly defined and positioned before development began. The corporate engineering and corporate manufacturing organizations were joined to form the Product Generation Team and adopted a broader view of their task. Information systems, once viewed in separate functional domains, were integrated so that manufacturing and R&D no longer maintained different product databases.

The order fulfillment process was defined as that beginning with a customer order and ending with delivery and installation of the product at the customer site. Inventory turnover and order fulfillment rates were used to measure supply chain performance (Davis 1993). Corporate logistics took primary responsibility for the order fulfillment process, collecting and reporting performance data, benchmarking against other companies, and providing guidance for improvement. Once again, functional managers and white-collar personnel learned that they could not optimize performance on their own. R&D, for example, started to evaluate effects of their product designs on inventory requirements.[29] Manufacturing and marketing worked more closely together to determine the optimal location of localization activities—at plant sites or in distribution centers.

In recent years, several group manufacturing managers (see later description) have taken on responsibility as order fulfillment managers, changing their titles to reflect the shift. These managers, rarely given solid line responsibility for all the involved activities, are held responsible for the improvement of supply chain performance in their organization. Through influence and consensus decision making, they involve players from all functional areas in the improvement effort. In this radical departure from their functionally focused role, managers have become more customer-focused and broadened their strategic perspectives.

These three changes—consolidation, vertical disintegration, horizontal process management—have created a substantively different environment for manufacturing managers and white-collar professionals. That environment is more networked externally, with more critical vendor relationships and tighter outbound partnerships, as well as internally, across both functional and divisional boundaries. Organization of the manufacturing function has evolved commensurably, roles and responsibilities have been redefined, and human resources management systems changed to better match the needs.

Changes to Managerial and White-Collar Roles

The lives of manufacturing managers and white-collar professionals have changed rather radically over the past decade, although many currently in these roles have trouble articulating the ways in which their jobs differ from what they were 10 or even 20 years ago. Consistent values and overall strategic direction have allowed managers to accommodate vast change as a part of their everyday work. This section describes the roles of manufacturing managers and manufacturing professionals in 1984, changes made to those roles over the subsequent decade, resulting roles played in 1994, and the evolution of the supporting organizational infrastructure—rewards, pay, evaluation, career paths.

Manufacturing managers in the divisionalized structure of 1984 reported directly to the general managers of their divisions, participated heavily in business decisions for their product lines (albeit not necessarily as equal partners),[30] and had little allegiance to their functional area outside the division. They were operationally or tactically focused, spending their time on day-to-day management issues, many regarding direct labor. They were also internally focused, rarely benchmarking their performance against other HP divisions, much less companies outside HP. On an erratic basis, worldwide manufacturing managers' meetings were convened to discuss issues of common interest, but agendas were as much informal and social as business.

Other manufacturing professionals, including manufacturing engineers, procurement specialists, and production managers, similarly found little need to interact with their counterparts from other divisions. They focused their efforts on improvement of their own division's bottom line, often reinventing processes already developed and implemented at the division next door.[31] Competition among the divisions encouraged continuous improvement of manufacturing processes; developing a better process than the division next door was a source of considerable pride. Roles and responsibilities were clearly defined, as product line profitability was the division's singular objective and all activities focused on that outcome. Colocation in a campus setting with R&D and marketing counterparts allowed for significant communication and a shared understanding of divisional objectives.

Manufacturing managers' pay in the early 1980s was based largely on manufacturing head count; the larger the number of people in a manager's organization, the greater his or her "scope" which determined potential pay. Evaluated annually[32] by their divisional general managers, manufacturing managers were (loosely) ranked against other managers, including other functional (R&D, marketing) managers, who were on the same pay scale. Although all manufacturing managers were informally ranked against one another by the vice president of manufacturing, this input had less impact on the managers' pay than that of their own bosses, the divisional general managers. Careers were functionally oriented, although there was some crossing of boundaries.[33] As new divisions were created, opportunities arose to move to new sites and take on increased responsibility, which many did. Such moves typically entailed promotions.

Pay for manufacturing professionals was determined in much the same way as that for their managers. Employees were first "scoped" to determine the pay band on which they resided.[34] Their pay within this band was determined by their ranking relative to all others within the division on that same band. Semiannual ranking sessions, in which managers convened to argue the relative merits of each of their employees, determined an individual's ranking and, therefore, pay. Career trajectories, once again, were largely unifunctional, although frequent movement among divisions at a single site occurred.[35] Generally, the objective of a white-collar professional on joining HP was to climb the management ladder, eventually gaining a divisional general manager position that in essence allowed her or him to run a small, self-contained business.

Development of the Manufacturing Function from 1984 to 1994

Between 1984 and 1994, the organizational form of the manufacturing function at HP changed radically. To facilitate and expedite the changes described earlier—consolidation, vertical disintegration, and horizontal process management—the corporate and group manufacturing organizations were strengthened. The 500-person corporate manufacturing organization housed several functions including procurement (negotiation of companywide purchase agreements for commonly used parts), new process development and standardization (specifically for surface mount technology), manufacturing information systems development (which adapted manufacturing systems products developed by the Manufacturing Productivity Division and other external sources for internal use), and a small consulting group that supported strategic decision making (e.g., regarding consolidation) and organizational redesign.

Historically, the corporate organization (as is true in many companies) was regarded as lightweight and a place to which burned-out managers retired. Divisions viewed it as a source of unnecessary overhead and, if given their way, would have done away with the entire organization. The vice president of manufacturing, with 25 years of HP experience,[36] was determined to turn the situation around, and hired an entirely new staff from outside the company. These managers, in turn, staffed their organizations with professionals in their respective fields, offering training to those who needed to upgrade their skills. The result was a much stronger corporate organization that over time gained credibility with the divisions and set new professional standards throughout the company.[37]

Strengthening the corporate organization alone was insufficient to effect much needed change in the manufacturing function, so the vice president began convincing group general managers throughout the company to add group manufacturing managers to their staffs. The Computer Manufacturing Operation was already led by a group-level manufacturing manager who was put in place to coordinate the rollout of the new Spectrum product line. He was responsible for balancing worldwide demand and capacity, standardizing parts, processes, and information systems so that products could be easily manufactured at any of the sites, and representing manufacturing concerns to his business partners in R&D

and marketing. Between 1987 and 1989, armed with this model and a list of the tasks that a group manufacturing manager might undertake,[38] the vice president was able to convince all group general managers to add such a position.

The roles that the new group manufacturing managers played varied considerably from group to group. The group manufacturing manager for the Computer Systems Operation had direct line responsibility for all manufacturing in his sector, although it took some time to evolve to this point as division general managers gave up their manufacturing responsibilities slowly.[39] Multiple group manufacturing managers in the Measurement Systems Operation[40] often had direct responsibility for the consolidated fabrication functions, but only indirect responsibility for activities carried out within the divisional manufacturing organizations. And, in the Computer Products Operation, the sole group manufacturing manager acted more as an advocate for the collective view of the manufacturing contingent in his sector and less as an enforcer of standards and corporate policies.

Group manufacturing managers were empowered[41] through a gradual process of gaining control over corporate manufacturing budgets. Cautiously, the vice president yielded authority to the group manufacturing managers (who collectively formed the corporate manufacturing council) to set direction and, thus, investment levels for the corporate organization. A long education process accompanied this shift as group manufacturing managers learned about the activities performed in corporate, the needs of their divisional constituents, and how those needs might be integrated.

Through this process, divisional manufacturing managers saw their freedom and autonomy erode as they were forced to standardize activities[42] across their groups and jointly make strategic decisions for the good of the group rather than just their own division. Each sector or group found its own equilibrium point between central (corporate or group) control and divisional autonomy; the Computer Systems Operation developed the most, and the Computer Products Operation the least, centralized structure. Today, manufacturing managers in the Computer Systems Operation all report directly to the group manufacturing manager (shown in Figure 6-3 as the computer order fulfillment and manufacturing manager) and spend considerable time working with one another to coordinate and jointly manage worldwide computer manufacturing operations. Computer Products Operation's manufacturing managers, on the other hand, report to division general managers, and remain closely tied to their business partners (R&D and marketing) striving to optimize the performance of their particular product line.

The new group management organizational structure facilitated consolidation, vertical disintegration and horizontal process management implementation activities by providing focal points for their execution and adding a supportive voice at senior management levels. Other organizational changes, some well-documented in the literature, also accompanied the consolidation, vertical disintegration, and horizontal process management efforts.

The oft-cited effect of consolidation and downsizing—fewer management positions (e.g., Miles, 1989)—occurred at HP also, resulting in a large proportion of the direct savings.[43] Some managers left the company, perceiving that the opportunities apparent to them on joining HP—such as running their own independent divisional operations—were no longer available. Other remained within the company, often adopting newly defined roles that they might not have considered previously.[44] Managers who stayed to oversee consolidated manufacturing operations found themselves in different roles as well. Now responsible to the general managers of multiple (at least two) divisions, they had to think more strategically and explicitly about how to serve their customers. Not only did they have to learn about the business directions of *all* of their customers, but they had to be able to balance differing needs with a limited investment budget and then sell the resultant compromises to sometimes reluctant buyers.

Other manufacturing professionals, such as manufacturing engineers and procurement specialists, were similarly affected. They, too, had to learn about the different needs of their multiple customer divisions and to think about how those needs might be concurrently met by the processes on which they worked. Increased standardization of processes and components across product lines, often enforced by group manufacturing managers, forced manufacturing engineers, and procurement specialists to become more aware of activities in sister divisions and to make decisions in concert with those activities.

Consolidated organizations were usually larger than the typical divisional manufacturing activity, creating both problems and opportunities for white-collar workers. In the Computer Systems Operation, where manufacturing was centralized, divisional ties were severed and it became more difficult to judge one's work directly in terms of divisional bottom-line results. In organizational designers' terms, the line of sight between one's daily work and measurable outcomes was lengthened. In other cases, however, consolidation provided larger critical mass and thus ability to invest more in development of manufacturing processes. Professionals in these operations, although part of a larger group, were often able to experiment with more interesting, state-of-the-art activities.

At all levels of the organization, insecurity about jobs and job prospects increased. Open communications about the objectives of consolidation and about programs to facilitate finding new jobs either within or outside the company helped ameliorate some of the new concerns. Nevertheless, the historical sense of employment security and company loyalty was greatly disturbed.[45] Career opportunities were perceived as more limited, due to a smaller number of manufacturing management positions HP-wide to which to aspire.

Literature on vertical integration and networked organizations suggests that organizations become more networked as they vertically disintegrate (e.g., Perrow, 1992). Results in HP's case are mixed. Many of the processes that were spun out were replaced by only one or two vendors managed at arm's length. The sheet metal operation in Andover, for example, was turned over virtually intact to two external vendors thus reducing the number of relationships managed to a single liaison point between HP and the vendors. The low level of importance given to the "noncritical" parts being purchased meant that the vendors could be managed at arm's length, rather than as close partners in new product design or production.[46] In these cases, the organization became less networked as it reduced the number of relationships it had been managing internally to one or two external relationships managed by a procurement specialist.

When the process and parts are still considered critical, such as the machining operations spun out of the Avondale Division, tighter relationships are maintained. And new relationships, developed for strategic business reasons, increased networking. HP's relationship with Canon to acquire the LaserJet engine is a tight and highly managed relationship as are many of the new relationships developed with OEM's and other value-added partners to deliver systems solutions to end customers. In these situations, relationship managers may be designated to directly manage the partnership. Many throughout the organization, from the engineers who travel to Japan to visit with Canon to the manufacturing manager who meets with engineers who travel to Japan to visit with Cannon to the manufacturing manager who meets with the OEM to determine distribution strategies, are involved in the partnership.

Manufacturing managers and professionals involved in the new partnerships have very different roles than in the past. No longer managing a large group of internal employees, particularly blue-collar workers, they focus instead on managing one or more external partnerships. Once able to control outcomes through direct control of resources, they must now use personal influence and market forces to obtain similar ends. Broader, more strategic perspectives are required of them as they must monitor all aspects of the external business and fit that with an understanding of their own business direction. One manager suggested that the "organization chart just be thrown away" except for tax or formal financial reporting purposes, as his work today is largely done through informal internal and external networks.

Horizontal process management, the most recent of the three changes, has resulted in significant role redefinition for a number of manufacturing managers many of whom are now called order fulfillment managers. Adopting either the product generation or order fulfillment perspective mandates a broader perspective and formation of tight partnerships with other functional (e.g., R&D and marketing) players. As in the management of external technology partnerships, horizontal process management entails less direct resource control and more indirect, influential control. Order fulfillment managers, for example, are held accountable for inventory reductions and increased order fulfillment rates in their organizations, but rarely directly control forecasting, order entry, distribution, and other activities associated with accomplishing these ends. Learning to manage through influence has been a great challenge for many of them.[47]

Managers and White-Collar Professionals in 1994

It is difficult to describe a typical manufacturing manager in 1994, as the role has taken many forms throughout the HP organization. Some, particularly in the Computer Products Operation, have become integral members of the business team, working intimately with the R&D and marketing organizations as well as with a small set of external vendors to accomplish extremely rapid new product introduction and ramp cycles.[48] Others, especially those managing systems product lines (e.g., computer systems, medical systems) have adopted order fulfillment management roles in which they concentrate on internal functional integration (particularly with marketing) to improve customer satisfaction at reduced inventory costs. A focal point of their work is global information systems integration to facilitate rapid transmission and fulfillment of orders and payments worldwide. And others have no manufacturing at all reporting directly to them; rather, they manage only external vendors in support of large and growing new market segments.

Although quite different from one another in the roles they play, many manufacturing managers in today's environment share the need to accomplish their objectives through influence rather than direct control. Forced to operate in teams, either with internal R&D and marketing partners or with external operators, they must learn to take others' perspectives and to think strategically in integrating others' needs with their own. Interpersonal, negotiation, and business skills are far more critical than technical skills in accomplishing 1994 objectives.

White-collar professionals similarly have fewer boundaries around their work, more dynamic work environments, and a need for greater influence skills. As more manufacturing is outsourced, procurement activities increase in importance, manufacturing engineering is charged with optimizing a process at a vendor's site, and product disappears. Much of what applies to management roles applies for white-collar professionals as well.

New roles and responsibilities require new human resources management practices as well. These, too, have evolved slowly in response to the changing environment of the past 10 years. Team-based management and reward systems have become more prominent in the last decade as work has been restructured on the factory floor and cross-functional teams have attacked horizontal process management. Implemented through a series of organizational experiments,[49] team structures took on various forms throughout the company: A workstation development team was rewarded for delivering on time; a pay for knowledge system was implemented in a new factory; and several experiments allowed cross-evaluation and reward allocation by team members. Companywide, team-based criteria were added to the standard personnel evaluation form, reducing the proportion of the evaluation based on technical skills alone. Nearly two-thirds of a manufacturing manager's evaluation today is based on input from customers and employees, whereas 10 years ago it was based primarily on technical criteria. Many consider this a major change.

Manufacturing managers' pay, once based on the total number of people reporting to them, was changed to reflect other important characteristics of their jobs, such as revenue base supported or gross margin achieved. Their objectives became more "results" oriented with results defined along a number of dimensions. Some individual contributor and staff positions were recognized as equivalent in value to management positions, and pay ranges adjusted accordingly. Several critical manufacturing jobs, such as procurement specialists, were recognized with higher "scoping" and thus potential for higher pay. Each of these changes was made in response to a different set of needs; they were not made as a group or even necessarily considered as an integrated package by those proposing them.

Skill sets in the white-collar community have also evolved over time in response to needs. One manager described the new environment as requiring the "same academic skills, but with more emphasis on personality." He, and others, went on to say that it was critical in the (networked) environment to be able to create a picture of where the organization was to go, get people lined up behind that vision, understanding where various people fit, and then get them to execute against it. Some saw the role of managers as managing linkages, putting in place required checks and balances, to keep the entire system working. Clear definition of processes and process owners was seen as critical.

Other specific skills expected of white-collar professionals are supplier management, increased participation with members of other functional areas and ability to remain highly tuned to the customer base (including as many visits to customers for manufacturing people as are made by R&D and marketing.) Business management and leadership skills are expected not only of managers, but of individual contributors who are expected to have vision and change management skills to carry out that vision. Increased investments in white-collar education— the Medical Products Group has its own "college" on the Andover, Massachusetts, site—focus on developing skills in communication, systems thinking, planning, and strategy development (referred to by one manager as "obstacle management.") Quality methods and the ability to collect, analyze, and make decisions with data continue to be emphasized throughout.

So, how have managers and white-collar workers responded to all this change? The initial response of those interviewed, many of whom have been with HP for over 20 years, was that they really didn't do their jobs differently, but rather they had different jobs, and this was an expected part of growth and change. Many identified factors other than increased networking for their different approach to work in the current environment (e.g., one manager thought he had mishandled a political situation leading to his current positioning). But, there were some changes identified.

There is no question that these people find the fast pace of their present environment challenging. And, they certainly confess that getting things done through influence rather than through direct control is different.[50] (One manager says that he has learned that "Sometimes you have to go slow to go fast today.") They have all learned a lot over the past 10 years, particularly about the role of manufacturing in the overall business strategy, and how to make change in an organization. Miles' (1989) notion that "there is increasingly an opportunity for those retained to use more of their capabilities, to be closer to the core of operations, to be less burdened by lengthy communications and control system, and to be more directed by market needs" is borne out in the experiences of those interviewed. All seemed interested in and challenged by their present positions, albeit not necessarily any more so than they were 10 years ago.

HP's open culture, the dynamic organizational structure put in place by Hewlett and Packard 50 years ago, and the types of people HP hires all contribute to its ongoing ability to manage change gracefully. One manager likened the change process at HP to the creation of the Grand Canyon by the Colorado River. Slowly, over time, as the river wends its way through the canyon it chews away at the rock, forming and reforming the geography that surrounds it. HP's network organizational form continues to emerge in much the same fashion.

Conclusion

The networked, or virtual (Davidow and Malone, 1992), corporation is becoming a reality in today's business world, and Hewlett-Packard is one good example. But, the process of creating the networks is not necessarily as predetermined as some of the literature on the subject would lead us to believe. Hewlett-Packard never had a grand corporate plan to become more networked; rather, it responded to business needs as they presented themselves, making change as needed. The net result—after much consolidation, vertical disintegration, centralization and shifts to horizontal process views—is an organization that is more networked than it was 10 years ago.

Along with the gradual structural shifts have come gradual changes in the roles and responsibilities of white-collar workers, who have learned new skills in negotiation and cross-boundary management that were not required (as much) 10 years ago. But, these workers (at HP, anyway) see the evolution as just part of the natural change and growth patterns of the organization, and accommodate them much as they have accommodated many other changes in their careers.

While we still have much to learn about the networked organizational form, we must be careful not to treat it as a static form, but rather one that has evolved and will continue to evolve taking us along paths yet undiscovered.

Notes

This work was sponsored by the Sloan Foundation through a grant to the Massachusetts Institute of Technology to examine trends in white-collar and managerial work. First draft papers were presented and reviewed at a conference on white-collar work hosted by the Sloan School at MIT on July 20–21, 1994.

1. Hewlett-Packard is not alone in making the transition to being more networked. A cursory review of the popular management literature, particularly a recent spate of *Fortune* articles, suggests that many companies are engaged in the change. HP makes a particularly good case study as the company continues to be successful despite major changes in its industry. Many others have failed, or at best, just survived.

2. I was a graduate student at Stanford when I first became involved with HP in 1984 as a summer hire helping formulate manufacturing strategy at the Data Systems Division. Subsequently, I was given permission to administer an extensive survey to all HP manufacturing divisions (numbering 50–60 at the time) to collect data for my doctoral dissertation on the development of flexibility in manufacturing organizations. My data collection effort, which also entailed visits to most of the divisions, was the first attempt in the history of the company to create a comprehensive description of the company's manufacturing capability at the corporate level. On completing my dissertation, I joined HP's corporate manufacturing staff, reporting to the vice president of manufacturing to continue the strategic planning activities I had begun.

Over the following years, I had numerous responsibilities in the corporate function, the most pertinent to this chapter being the creation of the "Change Management Team," a group of 10–12 professionals who offered support to HP organizations for making strategic decisions (e.g., how many manufacturing sites, how vertically integrated), redesigning their organizations (e.g., establishing self-managed team structures), and developing manufacturing education programs. In addition, I managed the Surface Mount Technology program and the Environmental, Health, and Safety activities for the company.

I was involved in early manufacturing consolidation and vertical dis-integration decisions, working both with the divisions making the changes as well as with senior management to gain approval for the changes. I was also responsible for setting agendas for our Corporate Manufacturing Council meetings and helping run those meetings. These experiences provided me with a strong sense of the thinking that went on around the decisions made.

In January, 1993, I was given a voluntary severance package and reverted to research, teaching and consulting on a full-time basis.

3. Hewlett-Packard is rare among its U.S. counterparts in the breadth of its product line. Started as an instrumentation company in 1939, HP has evolved over the years to being a major player in the computer (and related peripherals) industry. In 1993, 77% of HP's revenues came from computer and peripherals products, 11% from its traditional test and measurement instrumentation businesses, 6% from medical products, 3% from analytical products (e.g., gas and liquid chromatographs), and 3% from components (e.g., LEDs and LCDs). Its largest U.S. competitors in the computer arena are Digital Equipment Corporation (DEC) and International Business Machines (IBM). Large players in the test and measurement market include Tektronix and Fluke. None sport a product line as broad as HP's. My discussion of the evolution of the industry in which HP competes will focus on the computer and peripherals industry, which I will refer to as the computer industry. Dynamics in the instrumentation world are somewhat different, due primarily to the larger number of small niche competitors, but in general lag the computer industry by a few years. Recent reductions in military spending are pressuring companies to radically rethink the structure of the instrumentation businesses; these pressures were felt earlier in the computer arena.

4. A number of industry surveys document the progress being made in the implementation of programs such as total quality management and just-in-time. Pittiglio, Rabin, Todd, and McGrath, a Menlo Park, California, high-technology operations management consulting firm, does an annual survey of these issues and jointly publishes the results with the American Electronics Association.

5. The extent to which quality improvement teams were truly cross-functional in their early incarnations is unclear. Although teams successfully operated for some time, many devolved to contain members from the immediate workgroup only, thus not truly increasing the amount of cross-functional networking in the organization. See Main (1994) for a fuller description of the evolution of the quality movement.

6. For an integrated view of how these various programs worked together in the auto industry see Womack, Jones, and Roos' (1990) description of the lean production system. It integrates shop floor improvements, such as just-in-time, with horizontal process management activities in the supply chain arena.

7. Relationships among companies in Japan have historically been formed more broadly and deeply than those in the United States (Gerlach, 1992). See Biggart and Hamilton (1992) for an interesting view as to why we have failed to better understand and possibly adopt the Japanese structure. Increased formation of partnerships in U.S. industry (particularly biotechnology [Barley, Freeman, and Hybels 1992] and computers [Saxenian,

1990]) causes it to appear, at least superficially, more like the Japanese model. This section concentrates on major changes in the U.S. model.

8. Of 1995 revenues, 44% are from the United States, 30% from Europe, and 20% from Asia Pacific, Canada, and Latin America. Employment figures from 1995 show 60,200 employees in the United States, 21,000 in Europe, and 21,100 in Asia Pacific, Canada, and Latin America.

9. This is an important distinction. Job security allows an expectation that one might stay in the same job throughout one's tenure at the company, whereas employment security provides a guarantee of a position somewhere in the organization, not necessarily in the job category of the employee's choice. It is unclear today that Hewlett and Packard ever explicitly offered job security, but the economic conditions under which the company prospered allowed them to effectively do so. As a result, at the time voluntary severance packages were offered, there was a strong sense that job security had been a part of the culture.

10. Pascale argued that HP's consensus management style and people-oriented culture would not allow it to make the tough decisions required to succeed in the very competitive computer marketplace it was entering. His predictions have not materialized, as HP has undertaken voluntary severance programs to resize and redeploy its workforce, put in place a "no nonsense," hands-on CEO (Lew Platt), and become rigorous in focusing activities throughout the company on bottom-line performance metrics. The company's performance in the tough economy of the past few years is substantial evidence that the traps Pascale perceived were not sprung.

11. Not only did the number of divisions get too large, but numerous "charter wars" appeared as divisions developed similar products. In Corvallis, Oregon, for example, inventors of the HP calculator grew their product to approximate a desktop personal computer while the terminals division in Sunnyvale, California, added functionality to convert their product to a personal computer as well. Although Hewlett and Packard saw benefit in allowing divisions to compete with one another, often encouraging it, eventually greater strategic integration was felt to be needed. Ultimately, customers and expensive technology investments required divisions to work more closely together.

12. In order to create a new job description or position, for example, divisions were expected to appear before a corporate review board that subsequently made "behind closed door" decisions to approve or deny the division's petition. This "closed door" approach was in stark contrast to all other processes at HP, leaving the hapless participant with a strong sense of power withheld.

Careers in the finance community were tightly, centrally managed so that young controllers might be moved from division to division, gaining experience with new and broader management issues in the process. Divisional general managers often had little say in the placement of a controller in his or her division, a sharp departure from other employee choices in the division.

13. Pascale (1990) notes both "perils of split"—integration and duplication—in his book (pp. 48–50), spelling out some of the problems they caused for the company at the time.

14. This sector has now been broken into two: Measurements Systems now contains the medical, analytical, components and mass storage businesses, and Test and Measurement contains the more traditional instrumentation business as well as a new foray into the communications market.

15. R&D, long considered the premier resource at HP is often the last organization to be changed. Marketing, on the other hand, has evolved continually as the marketplace has required closer attention, enhanced advertising, finer segmentation, and more responsive

service. Changes to the marketing organization have been more complex and far-reaching, making them harder to describe concisely. Managers and white-collar workers in the marketing organization have faced changes similar to those dealt with by manufacturing managers. Thus, understanding the manufacturing function provides insight across the organization.

16. Reduced Instruction Set Computing (RISC) was an important new technology in the computing world. HP took advantage of the shift to this new architecture to develop a family of compatible computers, thus consolidating its offerings. This family was developed by a single R&D organization drawn from the membership of several existing computer divisions. Arguably, although not a true consolidation of resources, this preceded the first manufacturing consolidations.

17. It is this number that was the most help in convincing senior management of the need to consolidate. The thought that by consolidating two divisions, one might double the engineering effort applied to process development in the resulting division was greatly appealing.

18. A corporate procurement organization had been created prior to this time that was responsible for negotiating companywide purchase agreements for commonly used parts. Divisional purchasing organizations managed the release of purchase orders against these contracts, controlling the physical flow of parts to the division. Fortunately, a common part numbering system had been adopted early in the history of the company facilitating creation of a corporate database and common communication medium. Nevertheless, vendors not only delivered parts to HP's many sites independently, but also worked with the product and procurement engineers at those sites individually in the selection of parts for new products.

19. The computer manufacturing organizations were the first to be consolidated, as they faced the greatest competitive challenge in the 1980's. The instrumentation divisions followed, as they began to see their market erode with the shift in military spending of the late 1980's and early 1990's. The peripherals organization faced different challenges associated with the need to achieve rapid manufacturing ramps and very high volume production; they did less consolidation and more vertical disintegration to achieve their goals.

20. Each member of the team was assigned a cost category and asked to develop information for that category across all participating divisions. In this way, each of the individuals gained ownership of the entire project and avoided their singular identification with their own division.

21. It is not clear that vertical integration decisions were as well thought out when the computer manufacturing operations were set up, as more external capability was available by then. Rather, it seems, tradition prevailed as managers moving from instrumentation divisions to start new computer divisions replicated the organizations from which they had come. Basic return on investment analyses were rarely required by division general managers; rather, they followed the instincts developed through experience at other divisions in the company.

22. This was particularly true in those divisions trying to enter and compete in the dealer channel (e.g., the low-end printer and disk drive divisions). The margins commanded by dealers left little room for extra expenditure elsewhere in the organization, and division general managers looked to manufacturing to make up the difference. Other divisions, such as the Andover Division making ultrasound imaging devices, simply wanted money to invest in new product lines or businesses, and found that they could get that funding by cutting back on the number of manufacturing processes they supported.

23. *Business Week* ran a popular cover story about this time declaiming the "hollow corporation" thought to represent the future of the typical U.S. company whose manufac-

turing had all been outsourced to overseas locations. These notions were the source of considerable controversy inside HP.

24. In a sense this is an early failure of the attempt to become more networked. Divisional managers, unaccustomed to working with other HP divisions, perceived the performance of outside operations as better and were more comfortable working with them. As one of the group manufacturing managers commented, "when you own something, you'll bury your head; when you don't, you throw rocks at it." Another said, "Internally you were dealing with socialism and externally you were dealing with capitalism. And one works better than the other."

25. One of the largest fabrication shops resulting from a 1987 consolidation of three shops in the Greater San Francisco Bay Area, was finally closed in June, 1994, after attempts by several management teams to make it successful. Lacking support from internal customer, the remnants of the shop were sold.

26. A key benefit of selling the fabrication business as a whole is ease of people placement. When the Palo Alto Fabrication Center was sold, about half of the employees chose to move to the buying company. They retain jobs for which their skills are applicable, rather than a less relevant position in which HP might have placed them. Typically the sale price of the shops is low, averaging roughly the market value of the assets themselves and sale agreements entail a limited—one or two years—commitment on HP's part to purchase from the buying company. Ironically, this works better than comparable internal commitments.

27. The purchase of the Loveland, Colorado, printed circuit board fabrication center by Meric, a Portland, Oregon, based manufacturer was recently announced. Meric is a Tektronix spin-off that resulted as Tektronix went through the same vertical disintegration process.

28. Some compelling logic, particularly representative of the high-volume, low-margin businesses, underlies this trend. Figure 6–2 shows the rate at which new products are developed, introduced, and rendered obsolete. In 1993, HP earned revenues from new products alone that exceeded the total size of the company in 1985. For very high-volume products, production is started and nearly complete before the product is even introduced to the dealer channel. By the time revenues peak, the manufacturing organization is working on the next product. Developing sufficient technology to support this kind of product turnover is an onerous task, and is virtually impossible to successfully manage within one firm. Thus, HP increasingly relies on others to develop and produce new technologies, and focuses its internal efforts on the critical few it views as important to long-term success. Recent attention to return on assets measures throughout the company—traditionally HP focused almost exclusively on profits—will also drive additional outsourcing.

29. DeskJet development engineers chose between a generic power supply and country-specific power supplies on the basis of inventory implications. Generic power supplies, although more expensive, allowed inventory to be used anywhere in the world. Less expensive country-specific power supplies would have to be stocked in single locations, and reworked if removed to others. See Lee, et al., 1993, for a detailed description of this decision.

30. In Hayes and Wheelwright's (1984) parlance, HP at the time was at best a Stage II or Stage III manufacturing organization. R&D was the preeminent function in the company, while marketing and manufacturing vied for a distant second. Often, manufacturing managers were considered to be heroes when they succeeded in producing a terribly designed product or made up for lost time when R&D delivered designs late. With significant work on the part of the vice president of manufacturing and organizational

changes made to elevate the manufacturing function, this began to change in the mid-1980s.

31. During 1985, for example, a visit to two divisions in Colorado Springs revealed that the Colorado Telecommunications Division had recently purchased new automatic insertion equipment for their printed circuit board assembly process—without conferring at all with the Colorado Springs Division, which had extensive experience with said equipment and was located a mere few hundred feet away. The vice president of manufacturing for the company at the time joked that divisions *did* share with one another—and then returned home to attempt any approach that would be different (albeit presumably better) than the one they had seen.

32. Written performance evaluations were (and still are) required for all personnel on an annual basis. In the early 1980s, this standard was less stringently enforced resulting in many manufacturing managers who had not been formally reviewed in years. When the company entered its downsizing phase, this became a problem as there was scant support for feedback to poor performers.

33. Transfers occurred from R&D to manufacturing and marketing, but never in the other direction. For all practical purposes, a transfer out of R&D was considered a step down. At management levels, transfer occurred more frequently between accounting and manufacturing; several divisional controllers subsequently became manufacturing managers.

34. "Scoping" entailed placing all comparable jobs—from a value-to-the-company perspective—on the same pay curve. There might, for example, be two scoping curves for manufacturing engineers, one for entry-level engineers, and one for more experienced engineers. The curves for manufacturing engineers were usually the same as those for R&D engineers, although this was not always the case. Periodically, arguments were made that R&D engineers belonged on a higher pay curve as they were assumed to have higher value to the company. This argument was usually fought down by the manufacturing community.

35. One materials manager started his career by gaining experience in the various aspects of materials management—production scheduling, inventory management, purchasing. To do so, he moved among the various manufacturing operations at the Boise, Idaho, site. Well-versed in all aspects of materials management, he became a materials manager and thus a target for transfer to other HP divisions. He took on additional responsibility in each of two moves to Greeley, Colorado, and then Cupertino, California, still focused in the materials arena.

36. Hal Edmondson was named vice president of manufacturing and asked to lead the corporate manufacturing function in 1983. He brought to the job extensive experience managing R&D, marketing, and manufacturing, as well as general management experience in the test and measurement sector. More important, perhaps, was his willingness to entertain suggestions for change and to champion them against tough odds with both senior management as well as manufacturing managers soundly opposed to his ideas.

37. For a more detailed description of the corporate manufacturing organization, as well as of the council structure used to manage the corporate resource, see Harvard Business School case no. N9–691–001—Hewlett-Packard: Corporate, Group, and Divisional Manufacturing.

38. The list of the possible activities that group manufacturing managers might perform included: manage global expansion of manufacturing capability; develop standard processes across the group; enforce parts standards across the group, particularly with the R&D organizations; consolidate manufacturing organizations as needed; educate R&D and

marketing regarding manufacturing concerns; include manufacturing in business strategy development.

39. Note that this position is the only manufacturing role to show on the corporate organization chart (Figure 6–3). The computer order fulfillment and manufacturing manager for the Computer Systems Operation, has played this role with increasing responsibility since the Spectrum rollout in 1985–86.

40. There were five group manufacturing managers in the Measurement Systems Operations, one for each group: Medical, Analytical, Components, Electronic Instruments, and Microwave and Communications.

41. One of the group manufacturing managers interviewed described his position as one in which he had to use lateral influence rather than having direct control over the business. He emphasized that this is the way it should be, allowing the divisions the freedom to meet the needs of their own individual businesses.

42. Specific programs were undertaken to standardize in three primary areas: Common processes (typically printed circuit board assembly) were identified and shared development efforts undertaken. Databases of common parts, especially surface mount parts, were established and shared with R&D. Information systems, particularly database elements, were standardized so that divisions could more readily communicate with one another and less investment be made in information systems development. One process center manager described the standardization programs as follows: "That really is, I think, part of the changing paradigm. That kind of central management was a message to the divisions that the old big bang theory of HP where divisions grew by exploding off other divisions and they were vertically integrated wasn't going to continue and we were going to have these central programs with standard processes and standard materials and standard equipment sets and so on."

43. Management ranks were most affected, as they were typically reduced by half in a consolidation. Only one manufacturing, production, procurement, and manufacturing engineering manager would be required where there had been two. The procurement organization was also greatly affected, as high levels of part commonality among products from consolidating divisions allowed reduction of duplicated procurement effort. Least affected was the manufacturing engineering community, as many were kept to work on more advanced process development in the new critical mass manufacturing organization. Similarly, direct labor was not significantly affected, as the total amount of hands-on work was not changed.

44. The production manager of the Sunnyvale sheet metal shop, for example, became the implementation manager for the rollout of new technology from the Surface Mount Development Center. He went from being a hands-on manager of primarily blue-collar workers, to flying around the world with a team of manufacturing engineers implementing new technology at the various Surface Mount Centers.

The manufacturing manager of the Data Systems Division, after consolidation of his activities, was challenged with starting a new marketing organization to sell computers to potential manufacturing-oriented customers. He used his many years of manufacturing expertise to develop a consultative selling approach to delivering systems solutions into manufacturing companies. Creative use of his talents strengthened HP's position in an important market.

45. One of the earliest voluntary severance programs was offered in Northern Colorado as part of the closure of a fabrication shop there. Psychologists from Denver were recruited to help with the implementation. They reported afterward that the problems with which they dealt at HP were more severe than those experienced when Storage

Technology (a Boulder-based mass storage company) declared bankruptcy. Despite the voluntary nature of the programs (and they were fully voluntary in their early implementation), they were considered to be a major revision of HP's full employment policies.

46. This treatment of vendors is corroborated by the vendors themselves in many cases. The CEO of a small turnkey machining and assembly manufacturing business in Menlo Park, California, has found his strategy of becoming a "manufacturing partner" to companies that have chosen to vertically disintegrate difficult to implement. He finds that companies expect the services he offers (e.g., product redesign, process optimization, electronic data interchange) to be provided for the same price as the basic manufactured part. Unable to place a value on all of the functions that accompanied their internal manufacturing activities, they see no need to invest in the development of those capabilities elsewhere either. This has interesting implications for the future development of fundamental manufacturing capabilities.

47. Horizontal process management has elicited a more positive response to working across organizational boundaries than did earlier attempts to develop relationships with internal fabrication centers. Whereas manufacturing managers previously found it expedient to work with outside fabrication vendors rather than internal functions, they now consent to working closely with marketing and R&D personnel on horizontal process management.

48. The HP LaserJet division is an excellent example. The manufacturing manager, now fluent in strategic business conversation, is charged with managing the critical Canon partnership, with respect to manufacturing and distribution. No longer focused on operations within his factory (which has converted to a fluid, self-managed team environment) he is concerned with the dynamics of ensuring that manufacturing—internal or external—supports each subsequent product release.

49. Corporate personnel was reluctant to undertake wholesale change throughout the HP organization, and so authorized experiments in selected sites to allow learning to take place before widespread dissemination. Several experiments developed "self-managed" team structures on the factory floor, while others integrated manufacturing and design for rapid new product introduction. Subsequent experiments with team-based evaluation and reward systems were coordinated and monitored centrally.

50. One manager described the classic model as "think of an idea, make a decision, implement the decision," and contrasts it with the process management model of "several process owners, decision entails lining up the values of the different constituents, end results take longer but are better." One of the most difficult aspects of the process management model as far as he is concerned is the question of who really gets to decide in the end. In the hierarchical, more autocratic system the final decision-making point was more clear.

References

Baker, Wayne E. 1992. "The Network Organization in Theory and Practice." In *Networks and Organizations: Structure, Form and Action.* Nitin Nohria and Robert G. Eccles, eds. Cambridge: Harvard Business School Press.

Barley, Stephen R., John Freeman, and Ralph C. Hybels. 1992. "Strategic Alliances in Commercial Biotechnology." In *Networks and Organizations: Structure, Form and Action.* Nitin Nohria and Robert G. Eccles, eds. Cambridge: Harvard Business School Press.

Biggart, Nicole Woolsey, and Gary G. Hamilton. 1992. "On the Limits of a Firm-Based Theory to Explain Business Networks: The Western Bias of Neoclassical Economics."

In *Networks and Organizations: Structure, Form and Action.* Nitin Nohria and Robert G. Eccles, eds. Cambridge: Harvard Business School Press.

Burns, Tom, and George M. Stalker. 1961. *The Management of Innovation.* London: Tavistock.

Davidow, William H., and Michael S. Malone. 1992. *The Virtual Corporation: Structuring and Revitalizing the Corporation for the 21st Century.* New York: Harper Collins Publishers.

Davis, Tom. 1993. "Effective Supply Chain Management," *Sloan Management Review* 34, no. 4 (Summer): 35–46.

Deutschman, Alan. 1994. "How HP Continues to Grow and Grow," *Fortune* 129, no. 9 (May 2): 90–96.

Galbraith, Jay R., 1973. *Designing Complex Organizations.* Reading, Mass.: Addison-Wesley.

Gerlach, Michael L. 1992. *Alliance Capitalism: The Social Organization of Japanese Business.* Berkeley: University of California Press.

House, Charles H., and Raymond L. Price. 1991. "The Return Map: Tracking Product Teams," *Harvard Business Review* 69, no. 1 (January–February): 92–101.

Kanter, Rosabeth Moss. 1983. "Variations in Managerial Career Structures in High-Technology Firms: The Impact of Organizational Characteristics on Internal Labor Market Patterns." In *Internal Labor Markets.* Paul Osterman, ed. Cambridge: M.I.T. Press.

Lee, Hau L., Corey Billington, and Brent Carter. 1993. "Hewlett-Packard Gains Control of Inventory and Service through Design for Localization." *Interfaces* 23(4): 1–11.

Main, Jeremy. 1994. *The Quality Wars: The Triumphs and Defeats of American Business* (A Juran Institute Report) New York: Free Press.

Miles, Raymond E. 1989. "A New Industrial Relations System for the 21st Century," *California Management Review* 31, no. 2 (Winter):9–28.

Miles, Raymond E., and Charles C. Snow. 1986. "Network Organizations: New Concepts for New Forms," *California Management Review*: 62–73

Nohria, Nitin. 1992. "Information and Search in the Creation of New Business Ventures: The Case of the 128 Venture Group." In *Networks and Organizations: Structure, Form and Action.* Nitin Nohria and Robert G. Eccles, eds. Cambridge: Harvard Business School Press.

Nohria, Nitin, and Robert Eccles. 1992. "Face-to-Face: Making Network Organizations Work." In *Networks and Organizations: Structure, Form and Action.* Nitin Nohria and Robert G. Eccles, eds. Cambridge: Harvard Business School Press.

O'Reilly, Brian. 1994. "The New Deal: What Companies and Employees Owe One Another," *Fortune* 129, no. 12 (June 13): 44–50.

Ostroff, Frank, and Douglas Smith. 1992. "The Horizontal Organization," *McKinsey Quarterly* no. 1: 148–167. Packard, David, 1995, *The HP Way: How Bill Hewlett and I Built Our Company,* New York: Harper Collins.

Pascale, Richard Tanner. 1990. *Managing on the Edge: How the Smartest Companies Use Conflict to Stay Ahead.* New York: Touchstone.

Perrow, Charles. 1992. "Small-Firm Networks." In *Networks and Organizations: Structure, Form and Action.* Nitin Nohria and Robert G. Eccles, eds. Cambridge: Harvard Business School Press.

Piore, Michael, and Charles Sabel. 1984. *The Second Industrial Divide.* New York: Basic Books.

Prahalad, C. K., and Gary Hamel. 1990. "The Core Competence of the Corporation," *Harvard Business Review* (May–June): 79–91.

Rockart, John F., and James E. Short. 1991. "The Networked Organization and the Management of Interdependence." Chap. 7 of *The Corporation of the 1990's: Information Technology and Organizational Transformation*. Michael Scott Morton, ed. New York: Oxford University Press.

Sabel, Charles. 1991. "Moebius-Strip Organizations and Open Labor Markets: Some Consequences of the Reintegration of Conception and Execution in a Volatile Economy." In *Social Theory for a Changing Society*. J. Coleman and P. Bourdieu, eds. Boulder, Colo.: Westview Press.

Saxenian, AnnaLee. 1990. "The Regional Networks and the Resurgence of Silicon Valley," *California Management Review* 33, no. 1: 89–112.

Snow, Charles C., Raymond E. Miles, and Henry J. Coleman, Jr. 1992. "Managing 21st Century Network Organizations," *Organizational Dynamics* 20 (3): 5–20.

Stewart, Thomas A. 1992. "The Search for the Organization of Tomorrow," *Fortune* (May 18): 92–99.

Womack, James P., Daniel T. Jones, and Daniel Roos. 1990. *The Machine That Changed the World: The Story of Lean Production*. New York: Macmillan.

Redefining Success | 7

Ethnographic Observations
on the
Careers of Technicians

STACIA E. ZABUSKY
& STEPHEN R. BARLEY

A shadow of angst has fallen over the generation schooled to know "the color of its own parachute" (Bolles, 1981). After a decade of corporate layoffs, which for the first time in history have targeted managerial jobs, even the most well-packed parachutes now seem to fail with alarming frequency. The fear, of course, is the fear of not getting ahead, the broken promise of having a career that even an MBA may not mend. Speaking to aspiring managers, the author of a recent article in *Fortune Magazine* summarized the prevailing angst:

> Getting ahead wasn't supposed to be like this, was it? You thought you would start off at the bottom rung of the old career ladder and climb. The implicit promise: Do what you're told, wait your turn, and with seniority, you will be tapped to rise. But millions of Americans who hoped to grasp the next rung—or even hold on to the one they've reached—have discovered that they are grabbing air." (Richman, 1994, p. 46)

Two broad interpretations of the apparently dwindling opportunities for advancement are plausible. The most prevalent suggests that the world of work has become leaner and meaner, but that it remains essentially the same. From this perspective advancement is still possible, fewer people will simply succeed. Most commentators on the landscape of changing opportunity adopt this perspective. They counsel aspirants to gird themselves for lives in flatter organizations where assent will not only be precarious, but corporate ladders will look more like step stools. The watchwords of adaptation are flexibility, life-long learning, a willingness to take advantage of openings wherever they lead, and most importantly, increased self-reliance and self-reflection (see Henkoff, 1993; Kiechel, 1994; Sherman, 1994). The new rhetoric of adaptation sounds a familiar theme: rewards will come to those who take responsibility for themselves. Social Darwinists of the late 19th century would feel at home with such advice.

A second, less common interpretation of declining opportunities for advancement is that they signal a fundamental shift in employment structures. From this perspective, the shrinking internal labor markets on which so much attention is focused may reflect more than a reduction in opportunities for vertical mobility; the very nature of work itself may be changing for a sizable number of white-collar workers. Although one finds few analyses of how changes in the nature of work may be affecting careers, glimmers of recognition can be found in talk about "lateral" career moves. Commentators often note in passing that more people are moving between organizations and functional areas in search of opportunities that do not necessarily bring greater power or status. Why people should be willing to move "over" rather than "up" and what such moves entail, however, are rarely explored. One reason for the silence seems to be that our tendency to equate success with rung climbing has become so institutionalized that it is the only alternative we envision (Perlow and Bailyn, 1996). Evidence for this possibility can be found in the fact that most who comment on lateral career moves eventually conjecture that people move laterally to improve their odds of getting back on a vertical track. Regardless of whether such an interpretation accurately reflects people's motives, it points to how narrow our images of a respectable career may have become, and it is here that trouble lies. To the degree that definitions of success are bound to social and historical contexts, traditional images of what constitutes a respectable career may be inappropriate and even hinder adaptation when the context begins to change.

This chapter explores what a respectable career may mean in a world where a growing percentage of white-collar jobs no longer support definitions that equate success with vertical mobility. It begins by sketching the distinction between careers of advancement and careers of achievement and by suggesting why the letter may be becoming more prevalent. It then examines the careers of technicians, members of occupations in many ways paradigmatic of the shifting employment structures of most Western economies. The text focuses on how technicians make sense of their careers and examines the problems they face because their employers have a different understanding of work and success. Finally, the chapter explores what the spread of careers of achievement may mean for white-collar workers and the organizations that employ them.

Careers of Advancement and Achievement

A career, by definition, implies an ordered, coherent sequence of experiences, roles, statuses, or jobs. Coherence, however, is inherent neither in the career's sequence nor in the particular waystations that comprise it. Instead, incumbents and observers impute coherence by interpreting successive statuses against culturally prescribed milestones and criteria. For this reason, careers are best viewed as properties of collectives rather than of individuals (Barley, 1989). To be sure, careers are something that only individuals can experience, but they are not entirely of an individual's making. People may willfully choose between different courses of action as they progress through their careers. They may even dare to hope and plan with more or less success, but the options they foresee, the choices they make and, perhaps most important, the sense they make of where they have been and where they are going are always limited by collectively defined possibilities (Goffman, 1961; Roth, 1964; Van Maanen, 1977, 1980). The social context in which a career takes place thus serves as both blueprint and filter. It directs the paths that people forge through their lives while providing symbols and interpretations for separating meaningful from meaningless identities and activities.

One implication of the view that careers are contextually embedded and collectively defined is that observers and incumbents may interpret a sequence of statuses differently. As a result, incumbents may see a meaningful career where observers see no career at all, or vice versa. A second implication of contextualism is that there are more careers unfolding daily than most of us appreciate because we participate in different social contexts and orient ourselves to different reference groups. Not only may a sequence of jobs mean different things to people from different occupational subcultures (Van Maanen and Barley, 1984), but people may construct meaningful careers based on statuses and identities that have little to do with work per se (see Becker, 1953; Goffman, 1961; Farber, 1961; Roth, 1964).

Nevertheless, most recent career theory and nearly all popular images of a career presume that careers only make sense in the context of organizations. Moreover, managers and administrators almost always serve as the implicit reference group for defining success. Commentators and researchers usually measure career trajectories against the backdrop of vertically arrayed positions and compute success or failure in increments of power and authority.[1] Equating career success with vertical mobility has become so entrenched that most popular and academic discourse on careers would be incomprehensible without assuming a hierarchy. For instance, one cannot make sense of such phrases as "up and out," "career ladder," "plateauing," "promotion," or even "lateral move" without at least tacit reference to the vertical dimension (Schwartz, 1981). Successful careers are therefore almost always construed as "careers of advancement" in which identities are bound to organizations and attainment is parsed in increments of authority tied to formal positions in a chain of command.

There is, however, another model of a career that is sometimes acknowledged, especially in academic discussions, only to be bracketed as of secondary importance. One might call this second type of career a "career of achievement." Careers of achievement are stereotypically associated with professionals (doctors, lawyers, scientists, academics) and craftsworkers (carpenters, cabinet makers, electricians). Unlike careers of advancement, careers of achievement are usually played out against the backdrop of an occupation. Status attainment entails horizontal movement from the periphery to the center of an occupational community. Progress is scaled in terms of increments of skill, position in a network of practitioners and, sometimes, the setting in which one practices (Van Maanen and Barley, 1984). As in a career of advancement, success brings greater authority, but here authority is a form of moral leadership that rests more on expertise than formal position or the power to command. In fact, an occupation's most accomplished practitioners often have no right to tell other practitioners beyond their apprenticeships what to do. In careers of achievement, one may acquire considerable prestige, honor, and influence, one may even become known as a "sage," a "pro," a "guru," or an "old hand," but one does not become a "boss." Careers of achievement are largely horizontal affairs in which incumbents strive to move "in" rather than "up."

Careers of achievement are less salient than careers of advancement for at least three reasons. First, aside from the careers of doctors, lawyers, and a few other well-paid professionals, careers of achievement carry less status and prestige than careers of advancement. This is particularly true of craft careers that invoke images of manual labor. Second, careers of achievement are often hidden from view because they are phrased and phased in terms that are meaningful only to the members of an occupation. Outsiders generally have no knowledge of how the occupation's work is structured, what members count as expertise, or to what practitioners aspire. Even prestigious and visible occupations, such as medicine and law, appear to many outsiders as single statuses that offer "steady state careers" (Driver, 1980). It is widely known, for instance, that professors teach and do research, but even graduate students may fail to appreciate the fine distinctions by which academics judge success and failure. In comparison to careers of advancement, the criteria for a meaningful career of achievement are localized.

Most important, however, careers of achievement are less salient than careers of advancement because each is the product of a mode of production associated with a different historical era. Sociologists have long argued there are two broad systems for dividing labor in society. In a *vertical division of labor* tasks are organized hierarchically. Those who hold positions higher in the hierarchy not only have power over those below, they are generally presumed to have greater expertise. In a bureaucracy, the most well-developed instance of a vertical division of labor, superiors can legitimately exercise authority only to the degree that their knowledge encompasses, or is perceived to encompass, that of their subordinates (Weber, 1968/1922). Thus, a vertical division of labor presumes that knowledge and skills can be nested.

By contrast, in a *horizontal division of labor* tasks are allocated to groups of experts who have little direct authority over each other's activities. The logic of a horizontal division of labor rests on the assumption that knowledge and skills are too complex and domain-specific to be nested. Coordination, therefore, occurs not through a chain of command, but through the collaboration of members of different groups working jointly (Stinchcombe, 1959). Whereas organizations are usually the most relevant collectives in a vertical division of labor, occupations are the important collectives in a horizontal division of labor (Durkheim, 1933/1893). Since organizations and occupations are the primary contexts for careers of advancement and achievement respectively, it follows that the former should accompany a vertical division of labor while the latter should accompany a horizontal division of labor.

Scholars generally agree that a horizontal division of labor was more prominent before the late 18th century when most individuals worked in agriculture or the crafts. Agricultural expertise was divided according to the crops that farmers grew. Farm tasks were distributed by age and gender, but roles were otherwise undifferentiated. Farmers engaged in roughly the same activities regardless of whether they worked their own farms or pooled their labor on the estate of a lord (Applebaum, 1992). Commerce was an entrepreneurial activity pursued by shop-keepers, innkeepers, and local merchants who either worked alone or employed a handful of individuals, often members of their own family. Most other productive activities were organized as crafts whose domains were secured by guilds. Al-though the division of labor in preindustrial society had vertical overtones, these reflected either the relationship between master and apprentice or the workings of an omnipresent class structure, as in the case of serfs and their lords. Only in the military and the church were the rudiments of a vertical division of labor to be found.

After the middle of the 18th century, the vertical division of labor grew increasingly prominent. In fact, Durkheim (1933/1893). Tonnies (1957/1887), Weber (1968/1922), and Marx (1967/1867) contended that vertical models of organizing lay at the core of the Industrial Revolution. The logic of industrial production, as first articulated by Adam Smith (1937/1776), entailed the frag-mentation of tasks into increasingly simple jobs. Although fragmentation is some-times described as a functional (or horizontal) division of labor, its primary force was to narrow the scope of work sufficiently to allow administrative control (Weber 1968/1922; Braverman 1973; Edwards 1979). With the spread of mass manufacturing and the rise of large corporations in the late 19th and early 20th century, managerial, factory, and clerical work gradually overshadowed farming and craftwork as the primary forms of employment. Organizations replaced fami-lies and guilds as the locus of economic activity and the vertical dimension came to dominate relations of production. By the 1900s, management was not only widely recognized as a distinct endeavor (Chandler, 1977), but careers of ad-vancement had become more culturally prized than careers of achievement. To be sure, craft and professional careers remained available, but they were margin-alized because they employed relatively few people and because strong barriers precluded most people from entering these occupations. Respectable careers were now to be won in tournaments of mobility fought within pyramids of organiza-tional opportunity rather than in the slow development of mastery associated with occupational expertise. If you were an unskilled or semiskilled blue-collar worker, you might have no opportunity for a career at all (Thomas, 1989).

Most recent discourse on declining opportunities for careers implicitly as-sumes that a vertical division of labor will continue to dominate society. Although vertically organized work is unlikely to disappear, the assumption of its contin-ued dominance may be unwarranted. Just as the vertical division of labor gradu-ally overshadowed the horizontal during early 20th century, it is conceivable that changing modes of production may occasion a resurgence of horizontally orga-nized work. There is evidence that such a shift may have already begun.

In a paper on the changing distribution of employment, Barley (1994) shows that occupationally organized work has become more prominent since World War II. Since 1950, the percentage of Americans employed in professional and technical occupations has grown from 8% to 17% of the workforce. As of 1991, professional and technical workers had become the largest of the occupational categories charted by the U.S. census (see Table 7–1). Professional and technical

Table 7-1. Occupational Categories as a Percentage of the Labor Force: 1900–91

Category	1900	1910	1920	1930	1940	1950	1960	1970	1980	1991	Net change
Farmworkers	38%	31%	27%	21%	17%	12%	6%	3%	3%	3%	−36%
Professional/Technical	4	5	5	7	8	8	10	14	15	17	12
Craft and kindred	11	12	13	13	12	14	14	14	12	11	0
Operatives/Laborers	25	27	27	27	28	26	24	23	18	15	−10
Clerical and kindred	3	5	8	9	10	12	15	18	17	16	13
Service	9	10	8	10	12	11	12	13	13	14	5
Managerial/Administrative	6	7	7	7	7	9	8	8	10	13	7
Sales workers	5	5	5	6	7	7	7	7	11	12	7

Note: Percentage employment by occupational category from 1900 to 1970 was calculated from employment data presented in *The Statistical History of the United States from Colonial Times to the Present* (U.S. Bureau of the Census, 1976, p. 139). Data for 1980 were taken from Klien's (1984) article which transforms 1980 data using the Census Bureau's category system developed in 1983. Data for 1991 are taken from the *Statistical Abstract of the United States* (U.S. Department of Commerce, 1991.

workers now outnumber even "clerical and kindred workers" and "operatives and laborers." Although the proportion of Americans employed in managerial, sales, and low-level service jobs has also grown, they have increased at a much slower rate.

If one assumes that professional, technical, and craft employment is an imperfect but defensible proxy for the number of individuals in horizontally organized lines of work, then the percentage of the American labor force participating in a horizontal division of labor grew from 15% in 1900, to 22% in 1950, to 28% in 1991 (Barley, 1994). Forecasts suggest that this percentage will grow to 29% by 2005 (Silvestri and Lucasiewicz, 1991). Thus, it seems relatively conservative to claim that at least a quarter of all Americans are now working in jobs that are horizontally structured, and there is reason to believe that census data actually underestimate the importance of horizontally structured lines of work.

For instance, the census classifies accountants as managerial and administrative workers even though sociologists generally consider accounting to be a strongly organized profession. Accountants now represent 0.8% of all employed Americans. Census data also overlook what might be called the "occupationalization" of management (Barley and Tolbert, 1991). Since World War II, managerial tasks have undergone considerable specialization. Marketing and finance, in particular, have become distinct specialties. Not only can business students now major in each of these areas, but each has its own journals and professional organizations. Because researchers have paid little attention to the professionalization of management, we do not know how many people play out their careers entirely within a managerial specialty. It seems plausible, however, that business is evolving its own set of proto-occupational communities.

All else being equal, careers of achievement should become more viable as work organized along occupational lines expands. Such a development may partially explain why a growing number of managers are willing to accept lateral moves. But even if occupationally organized work in expanding, it would be a mistake to assume that people will find it easy to substitute careers of achievement for careers of advancement. The subcultures of the professions and crafts, where horizontal careers are well accepted, arose in an era when occupational and organizational forms of organizing were more easily separated. Medicine and law, for instance, solidified their occupational monopolies under a regime of self-employment. Today, organizational and occupational contexts are inextricably entwined, even for the established professions (Barley and Tolbert, 1991). Less than one-third of all lawyers in the United States now work as private practitioners, whereas in 1950, over one-half were so employed (Spangler, 1986). The employment of physicians has followed a similar path (Derber and Schwartz, 1991). The percentage of practitioners employed in organizational contexts is often near 100% for occupations of more recent origin. Technicians are a case in point.

Technicians are in many ways paradigmatic of the organizationally based occupations formed over the last several decades. Although one can trace the history of a handful of technicians' occupations to the turn of the century, most have come into being since World War II.[2] The term "technician" was not widely used to label occupations until after the late 1940s when it diffused from the military into civilian culture. Although the vast majority of technicians work in organizations ruled by cultures of advancement, most also participate in an occupational community of one sort or another (Whalley and Barley, 1996). Some are nearly as well organized as the professions themselves. For instance, radiological technologists and chemical technicians have their own journals, training programs, licensing procedures, and professional societies. Other technicians, such as microcomputer support specialists, participate in more loosely structured occupational communities that resemble a weak network of sociometric cliques. Yet, as we shall illustrate, even technicians in loosely structured occupational communities partake of subcultures that value careers of achievement more highly than careers of advancement. For this reason, the experiences of technicians offer a window on the dilemmas that may arise when cultures of achievement and advancement clash over the meaning of work and a respectable career.

Data Sources and Methods

Our analysis of technicians' careers draws on field notes collected by members of Cornell University's Program on Technology and Work. Between 1990 and 1994, PTW undertook a series of coordinated ethnographies of technical jobs. Each study focused on a single occupation and entailed both participant observation and extensive interviewing in one or more work sites over periods ranging from six to 12 months. Members of the research team studied emergency medical technicians (Nelsen, 1996), science technicians (Barley and Bechky, 1994), medical technologists (Scarselletta, 1996), microcomputer support technicians (Zabusky, 1996), engineers and engineering technicians (Darr, 1994). The study also made use of ethnographic data on photocopier repair technicians and radiological technologists collected respectively by Orr (1996) and Barley (1990).[3] Our remarks concerning technicians' careers are, therefore, comparative and span several lines of work.[4]

The researcher responsible for each ethnography culled from his or her field notes and transcripts all passages containing information on technicians' careers or technicians' assessments of their jobs. We divided the resulting body of excerpts into two sets: passages that pertained to a technician's "objective" career and passages that pertained to the technician's "subjective" career.[5] An "objective career" refers to the public and structural aspects of a career, the stream of more or less identifiable jobs, positions, statuses, and situations that serve as landmarks for gauging a person's movement over time. A "subjective career" denotes the meanings that an individual attributes to such movement in order to lend coherence to his or her biography. We used the data on objective careers to develop a typology of the career paths that technicians followed. We used the data on subjective careers to determine how technicians made sense of each path.

To identify career paths, we coded the data on objective careers for information pertaining to (1) educational background and training, (2) previous jobs, and (3) pay, benefits, and other working conditions. The analysis revealed several recurring patterns among the technicians' educational and work histories. We treated patterns traced by the biographies of more than three technicians as a distinct path. After identifying career paths, we coded the technicians' interpretations of their careers for talk about (1) what they liked and disliked about their jobs, (2) their reasons for entering the occupation, (3) their reasons for changing jobs, and (4) the kinds jobs they wanted in the future. The intent was to discover how technicians understood the choices they had made.

In the process of analyzing the technicians' subjective careers, we discovered that their interpretations were often tied to their perceptions of the organizations where they worked and to how other members of the organization perceived them. Specifically, we found that technicians used a discourse of "respect" to make sense of their professional lives. To better understand the relationship between technicians' careers and their notions of respect, we culled from each study passages in which technicians spoke of their relationship to and their feelings about the organizations that employed them as well as passages in which nontechnicians spoke about technicians. This data allowed us to better grasp the dilemmas the technicians faced as incumbents of occupational communities embedded in an organizational context.

The Objective Careers of Technicians

Despite diversity in the substance of the technicians' work, their objective careers traced a surprisingly limited number of patterns. These patterns were defined by the structure of the technicians' careers prior to entering the occupation and, in larger part, by the topography of their careers after entry.

Paths of Entry

Technicians differed by whether they had entered their line of work through an "orderly" or "disorderly" path (Wilensky, 1961). Orderly entry was particularly common among medical technicians, medical technologists, and radiological technologists. As is true of most health care occupations, these three were regulated by state agencies that restricted entry by licensing requirements that, in turn, dictated the kind of education a practitioner was to possess. To practice as a radiological technologist or medical technician one had to hold an associate's degree from a program recognized by both the state and the relevant medical authority, such as the American College of Radiology. Medical technologists were required to obtain a bachelor's degree in either medical technology or a related science, such as biology or chemistry. Because paths of entry were so well defined, most medical technicians, medical technologists, and radiological technologists had entered a degree program immediately after high school and had begun to practice as soon as they completed their degree. Although a few medical technicians and radiological technologists had worked in unrelated jobs before entering a training program, orderly school to work transitions were the norm.

In occupations free of regulation, paths of entry were more varied. To be sure, among science technicians, engineering technicians, and microcomputer support specialists were individuals with early careers as neatly structured as those of medical technicians. These practitioners had entered a degree program related to their line of work after high school and had become a technician immediately on graduation. The majority in these occupations, however, had traversed paths of entry that would appear nearly random to anyone but themselves. Most had not only held jobs that were unrelated to their present work, but many appeared to have had "disorderly educations."

One-third of the science technicians began their careers in jobs unrelated to science. One, for example, had been a water plant operator for six years prior to joining a lab, another had been a carpenter for over a decade. Although the personnel department of the organization that employed the science technicians claimed to require at least an associate's degree in a relevant scientific discipline, nearly one-quarter of the technicians had no more than a high school degree. In fact, educational credentials seemed to be largely unrelated to the type of work that the science technicians performed. Technicians with high school, associate's, bachelor's, and master's degrees held similar jobs in the laboratories we examined. The only commonality was that all science technicians had pursued a science-oriented curriculum regardless of the degree they possessed.

Paths of entry were even more disorderly for engineers, engineering technicians, and microcomputer support technicians. Computer technicians were as likely to have majored in the humanities or social sciences as in computer science. Their academic past was often checkered, replete with poor grades and unfinished degrees. Many engineers and technicians in the small start-up companies studied by Darr (1994) also followed disorderly paths into their occupations. The president of one company that manufactured computers had begun a bachelor's in engineering, but had dropped out before completing his degree. A software engineer who founded another company had studied theater and had worked as a professional musician for 10 years before becoming interested in computers. Perhaps the most colorful story of prior wanderings occurred among Orr's photocopier technicians:

> She left home at 16, taking her younger brothers with her, and did some logging with an old Indian and a horse: she felled and trimmed the trees, hooked the horse to a log and sent it on down the trail. . . . After that she got a job as a laborer in a sawmill and worked her way up to millwright (responsible for maintenance and adjustment of all the machinery). Then the mill shut down. She apprenticed as an electrician and worked her way up to journeyman before the construction industry around Laramie collapsed. She wanted to stay in Laramie since that's where her husband's job was and happened to see an ad for the Company down at the employment office. (Orr, personal communications)

That orderly paths of entry largely reflected legal rather than substantive requirements grains further credence from the careers of emergency medical technicians, which combined aspects of both trajectories. Like other health care technicians, EMTs had to be certified by the state. However, unlike medical technicians and radiological technologists, EMTs were not required to possess a postsecondary degree. Instead they had to pass a graded series of examinations to administer successively more risky treatments. Although EMTs learned these skills through a combination of coursework and supervised practice, the training was offered through adult education courses and led to certification but no formal degree. Consequently, most professional EMTs began their careers as volunteers with local rescue squads while attending high school or college or while employed full-time in another occupation. Among the EMTs Nelsen encountered during her study were a former broadcast journalist, a former sociologist, and a former insurance salesmen. Although all EMTs had taken courses to become certified, only one possessed a degree in a medical field and only two had originally set out to become paramedics. Most had wandered into the occupation.

Career Paths After Entry

Regardless of path of entry most technicians' careers became more orderly after entering their occupation. In fact, their subsequent careers generally evinced one of three patterns: stability, movement through a series of positions in substantively related, but distinct, occupational communities, and movement through a series of positions in a single occupational community. Unlike the difference between orderly and disorderly entry, these three trajectories were more evenly distributed across technicians in the various occupations.

Stability   Technicians with stable careers remained employed in the same position in the same organization for long periods of time. Some appeared to have had stable careers simply because few firms employed members of their occupation. For instance, Orr's (1996) photocopier repair technicians worked for a corporation that manufactured and serviced copiers. Because the corporation's technology was proprietary, it trained its own technicians. In-house training limited the technicians' mobility because their expertise revolved around the machines the company manufactured.

Other technicians had stable careers because they were tied to a geographic location. This reason for stability was common in hospital settings where a sizable minority of medical technicians and radiological technologists had worked in their departments for as long as 20 years. Geographic restrictions were also voiced by a number of science technicians and EMTs. Many of these technicians had grown up in nearby communities and wished to remain close to their relatives. Others had come from elsewhere, but now had spouses whose careers were bound to local employers. As might be expected, geographical reasons for stability were more common among medical technicians in the rural hospital Scarselletta studied than among the radiological technologists in the urban hospitals where Barley conducted his field research.

The third group of technicians with stable careers consisted of medical technicians, radiological technologists, and a science technician with no formal credentials. Compared to other technicians with stable careers, this group was small and consisted of practitioners who had entered the field before degrees were mandatory. Although they were grandfathered by their employer's personnel policies, they would have been unable to continue to practice if they left their current job.

Movement Between Related Occupational Communities   The second postentry career pattern involved movement through a series of substantively, but not hierarchically, related occupations. Several medical technicians at the hospital Scarselletta studied had shifted into nursing after working as technicians for a number
of years. Other medical and radiological technologists left hospital settings altogether for jobs as trainers and salespeople with companies that manufactured
laboratory and radiological devices. The technical supervisor in a computer department at a university had worked in series of jobs, all of which involved
repairing or servicing microelectronic technologies. Since 1976, he had debugged
controllers for a manufacturer of minicomputers, served as a field engineer for
two other computer companies, worked as a product support specialist for a firm
that made computer-controlled chromatography equipment, done a stint as a
manufacturing engineer in a ceramics operation, and served as a customer service
representative for a microcomputer company. Movement into substantively related occupations was especially common among emergency medical technicians.
There were few veteran EMTs in the sites that Nelsen studied. Many former EMTs
had become nurses, physician's assistants, police officers, and firefighters. These
choices suggested that EMTs viewed their work as a way of entering two larger
occupational domains: the world of health care and the world of protective
services.

Occupational changes in domain-oriented careers entailed no vertical advancement since work in one occupation was never prerequisite for the other.
Nevertheless, the pattern evinced a clear logic: those who moved into substantively related occupations oriented themselves to thematic content when changing jobs rather than to the occupational or organizational context of their work.

Movement Within One Occupational Community   The third postentry career pattern entailed movement through a series of positions in the same community of
practice. Sometimes this meant that technicians had held a number of positions
with the same employer. This pattern was especially common among science
technicians and research support specialists. For instance, all the cell culture
specialists that Bechky interviewed had worked in three or more labs in the same
university doing roughly similar work. Although such job changes usually
brought a larger salary, this was not always true and in most cases increments in
salary were marginal.

The careers of other technicians consisted of holding the same or similar jobs
in different organizations. A number of medical technologists, emergency medical technicians, programmers, and radiological technologists had held nearly
identical jobs in several organizations. Many had done so because they had
moved from one locale to another in search of higher salaries and a better
environment or because a spouse had been transferred.

Slightly different yet were technicians who remained in the same occupational community while pursuing a series of different jobs in a number of organizations. For instance, one science technician began her career as a quality control
technician in the food industry, moved on to become a serologist in a veterinary
lab, and later became a technician in a flow cytology lab in a biotechnology

center. Although she had worked in three otherwise unrelated contexts, each job built on her knowledge and skills in microbiology. Strings of jobs in a single occupational domain were particularly common among computer technicians who seemed to change positions every two or three years. Several technicians had held jobs as lab attendants or computer operators while in college, had subsequently worked as workstation technicians, were then employed as programmers, and ultimately moved on to become network administrators and systems analysts. Although each job in the sequence complemented the technician's previous experience, all involved overlapping duties and none entailed an increment in formal authority.

Despite diversity of career patterns, a common thread cut across the careers of most technicians: the virtual absence of vertical movement. Few technicians had attempted to climb an organizational hierarchy and those who did were typically first-level technical supervisors who downplayed their authority. In several studies, we encountered technicians who had once held supervisory positions, but who had abandoned them to return to more technical jobs. None of these technicians were forced to step down. Several had renounced their authority so that they could relocate, the others were still employed by the same organization. Because the latter were held in high regard by their colleagues and employers, it seems likely that their "demotion" was a matter of choice.

One might counter the claim that technicians' careers showed no vertical movement by arguing that ethnographers do not usually encounter people who no longer work in the settings they study. Although the objection has merit, each researcher made an effort to elicit information on technicians with whom informants had previously worked. Such questioning uncovered two individuals who had embarked on a vertical career by leaving technical work, but the majority of stories about former colleagues told of careers consistent with the patterns outlined above. It therefore seems reasonable to entertain the hypothesis that technicians' careers are usually devoid of vertical movement. From the perspective of a culture of advancement, technicians' work could be said to offer, at best, opportunities for lateral moves and, at worse, the specter of a dead-end job. Technicians, however, viewed their careers from an entirely different vantage point: for them, careers centered on work, not advancement. Consequently, they saw their careers as thick with opportunities and challenge.

The Subjective Careers of Technicians

Love of Work

The stories technicians told about why they entered their occupations always centered on their attraction to the technical content of the work, an attraction they often referred to as "love." Computer technicians were particularly eloquent on this score. One programmer talked about how he had become infatuated with computers as a boy. His parents had given him and his sister a choice between going to Disney World and getting a computer. They chose the computer. Another workstation technician talked about how he discovered computing during his senior year in high school: "I picked up a computer manual and started playing. In three days I taught myself more than the teacher had taught me in three weeks. It came naturally, I went to town with it."

Early fascination with computers and the experience of quickly learning more than a mentor were common themes in the stories computer technicians told about themselves. So was the language of entertainment. Programmers and workstation technicians referred to their computers as "toys" and often used the verb "play" as synonym for "work." Expressions of enthrallment with new hardware and software were sometimes graphic, as when a technician who had been waiting anxiously for a release of a new program, proceeded to caress the shrink-wrapped package upon its arrival to the amusement of his colleagues. At times, the technicians expressed amazement that people would pay them to pursue something they loved. As one network administrator put it when explaining the source of his job satisfaction: "As long as [my employers] give me exciting things to mess with and keep giving me money to play with, I'll be happy." So powerful was the excitement of technology for these technicians, that several had shirked their studies and even quit college to work for minimum wage in a computer lab. Orr (1996) referred to a similar orientation among copier repair technicians as "a propensity to tinker." Copier technicians told stories about how they helped tune the family car or rebuilt bicycles from junk parts in their younger days. For them, working with photocopiers was an extension of a long-held interest in machines.

Medical technologists and EMTs also told stories about loving their work. Their stories, however, focused less on technology than on the larger context of health care. EMTs talked about the satisfaction that came from using their knowledge and skills to save lives. Some spoke, as well, of the excitement and danger of emergency medicine, admitting that they were "trauma junkies." All insisted that because pay was low and the hours bad, "anyone in this line of work [does] it because they love it." The medical technologists that Scarselletta interviewed echoed similar sentiments. Consider the testimony of one:

> I can remember exactly what it was [that attracted me to the occupation]. I was in biology class watching a film on blood cells going through capillaries and I thought, "this is truly amazing." That's when I decided I didn't want to talk about anything else. . . . You know I just loved it and I wanted to make a career of it.

In these and other stories that technicians told about entering their occupations one hears not only a sense of excitement but a sense of calling. The technicians' terms of discourse were affective and personal, never instrumental. For most technicians, entering the occupation had something to do with finding one's self and one's identity.

Growth and Learning

Technicians sounded similar themes when making sense of their subsequent careers. All the technicians we studied had an abiding interest in growing and staying current in their field. All spoke of the constant learning that came with their jobs and demonstrated their commitment to the ideal of continual learning in a variety of ways. Most science technicians, EMTs, and computer technicians had either recently taken or were currently enrolled in a workshop, a refresher course, or a college course related to their work. Technicians in all the occupations we studied read the literature in their field, often on their own time. A number of computer technicians, science technicians, and medical technologists participated in networks of other technicians who met formally and informally to talk about problems and issues they faced in common. All participated daily in casual discussions with their colleagues that carried considerable information about what each had read or heard and about their encounters with and solutions to problems. Even the technicians who did not have formal credentials actively sought to enhance their knowledge and improve their expertise. As one science technician put it, a good technician "works to keep on top of the cutting edge information . . . trying to experiment, trying new things. You have to stay on top or you get left behind."

Expanding one's skills and encountering new challenges were primary reasons technicians gave for changing jobs. A computer technician oriented to hardware explained that he had begun his career as a computer operator tending a mainframe, but after a year he had learned all he thought he could learn, so he began looking for work supporting microcomputers. He quickly found such a job, but after working as a workstation support specialist for three years, he had taken a training course in network technology and was now searching for yet another position that would allow him to expand his knowledge by installing and managing his own network. He also wanted to move out of educational organizations where had he worked up to this point in time because "here, things are kind of static, you just come, you do your job, you go home. You do what's required and that's it." The technician felt that a business environment would provide "more technical avenues to follow." In a similar vein, a network administrator matter-of-factly noted that his tenure in his present position was limited and that he would leave as soon as "it reaches a point of saturation"; that is, when his work began to be little more than simply maintaining what he already created.

The quest for growth and challenges also figured prominently in the tales of technicians who moved between related occupations. The technician who had made a career of mastering a string of microelectronic technologies spoke with pride of his foray into materials science as a manufacturing engineer:

> What a difference [his experience as a manufacturing engineer had been from his earlier jobs]! But, I had a lot of on-the-job training. There was a guy there who had a master's in material science, a plastics engineer. So they brought me up to speed on material sciences, plastics technology, and ceramics technology. After a year, I could actually work with professors at different universities, intelligently conversing with them on mechanics of stress and things like that.

Even technicians who had stable objective careers saw themselves as continually accumulating expertise. In radiology departments and medical laboratories, long-tenured technicians were known as rich sources of tacit knowledge about how to solve problems and were treated as technical virtuosos. Many of these individuals saw their work as a trade that involved a never-ending journey toward the status of a master craftsman.

Although technicians valued constant learning, most took a dim view of credentials. Technicians explained that credentials mattered only to managers. What really counted was "what you could do and how your peers evaluated your expertise." The general disdain for credentials was particularly strong in computer subcultures. A network administrator and technical supervisor, for instance, displayed on his door alongside a collection of cartoons a certificate that announced that he was a "Certified Novell Engineer." Zabusky commented admiringly on the certificate, which indicated that the technician had been formally trained to install and maintain Novell networks, only to find herself rebuffed. The technician explained that he had put the certificate on his door "with all the other jokes" to signal the value of the "piece of paper." To be sure, the certificate had been critical to his promotion because it had impressed the administrators. But as far as he was concerned, the certificate was meaningless: what mattered to him and his peers was "whether you can get the work done."

The belief that formal evaluations were irrelevant was echoed by technicians in all fields we examined. For instance, an EMT who had taken an examination to be promoted to a senior technician told the researcher that he had "been really ambivalent about taking the test" and had only done so because his partner was leaving and he "didn't want to be stuck with a lousy partner." The EMT explained that the test was "outdated and full of dumb questions" and that it did not test what he knew. He had taken the test not because he wanted the title it conferred, but because he saw it as the only way of guaranteeing a partner on whose expertise he could rely.

Experience was the source of know-how that counted among technicians. Nelsen (1996) describes how new EMTs were taught, in training courses, to follow official protocols for delivering care. However, to advance beyond being a novice in the eyes of their peers, EMTs had to demonstrate that they could extrapolate from protocols and do whatever the situation demanded with finesse. Photocopier repair technicians (Orr, 1996) viewed repair manuals, with their step-by-step procedures, as no more than a starting point for effective repair. Even science technicians, who were more prone than other technicians to find value in their training, claimed that only by experience could one become an accomplished practitioner. The science technicians deemed experience critical for two reasons. First, considerable information was carried by subtle differences in the colors, sounds, and patterns produced by assays and test equipment. Second, like spoken languages, technological codes exhibited "dialects" or local variations. These variations were often tied to peculiarities of specific cell lines, machines, and experiments. Experienced technicians therefore made use of signs that could be found in no textbook and that were difficult to define except ostensively. Partially for this reason, practices successful in one lab often failed in another unless technicians from the first trained technicians from the second (for similar observations see Cambrosio and Keating, 1988; Jordan and Lynch, 1992).

Expertise, Reputation, and Achievement

Love of work and the search for challenge underwrote the technicians' perception of what constituted an honorable career. Success had little to do with ladder climbing. Not only did technicians' careers lack objective indices of vertical mobility, most technicians did not appear to desire advancement. Technicians' narratives of work *never* included statements about wanting to move up an organizational hierarchy. Technicians *never* talked about gaining more authority or control over the work of other people. If anything, they portrayed organizations and management as potential barriers to getting the work done. As one software engineer put it, "management always puts obstacles in the way of engineers because they do not understand or care about what is involved in getting software to work." Computer technicians unanimously referred to organizational matters disdainfully as "politics," by which they meant that the "irrationalities" of organizational life frequently interfered with their efforts to bring their expertise to bear on technical problems.[6]

Even technicians who had assumed supervisory positions belittled their authority and expressed little interest in further vertical mobility. An EMT who had abandoned a management position in another emergency medical service company indicated that he had left the position because he "wanted to get back on the street." A supervisor of a medical laboratory said that she had taken the job because she had convinced herself that such a position would allow her to become involved in the "people end of things" without losing contact with laboratory work. She indicated that she had no desire to move further into hospital management, although such opportunities were available, because doing so would distance her from the lab. A systems analyst who had responsibility for supervising the work of programmers, echoed the attitude of most of the technicians and technical supervisors we encountered by pointing directly to the irony of her situation.

> Its very interesting looking at my position as opposed to Tom's (a programmer). If you're supposed to know more because you're higher up on the corporate ladder or whatever—that's definitely not true. I mean when it comes right down to it, Tom knows a hell of a lot more about programming and more about the nitty gritty of setting up complicated databases. I wouldn't know where to begin doing something like that. So it seems reversed. Why should I be his supervisor? . . . It would be foolish of me to try and tell him exactly what to do. About all that I can do is work with him to set priorities.

Technicians shunned vertical careers because they believed that advancing through an organization would take them away from the work they loved. They devalued positions of authority, even when it was their own, because they felt that legitimate authority should come from only one source, demonstrably superior expertise. But to say that technicians eschewed careers of advancement and denigrated organizational authority is not to say that they had no notion of success. Indeed, technicians had fairly well developed criteria for judging the meaningfulness of their professional biographies.

Technicians measured career success in terms of accumulated expertise, accomplishment in the face of a new challenge, and the gradual acquisition of a reputation for skill. The trajectory of successful careers moved from a peripheral to a more central position in a community of practice. Such movement rarely resulted in greater organizational status as evinced by titles, higher pay, or formal authority. Instead, what technicians sought were autonomy and respect, not only from their peers, but from their employers.

At the center of the social networks in each of the technical communities studied stood technicians who were widely known for their technical prowess. These individuals had developed an especially extensive and contextualized understanding of their work and their proficiencies placed them in great demand. It was to these individuals that other technicians turned for advice and counsel. Although many central technicians had considerable experience and seniority, a significant minority were quite young. The fact that it was possible for young practitioners to become acknowledged "gurus" demonstrated that it was expertise rather than experience or seniority per se that technicians valued.

The technicians' tales of their search for challenge were often tied to stories about a quest for respect. A programmer, for instance, explained that he had left a previous position in a company that had paid more money because his employer made "unreasonable technical demands even though he had no idea of what we were doing." A network administrator had left a previous job that he admitted was "quite challenging" because "the boss who started the company was very insistent on doing it a certain way and it turned out to be his way." Quests for respect and autonomy were particularly prominent among science technicians. The career histories of all the research support specialists that Bechky interviewed included a story of how they had moved from lab to lab until they found a scientist willing to grant them the autonomy, flexibility, challenge, and respect they believed they deserved.

Although many technicians found they had to move from organization to organization to gain challenge and respect, this was not always the case. Becoming central was also possible for technicians who had organizationally stable careers. In stable careers, movement from the periphery inward was more about acquiring depth than breadth of knowledge. Scarselletta (1996) described the case of a medical technician in a medium-sized hospital who "was revered by his colleagues for his ability to troubleshoot hematology's analyzers with uncanny speed and accuracy," an ability he had developed largely on his own through his experience with the machines. His troubleshooting ability had enhanced his standing among hematology's technicians: other technicians consulted with him whenever things went wrong. Even the pathologists recognized his expertise. Yet, the technician's reputation for expertise among his colleagues was largely invisible to the organization. It brought him no increment in pay or status and, most important, no respect from those who managed the hospital. According to most technicians, here lay the rub: the organizations in which they worked appeared either incapable or unwilling to recognize them for their achievements.

Achievement-Oriented Careers in Subcultures
of Advancement

Institutionalized Disrespect

Complaints about lack of respect were as characteristic of the technicians' stories of their careers as expressions of commitment to the work itself. Technicians found a lack of respect in the policies, the benefits, and the practices of their employers. Pay was perhaps the most symbolic reminder. Most of the technicians studied earned between $18,000 and $27,000 a year. Starting salaries for medical technicians and engineering technicians with an associate's degree averaged $22,000 in the region where the studies were conducted (Kmetz et al., 1994). Almost every technician interviewed felt underpaid.[7] Although technicians certainly desired to make more money for instrumental reasons, personal finances were not the only, or even the primary, reason that technicians complained about pay. Technicians interpreted their low salaries as signs of disdain. They believed their low wages indicated that employers valued neither the contribution they made to the organization nor the knowledge they had acquired though years of experience and continued learning.

Technicians frequently remarked on the discrepancy between their wages and their level of expertise. One computer technician indicated that he had immersed himself in learning a new technical area (desktop publishing) because he thought, "if I do more work that requires more knowledge, maybe I'll get paid more, [but I found out] this was not necessarily true." Like most other technicians, this technician now believed that employers paid for credentials, not for skill or for what people actually contributed. Medical technicians in the community hospital that Scarselletta studied had mounted a poster in the staff's break room that spoke to the same issue. The poster depicted several puppies in a basket beneath which a caption read: "they can't fire us—slaves have to be sold."

Technicians believed low pay was the primary reason why young people were hesitant to enter their fields. This was particularly true in medical technology where a labor shortage has existed for several decades (Franke and Sobel, 1970). According to one laboratory supervisor:

> You get out of school after working hard for four years, and you want a decent salary to make a decent living. That's one of our problems. A starting salary is 22 [thousand] for a four-year tech. Yet, an engineering student who probably took comparably complex courses starts out easily at 32. So [they get] $10,000 more for basically going through a similar program. When we go and interview or attend student career fairs that's one of the first questions: "How much money do you make?" When we say you start off at $22–24,000, a lot of kids just completely turn off. If they have to put in the effort, they want to reap the benefits as soon as they're out of school.

EMTs, whose primary complaint was pay, echoed similar sentiments. Indeed, pay had become such an issue in one company that the EMTs were trying to unionize. One full-time EMT explained that even top wages for a paramedic were "pretty low" considering the paramedics' expertise:

> $30,000 is a good living for a paramedic, pretty close to top of the line. That's not much for paramedics who've gone through a lot of training and a lot of years. You know, people don't just go from basic EMT to paramedic. I know a lot of people who took four to eight years to become a paramedic. And there's continuing education that you must go through. So it's really not right that they're paid so low. Granted, fire fighters and police aren't paid a lot either, but (paramedics) are medical professionals.

Some EMTs viewed low wages as part of a strategy to "encourage high turnover." Two full-time EMTs told Nelsen that their company had a "policy of hiring new people, particularly green medics with little experience to take the place of frustrated old-timers." They believed the practice was dangerous:

> So much of an experienced medic's knowledge is picked up on the street. This knowledge can't be gained during the two-week orientation, which includes the seven ride-outs that all new [EMTs] go through. When an experienced medic leaves, his knowledge goes with him, and it isn't replaced by the addition of a medic fresh out of school. . . . No occupation can survive and flourish very long if its best people are always leaving and the people who use the emergency care system are the ones who suffer for it.

Although technicians considered experience to be more critical than formal training, they also thought that continued education merited some reward. Technicians, as we have noted, spent considerable time keeping up to date by reading, taking courses and becoming involved in professional activities. One programmer explained that "if you don't keep up you'll be out of a job; [and a lot of the learning that keeps you busy] takes place outside of the actual work environment." Yet, employers neither directly rewarded nor recognized the time that technicians spent furthering their knowledge unless it resulted in a degree.

Supervisors of technicians were particularly troubled by their organizations' inability to reward demonstrated expertise. The supervisor of a large urban laboratory described for Scarselletta the case of a 25-year veteran with "a wealth of information," someone who could "look at chemistry results and pinpoint what a patient is going through in the emergency room, just based on her job experience." The supervisor lamented, "But, I can't do anything for her, as far as increasing her pay, because she doesn't have the education." A supervisor of computer technicians recounted how he managed similar problems. He claimed that the university paid on the basis of job descriptions and degrees, not on the basis of what technicians knew or actually had to do on the job. Thus, when hiring a new person, he felt he had to manipulate the official job descriptions he sent to the personnel office so that they reflected, "not exactly what [the technicians] do, but what I want to be able to pay them." The supervisor claimed that the best computer technicians were often not those with the best credentials. A computer technician employed in a commercial setting echoed this view: "it is difficult to keep abreast of developments in the field, which move at a staggering pace and be in school [at the same time] . . . so a lot of people with computer science degrees aren't always at the forefront of the technology."

The experience of a computer programmer who had learned to program in a machine shop illustrated the inability of organizations to reward technical skills learned and practiced on the job. The programmer was originally hired into a lower level clerical position as a stockkeeper. When her immediate supervisor decided to computerize the office, he asked her to take a college-level course in programming. After taking the course, she continued to learn programming on her own and participated in building the databases to automate the machine shop's inventory and facilities systems. Despite her newfound expertise, she could not get a promotion. "I knew and liked everybody in the basement [where the machine shops were located]," she explained, "but they'd hire some guy out of [a vocational education program] for machining at a higher grade and they'd fight my upgrade. The guys thought I was intelligent, but 'upstairs' they didn't."

Interpersonal Disrespect

It was not only institutionalized forms of disrespect that irked technicians. They were troubled, too, by interpersonal evidence that managers and other non-technical people held them in low esteem. A computer technician in a professional school explained his anger at how rudely he had been treated during a training program he had developed for faculty and staff: "It became clear what our status was. . . . People tried things they wouldn't try with someone they thought was professional. . . . [It was as if] nobody could decide whether we were librarians, janitors, or faculty. It still comes as a surprise to the faculty that people in this department can use words of more than one syllable." An analogous lack of regard disturbed copier technicians. Although copier technicians did not complain about pay, they did complain of being "insufficiently respected" by management and by the customers whose machines they serviced (Orr, 1996). For instance, one technician recalled that while working on a copier in a secretarial area, a manager came out of his office and literally stepped over him without acknowledging his presence.

For most technicians, management was a sore point. Technicians complained about managers' attempts to limit their autonomy and discretion. Technicians interpreted such actions as a sign that managers had no appreciation for their sense of professionalism. Technicians expected to be trusted to do their work well. They resented any implication that they needed to "be watched over by a mother hen" as one science technician put it. An incident from a medical laboratory illustrated why technicians grew to resent the attitudes of managers and other superiors. Scarselletta arrived one day to find a technician carefully checking and rechecking a set of results. When asked why he was taking such extraordinary care, the technician replied:

> Well, this doctor I'm dealing with here can get real irate. After [I reported the results], the doctor . . . actually came down here and said, "You're full of shit;

where's the real result?" He was all over me like a cheap suit, which I thought was unprofessional. So I want to be sure this time that I've done everything possible to show that the results are right.

Although the results were indeed correct, the physician would not accept the technician's evidence until a pathologist vouched for the accuracy of the data.

Many technicians viewed such lack of trust as reason enough for moving on. An EMT described how he and his colleagues had left positions with another company because they felt that their responsibilities were gradually being diminished. The EMTs were allowed to do less and less because of a jurisdictional dispute with emergency room nurses. Eventually, he became so frustrated that he quit "to find something else in EMS that interested him." An engineer described how a small start-up company he had worked for "went crazy and tried to build those little hierarchies, like you study in business schools. All the good people said, 'thank you very much,' and left the company." A science technician said that she had moved from three previous positions because her supervisors had not respected her. She said that she was unlikely to leave ever her present lab unless unforeseen events arose because, "you can't beat the flexibility and trust I get here. I just don't think it's going to get any better, as far as supervisors go." Most technicians viewed the lack of trust and respect they experienced as evidence of a systemic problem. Managers who recognized and appreciated a technician's expertise were thought to be exceptional individuals and a rare find.

Our interviews with managers often corroborated the technicians' worse fears, many managers did not seem to respect the technicians or their work. An administrator responsible for a computer department, but who had no technical training, revealed his reluctance to accord technicians the status of professionals. He told a story about "supervisory problems" he had with a technician he had previously employed and claimed that administrators in the central personnel office had told him that "compliance problems" were "typical of computer staff." "They look at themselves as professionals," he explained, "and feel that they alone have capacity to judge their work. But you can't regard them as professionals because they don't have the requisite capacity for judgment." An administrator in charge of another computer department similarly insisted that technicians lacked the organizational and social acumen required of professionals. He said that although technical problems might sometimes be "organizational problems," as the technicians often maintained, he did not want the computer staff to address them as organizational problems: "I don't want them to be change agents. They don't know how to see a big thing that requires the Dean to get involved. They don't kind of get the idea."

Some managers went beyond questioning the technicians' comportment and social judgment to dispute the value of their expertise. A pathologist in charge of the medical laboratory at the hospital where Scarselletta did his field work argued that clinical analyzers [machines] not only produced but largely interpreted test results automatically. Thus, he referred to medical technicians as "glorified button pushers." The pathologist further disparaged the technicians' expertise by referring to their professional journals as "throwaways, because I get them and I throw them away." Orr (1996) reported that corporate managers similarly contested the photocopier technicians' sense of themselves as professionals: "service management believed that the technicians . . . could be replaced by semiskilled labor with a good set of instructions. Many managers believed that technicians waste a lot of time [and] that any technician who [wasn't] . . . being controlled [was] going to goof off."

Ethnographic observations universally belied such views. For instance, the computer technicians we studied were acutely aware of the social dimensions of their work and regarded them as an integral part of their job (Zabusky, 1996). They were also aware that they could not always act on their knowledge of the social situation because of their subordinate status (Nelsen, 1996). Scarselletta, (1996) carefully documented the dedication and concern medical technicians showed for the accuracy of the data they produced. Medical technicians had clear norms against "goofing off" and subjected technicians who worked carelessly to embarrassing public ridicule. What the pathologists overlooked was the fact that medical technicians' work was not so much about the production of test results as it was about identifying and rectifying errors which required not only the ability to interpret the pattern of results in a patient's file but extensive knowledge of the hospital as a social system. Nelsen (1996) has shown that EMTs have strict moral codes regarding the welfare of patients. Finally, Orr (1996) and Barley and Bechky (1994) have documented how the wealth of contextual and tacit skills that copier technicians and science technicians bring to their work cannot be reduced to simplified manuals provided by management or to experimental protocols published in scientific journals.

Implications

We point to the discrepancy between our ethnographic assessments of technician's work and management's perceptions of technician's work not because we wish to suggest that the technicians were right and the managers wrong. Rather, we note the disjuncture to highlight the gulf that currently separates those who pursue careers of achievement from those who value careers of advancement. The difficulties technicians encountered in their careers signal a class of problems that may become more common as horizontally organized work proliferates in a world of organizations premised on a vertical division of labor.

We have shown that technicians ground their careers on the acquisition of substantive skill and knowledge within the context of a community of practitioners. As a result, they base their identities on the work they do and subscribe to an ethos of expertise that prizes commitment to and responsibility for the work they produce. Technicians value achievement, teamwork, and a healthy respect for individual differences in knowledge and skill. Most technicians have little interest in hierarchical advancement and even less interest in becoming managers. They want, instead, to be rewarded with more challenging tasks, to be trusted for their professionalism and to be accorded respect for their abilities. In short, technicians exemplify precisely the sort of values championed by much of the recent discourse on the "new economy." Like the new rhetoric of quality to which so many managers now give allegiance, technicians stress achievement, quality, responsibility, and continual learning.

Yet, technicians' careers suggest that organizations may be less ready for an achievement-oriented workforce than the business press suggests. The technicians' emphasis on substantive expertise seems to conflict sharply with the cultures of authority, control, and advancement in which they often find themselves working. The mismatch manifests itself in the technicians' complaints about the lack of respect they receive, in their low salaries, and in the disdain that managers express for the role technicians play in organizations. Indeed, it is partially this lack of respect that leads technicians to move from job to job and organization to organization in search of positions where they feel valued for the knowledge they have amassed, to have what others call lateral careers. Although some technicians eventually achieve the trust and challenge they desire, even these individuals are acutely aware that their good fortune rests on the idiosyncrasies of the particular people with whom they happen to work. Respect for technical expertise and careers of achievement are not yet central to most organizational cultures. Thus, at best, most technicians remain invisible to the organizations that depend on their work. At worst, they may be denigrated as incapable, narrow-minded "geeks" and "button pushers."

The situation contains several ironies. First, technicians are often better educated and are almost always more skilled in their substantive field than those who supervise them. This is true even if one uses credentials as a measure of expertise. The average technician in the United States has more formal education than the average manager (Carey and Eck, 1984). In fact, professionals are the only occupational group that is more highly educated than technicians. Yet, technicians are often treated as if they were low-level employees.

Second, because technicians build and maintain the infrastructures on which production systems rest and because they possess the skills necessary for generating the information that other knowledge workers use in their jobs (Barley, 1993), they are arguably among one of the most critical resources that organizations possess. Without competent and dedicated technicians, the production systems of many organizations would collapse (Barley and Bechky, 1994). Technicians are likely to have an even more important role in the future as production and control systems become more complex and dependent on integrated, microelectronic technologies. In such a world, managers are less likely to be able to step in and do the technicians' job as they might have done in the past with unskilled and semiskilled labor. Yet, many organizational authorities seem to be unwilling to accord technicians much esteem.

The third irony has linguistic roots. The rhetoric of vertical careers leads one to believe that advancement and achievement are coupled: those who achieve, advance. The technicians' experience calls the rhetoric into question. Their careers suggest either that advancement and achievement are not coterminous in cultures of advancement or that rewards are allocated only for achievement in a narrow band of activities. The difficulty seems to be that organizations simply do not know how to recognize and reward substantive expertise. Researchers who study engineers have often reached the same conclusion (Kornhauser, 1962; Ritti,

1971; Raelin, 1985; Von Glinow, 1988). The inability of organizations to reward expertise and substantive achievements may represent the Achilles' heel of current efforts to adapt to the "new economy."

Technicians' stories point to inequities that a growing number of white-collar employees are likely to encounter as the division of labor becomes more horizontal. If work becomes more occupationally structured but our models for making sense of work remain tied to a vertical division of labor, then it is likely that those who immerse themselves in occupational communities outside the established professions will be deemed failures and misfits. The low wages and lack of respect currently accorded to technicians despite their levels of education, skill, and commitment bode ill for a workforce increasingly composed of specialists. Unless we can expand our definitions of success beyond increments in formal authority and hierarchical advancement, we may wind up transforming a cadre of highly skilled, motivated individuals into the postindustrial equivalent of blue-collar labor.

Here lies the fourth and most bitter irony. Our research indicates that technicians evince precisely the sort of commitment and responsibility to work that employers now widely say they want from their employees. But if organizations cannot reward such commitment with trust and respect, then they may undermine the commitment they claim to desire so fervently. At the very least, repeated failure to appreciate the value of substantive achievements and technical expertise will likely engender dissatisfaction, turnover, and resentment. In the long run, it is likely to discourage young people from entering precisely those jobs that are most rapidly expanding. It is difficult to imagine parents and teachers urging children to enter technical occupations that require substantial education, extensive expertise, and continual learning, but that return little in the way of wages or prestige.

Moving from a culture of advancement to a culture of achievement is likely to require organizations to break dramatically with past practices. To support careers of achievement, those in charge of organizations must come to appreciate and recognize sometimes subtle differences in knowledge and skill. They must also understand what members of an array of occupational communities consider to be increasingly difficult challenges and then arrange opportunities to provide such challenges. However, as work becomes more technical and knowledge more balkanized, such knowledge is likely to become even less widely distributed that it is today. Consequently, if organizations are to support careers of achievement they may have little choice but to rely more heavily on occupational communities for assessing performance and allocating challenges to workers since managers unlikely to have the background necessary for making such assessments.

Rather than ignore or undermine occupational communities, organizations may actually need to strengthen occupational identities, occupational value systems, and ultimately the political influence of communities of practice. Although on the face of it such a suggestion may seem like heresy, especially given the role that organizations have played in the demise of the crafts over the last century, it would offer organizations several important advantages. First, occupational communities are best situated to define the sequence of experiences critical for building substantive expertise in technical fields. The chains of jobs that members of many technical occupations currently hold already resemble informal apprenticeships. Since firms see apprenticeships as a viable response to the critical shortage of skilled labor but few are willing to offer such apprenticeships (Zemsky, 1993), allocating the responsibility to a community of practice may be optimal not only for practitioners but for employers themselves. Second, because technical knowledge changes so quickly, communities of practitioners are better situated than managers to assess effective performance. Occupational assessment works reasonably well in medicine, law, and other established professions. There is no reason to believe that it would be impossible to build similar systems for other occupational groups. Finally, by strengthening the occupational community's hand in allocating challenges and rewards, employers may actually legitimate rather than undercut careers that span multiple organizations and that are predicated on the authority of expertise rather than the authority of position. In an era where hierarchical advancement is likely to become less widespread, legitimate occupational careers may provide a means of maintaining valued personnel as well as more flexible access to a shifting portfolio of knowledge and skill.

If nothing else, the trajectory of technicians' careers and their experiences in organizations reminds us that labor markets are embedded in a cultural matrix. The matrix tells us what we should and should not value. When cultural "oughts" become disconnected from structural realities, social disjunctures result. The last time the system of work diverged from cultural images of what work should provide, the world witnessed widespread labor unrest, the formation of unions, and the demise of the crafts. Although we would not venture to guess how the culture will eventually adjust to increasingly occupational patterns of work, we suspect that the adjustment will not be painless and that many who currently aspire to managerial careers will find themselves victims of the changes. On the basis of our examination of technicians' careers, it does seem safe to say, however, that expertise must come to wield the same respect as the authority of position. This is a tall order for an era preoccupied with shorter vacancy chains.

Notes

The work reported herein was supported under the Education Research and Development Center program agreement number R117Q00011–91, CFDA 84.117Q, as administered by the Office of Educational Research and Improvement, U.S. Department of Education. The findings and opinions expressed in this report do not reflect the position or policies of the Office of Educational Research and Improvement or the U.S. Department of Education. This work would not have been possible without the help of Assaf Darr, Bonalyn Nelsen, Julian Orr, and Mario Scarselletta.

1. A number of career theorists and researchers have actually made the notion of vertical movement a necessary condition for claiming that a individual has had a career (Wilensky, 1961, p. 523; Sofer, 1970, p. 5; White, 1970; Stewman and Konda, 1983, p. 643).

2. For instance, before 1950 there were no computer programmers, systems analysts, microcomputer support technicians, emergency medical technicians, sonographers, or

nuclear power plant technicians. Radiological technologists (Barley, 1990), science technicians (Shapin, 1989), and engineering technicians are among the handful of technicians' occupations formed before World War II.

3. We interviewed Orr to ensure the accuracy of the interpretations of his data.

4. To facilitate ease of reading, we shall sometimes speak from the perspective of the research team of which we were members. We feel justified in taking this stance because the ethnographers in our group worked closely throughout the course of the research and often assisted in analyzing each other's data. Moreover, our stance is consistent with the research team's norms: each member jointly owns the other's data. Nevertheless, when we speak of the specific technicians that "we have studied," the reader should keep in mind that neither of us may have actually produced the ethnography from which the data derive. Bonalyn Nelsen conducted the ethnography of emergency medical technicians. Mario Scarselletta studied medical technicians and technologists. Assaf Darr observed the work of engineers and engineering technicians. Beth Bechky conducted the study of technicians in science labs. The two of us jointly undertook the study of microcomputer support technicians.

5. The distinction originated with Hughes (1937) and is widely employed by career theorists (Schein, 1978).

6. This kind of rhetoric is also characteristic of scientists working in organizational contexts. At the European Space Agency, for instance, scientists regularly used the term "politics" to dismiss all organizational and interpersonal matters that interfered with efforts to solve technical problems according to scientific and technological criteria alone (Zabusky, 1992). Industrial engineers also tended to distinguish their own "real work" from the "politics" of the organization (Perlow and Bailyn, 1996).

7. Copier technicians were an important exception; they earned a reasonable salary as employees of a *Fortune* 500 company. As we shall show below, however, this did not mean that they felt respected in their work. Computer technicians posed another potential exception. The ethnographic study conducted by the authors focused on computer technicians working for a university, a nonprofit institution. These technicians felt seriously underpaid, not only with respect to the contribution they made, but with respect to what they could earn in the business sector. One programmer acknowledged explicitly that he "took a cut in salary" to come work for the university. When he had worked in industry he was well paid and, in fact, he suggested that: "maybe we got paid more because we had to work so hard and keep learning to stay up to date."

References

Applebaum, Herbert. 1992. *The Concept of Work: Ancient, Medieval, and Modern.* Albany, N.Y.: SUNY Press.

Barley, Stephen R. 1989. "Careers, Identities, and Institutions: The Legacy of the Chicago School of Sociology." In *Handbook of Career Theory.* Michael B. Arthur, Douglas T. Hall, and Barbara Lawrence, eds., 41–65. New York: Cambridge University Press.

———. 1990. "The Alignment of Technology and Structure Through Roles and Networks," *Administrative Science Quarterly* 35:61–103.

———. 1993. "What Do Technicians Do?," Working Paper, National Center for the Educational Quality of the Workforce, University of Pennsylvania, Philadelphia, Pa.

———. 1994. "The Turn Toward a Horizontal Division of Labor: On the Occupationalization of Firms and the Technization of Work." Working Paper, Program on Technology and Work, School of Industrial and Labor Relations, Cornell University.

Barley, Stephen R., and Beth Bechky. 1994. "In the Backrooms of Science: The Work of Technicians in Science Labs," *Work and Occupations* 21:85–126.

Barley, Stephen R., and Pamela S. Tolbert. 1991. "At the Intersection of Organization and Occupations." In *Research in the Sociology of Organizations* Pamela S. Tolbert and Stephen R. Barley, eds., 8:1–13.

Becker, Howard S. 1953. "Becoming a Marihuana User," *American Journal of Sociology* 59:235–242.

Bolles, R. 1981. *What Color in Your Parachute? A Practical Manual for Job Hunters and Job Changers*. Berkeley, Calif.: Ten Speed Press.

Braverman, Harry. 1973. *Labor and Monopoly Capital*. New York: Monthly Labor Review Press.

Cambrosio, A., and Keating, P. 1988. "Going Monoclonal: Art, Science and Magic in the Day-to-Day Use of Hybridoma Technology," *Social Problems* 35:244–260.

Carey, Max, and Alan Eck. 1984. "How Workers Get Their Training," *Occupational Outlook Quarterly* (Winter) 3–21.

Chandler, Alfred D., Jr. 1977. *The Visible Hand: The Managerial Revolution in American Business*. Cambridge: Harvard University Press.

Darr, Assaf. 1994. "Science, Art and Craft in Engineering." Presented at Organizational Behavior Workshop, April, Cornell University.

Derber, Charles, and William A. Schwartz. 1991. "New Mandarins or New Proletariat? Professional Power at Work." In *Research in the Sociology of Organizations*. Pamela Tolbert and Stephen R. Barley, eds., 8:71–96. Greenwich, Conn.: JAI Press. Driver, M.J. 1980. "Career Concepts and Organizational Change." In *Work Family and the Career*. Brook Derr, ed., New York: Wiley.

Durkheim, Emile. 1933/1893. *The Division of Labor in Society*. New York: Free Press.

Edwards, Richard. 1979. *Contested Terrain*. New York: Basic Books.

Farber, B. 1961. "The Family as a Set of Mutually Contingent Careers." In *Household Decision-Making*. N. Foote, ed., 276–298. New York: New York University Press.

Franke, Walter, and Irvin Sobel. 1970. *The Shortage of Skilled and Technical Workers*. Lexington, Mass.: Heath Lexington Books.

Goffman, Irving. 1961. "The moral career of the mental patient." In *Asylums*, 125–170. New York: Anchor.

Henkoff, Ronald. 1993. "Winning the New Career Game," *Fortune* 128:46–49.

Hughes, Everett C. 1937. "Institutional Office and the Person," *American Journal of Sociology* 43:104–143.

Jordan, K., and Lynch, M. 1992. "The Sociology of a Genetic Engineering Technique: Ritual and Rationality in the Performance of the 'Plasmid Prep'." In *The Right Tools for the Job: At Work in Twentieth-Century Life Science*. A. E. Clarke and J. H. Fujimura, eds. Princeton: Priceton University Press.

Kiechel, Walter. 1994. "A Manager's Career in the New Economy," *Fortune* 129:68–72.

Klein, D. P. 1984. "Occupational Employment Statistics: 1972–82," *Employment and Earnings* 20:13–16.

Kmetz, Rochelle, Freda McKinney, and Charles Walker. 1994. "Technical workers and the social organization of research and development." Unpublished manuscript. School of Industrial and Labor Relations, Cornell University.

Kornhauser, William. 1962. *Scientists in Industry*. Berkeley: University of California Press.

Nelsen, Bonalyn. 1996. "Work as a Moral Act: How Emergency Medical Technicians Understand Their Work." In *Between Science and Craft: Technical Work in U.S. Settings*. Stephen R. Barley and Julian Orr, eds. Ithaca, N.Y.: ILR Press.

Marx, Karl. 1967/1867. *Capital*. New York: International Publishers.

Orr, Julian E. 1996. *Talking about Machines: An Ethnography of a Modern Job*. Ithaca, N.Y.: ILR Press.

Perlow, Leslie, and Lotte Bailyn. (n.d. 1996) "The Senseless Submergence of Difference: Engineers, Their Work, and Their Careers." In *Between Science and Craft: Technical Work in U.S. Settings*. Stephen R. Barley and Julian Orr, eds. Ithaca, N.Y.: ILR Press.

Raelin, Joseph A. 1985. *The Clash of Cultures: Managers and Professionals*. Boston: Harvard University Press.

Richman, Louis S. 1994. "How to Get Ahead in America," *Fortune* 129:46–57.

Ritti, R. R. 1971. *The Engineer in the Industrial Corporation*. New York: Columbia University Press.

Roth, Julius A. 1964. *Timetables: Structuring the Passage of Time in Hospital Treatment and Other Careers*. Indianapolis, Ind.: Bobbs-Merrill.

Scarselletta, Mario. (1996). "The Infamous Lab Error: Education Skill and Quality in Medical Technicians' Work." In *Between Science and Craft: Technical Work in U.S. Settings*. Stephen R. Barley and Julian Orr, eds. Ithaca, N.Y.: ILR Press.

Schwartz, Barry. 1981. *Vertical Classification: A Study in Structuralism and the Sociology of Knowledge*. Chicago: University of Chicago Press.

Schein, Edgar H. 1978. *Career Dynamics: Matching Individual and Organizational Needs*. Reading, Mass.: Addison-Wesley.

Shapin, S. 1989. "The Invisible Technicians," *American Scientist* 77:554–563.

Silvestri, George, and John Lucasiewicz. 1991. "Occupational Employment Projections," *Monthly Labor Review* (Winter) 64–94.

Sherman, Stratford. 1994. "Leaders Learn to Heed the Voice Within," *Fortune* 130:92–100.

Smith, Adam. 1937/1776. *The Wealth of Nations,* New York: The Modern Library.

Sofer, Charles. 1970. *Men at Mid-Career.* Cambridge: Cambridge University Press.

Spangler, Eve. 1986. *Lawyers for Hire,* New Haven: Yale University Press.

Stewman, Shelby, and S. L. Konda. 1983. "Careers and Organizational Labor Markets: Demographic Models of Organizational Behavior," *American Journal of Sociology* 88:637–685.

Stinchcombe, Arthur L. 1959. "Bureaucratic and Craft Administration of Production: a Comparative Study," *Administrative Science Quarterly* 4:168–187.

Strauss, Anselm L. 1968. "Some Neglected Properties of Status Passage." Pp. 235–251 In *Institutions and the Person*. H. S. Becker, et al., eds., 235–251. Chicago: Aldine.

Thomas, Robert J. 1989. "Blue-collar Careers: Meaning and Choice in a World of Constraints." In *Handbook of Career Theory*. Michael B. Arthur, Douglas T. Hall, and Barbara Lawrence, eds., 354–379. New York: Cambridge University Press.

Tonnies, Ferdinand. 1957/1887. *Community and Society*. New York: Harper.

U.S. Bureau of the Census. 1976. *The Statistical History of the United States from Colonial Times to the Present*. New York: Basic Books.

U.S. Department of Commerce, 1991. *Statistical Abstract of the United States*. Washington, D.C.: Government Printing Office.

Van Maanen, John. 1977. "Experiencing Organization: Notes on the Meaning of Careers and Socialization." In *Organizational Careers: Some New Perspectives*. John Van Maanen, eds., 407–418. New York: Wiley.

———. 1980. "Career Games." In *Work Family and the Career*. Brook Derr, ed., 15–48. New York: Wiley.

Van Maanen, John, and Stephen R. Barley. 1984. "Occupational Communities: Culture and Control in Organizations." In *Research in Organizational Behavior,* Barry Staw and Larry Cummings, eds., 6:287–365. Greenwich, Conn.: JAI Press.

Von Glinow, Mary Ann. 1988. *The New Professionals: Managing Today's High Tech Employees.* Cambridge: Ballinger.

Weber, Max. 1968/1922. *Economy and Society.* Berkeley: University of California Press.

Whalley, Peter, and Stephen R. Barley. (1996) "Technical Work in the Division of Labor: Stalking the Wily Anomaly." In *Between Science and Craft: Technical Work in the U.S. Setting.* Stephen R. Barley and Julian Orr, eds. Ithaca, N.Y.: ILR Press.

White, Harrison C. 1970. *Chains of Opportunity.* Cambridge: Harvard University Press.

Wilensky, Harold L. 1961. "Orderly Careers and Social Participation: The Impact of Work History on Social Integration in the Middle Mass," *American Sociological Review* 26:521–539.

Zabusky, Stacia E. 1992. "Multiple Contexts, Multiple Meanings: Scientists in the European Space Agency." In *Knowledge and Society: The Anthropology of Science and Technology.* A. Rip, D. Hess, and L. Layne, eds. Greenwich, Conn.: JAI Press.

Zabusky, Stacia E. (n.d. 1996). "Computers, Clients and Expertise: The Negotiation of Technical Identities in a Non-Technical World." In *Between Science and Craft: Technical Work in U.S. Settings.* Stephen R. Barley and Julian Orr, eds. Ithaca, N.Y.: ILR Press.

Human Resources Practices and the Demographic Transformation of Professional Labor Markets

8

RENÉE M. LANDERS, JAMES B. REBITZER,
& LOWELL J. TAYLOR

Introduction

Professional occupations are in the midst of an unprecedented demographic transition. The ratio of men to women in professional schools was 23.4 in 1960 but 0.9 in 1988 (Goldin, 1992). This influx of women is not limited to traditionally female occupations. In 1979, women constituted only 10% of doctors, 13% lawyers, and 33% of accountants. Twelve years later in 1991, the comparable figures were: 20% for doctors, 18% for lawyers, and 52% for accountants.[1] These numbers are likely to understate the ultimate change in gender composition. For example, roughly 40% of students in law schools today are female (Rosen, 1992, p. 222).

The flood of women into previously male professions strains human resource systems designed for full-time men with stay-at-home wives. The cause of this strain is the gender based division of labor that prevails in many households. Even when working full time, women spend considerably more time on home and child related tasks than comparable men (Juster and Stafford, 1991; Leete-Guy and Schor, 1994). Thus women entering male professions are likely to demand a different mix of hours and income than earlier cohorts. The same will be true of the current cohort of men. These men are increasingly married to women with strong labor market commitments and find themselves under pressure to spend more time meeting household responsibilities.

Organizations that adapt to these changes in the workforce by offering shorter hours will find themselves better able to compete for critical talent than those that do not adapt. There is, however, little evidence that short-hour jobs are appearing in professional firms—indeed, aggregate statistics suggest that the work hours of college educated employees have been trending steadily upwards since the 1940s (Coleman and Pencavel 1993a and 1993b).

This chapter lays out a new framework for analyzing how firms respond to the demographic changes in the professional labor force. We argue that in many professional settings, long work hours (or other performance measures that entail long hours) are used to screen for valuable yet hard to observe characteristics of employees, such as commitment or ambition. Once introduced into work places, these norms can lead to a "long-hours trap" in which firms are unable to offer short hours to the growing proportion of professionals who might want them.

The causes of the downward inflexibility of hours that characterizes a long-hours trap is akin to the downward inflexibility of defense budgets that occurs in an arms race. In an arms race, all sides would be better off if they could simultaneously reduce their arsenals, but no individual nation would be willing to disarm unilaterally. Similarly employers and employees might be made better off if all firms simultaneously reduced hours. As we shall see, however, individual firms will not be willing to take this action on their own for fear of being inundated by short-hour workers.

The chapter proceeds in four parts. In section 2, we assess the current status of women in professions. Section 3 considers the determinants of work hours and identifies situations in which rigid and stringent work norms are likely to occur. In section 4, we present evidence for the existence of excessive hours norms in the legal profession and business consulting. Section 5 discusses the implications of these work norms for the distribution of economic opportunities and outcomes. The chapter concludes with a discussion of unresolved research and policy issues.

Women in the Professions

The Meaning of a College Education

The growing presence of women in previously male professions is part of a larger change in the role that college education plays in the lives of women.[2] Before 1940, the proportions of men and women who attended college were low. For those born between 1886 and 1895, 9.5% of men and 8.9% of women attended college for at least one year. The men and women who attended college took very similar classes because most institutions offered only two courses of study—classical and scientific. The job prospects for women who graduated college at this time were largely limited to teaching. The presence of marriage bars that prohibited the employment of married women forced college-education women to choose between having a family and a career—and many of these graduates chose careers. Goldin (1992, Table A2) estimates that for women who were 55–64 in 1940, 30.3% of those who attended college never married. In contrast, 8.1% of those with no college in this cohort had never married.

The significance of college changed dramatically in the post-war period. The demand for college-educated employees increased and the GI Bill of Rights made it possible for large numbers of men to attend college.[3] A college education substantially increased the lifetime earnings of men. College-educated women, whose job opportunities were still concentrated in teaching, nursing, and social work professions, received a smaller boost in lifetime earnings. The high ratio of men to women on campuses, however, offered an additional benefit to women—the possibility of marrying a man likely to earn a high income in the future. College-educated women were not only much more likely to marry college-educated men than women in other educational groups—they were also more likely to marry high-income men in other educational groups.[4] This indirect benefit of attending college, together with the dismantling of marriage bars and the general increase in fertility rates in post-Depression America, dramatically altered the labor market life cycle of college-educated women. Instead of choosing between family and career as their predecessors had done, women who graduated in the 1950s and early 1960s married and then (after their children had grown) returned to the labor market.

In the post-1960 period, new civil rights laws, the growth of feminism, and new norms of behavior for both sexes changed, once again, the significance of college in the lives of women. Women attended schools of higher education at roughly the same rate as men and they gained access to educational opportunities that had previously been denied them. These changes in educational attainment were accompanied by dramatic changes in labor force attachment. Women increasingly stayed in the labor force even as they married and had children. These cohorts of college-educated women, the first to balance career and family responsibilities simultaneously, were also the first to enter male professions in large numbers.

Hours of Work

The growing number of women and men in marriages where both partners are pursuing career and family building puts downward pressure on work hours. Very little is known about how the work hours of professionals changed as a result of these new entrants. What little we do know comes from aggregate data on part-time work and comparisons of the work hours of employees in different educational groups.

There is considerable evidence that firms have been successful in generating short-hour jobs in response to changes in workforce demographics in low-skill labor markets. Jobs scheduled for less than 35 hours per week, were virtually nonexistent prior to 1950. In the post-1950 era, a labor shortage prompted employers in the sales sector to began offering part-time jobs to attract married women into the work force (Goldin, 1990, p. 181). By 1970, 24.6% of women were working part-time. Since then, the number of female part-timers has increased at roughly the same rapid rate as the number of employed women (Blank, 1990, Table 1, p. 125). In 1987, 71% of all female part-time workers aged 20–65 were in low-wage sales, clerical, and service occupations—even though these occupations accounted for only 57% of female employment. In contrast, 22.4% of female part-timers were in the relatively high-wage professional, managerial, and technical occupations. These occupations accounted for 30.5% of female employment (Blank, 1990, Table 3).[5]

The increasing availability of shorter-hour jobs observed in the low-wage sector has not, by and large, been matched in professional labor markets. Com-

parisons of the work hours of college- and non-college-educated employees indicate that college-educated men and women work more hours than their counterparts with fewer years of schooling. More significantly, the trend of hours over
time differs across educational groups. White men with 15 or fewer years of
schooling exhibited a downward cohort trend in weekly and annual hours over
the period 1940–88. In contrast, white men with 16 or more years of schooling
exhibit a *positive* cohort trend for both these hours measures (Coleman and
Pencavel, 1993b, Table 14, p 280).[6] For white women with 15 or fewer years of
schooling, annual hours trended downward, but white women with 16 or more
years of schooling, like their male counterparts, display an upward trend in
annual hours worked (Coleman and Pencavel, 1993a, Table 13, p. 667).

Earnings Differentials in Professions

Studies of large, representative cross-sections of employees indicate that while
men earn more than women on average, the wages of college-educated, white
women moved closer to that of their male counterparts during the 1980s (Blackburn, Bloom, and Freeman, 1991; Blau and Kahn, 1992). Detailed studies of
individual professions suggest that differences in work setting and experience can
explain an important component of gender differences. Baker (1993), for example, finds that young, male physicians in 1991 earned, on average, 13% more
than young female physicians. Nearly 70% of this difference is due to the fact that
these women start in relatively low-wage specialties and practice settings. For
example, 18% of Baker's sample of female doctors were pediatricians compared
to 6.8% for men. In contrast, 18% of the men were in general and specialized
surgical practices compared with 6.8% of the women.[7]

Wood et al. (1993) examine a sample of graduates from the University of
Michigan School of Law classes of 1972–75. One year after graduation, women
earned $36,851 compared to $39,428 for men. Fifteen years after graduation this
earnings differential had grown enormously—with women receiving a salary of
$86,335 and men $140,917. Roughly 30% of the male/female earnings gap 15
years after graduation could be explained by cross-gender differences in legal
experience, and job setting. Women tended to accumulate a smaller portion of
their experience in private practice (the most profitable sort of experience). They
were also more likely to find work in relatively low-paying governmental jobs or
jobs in small, private practices. These regressions do not explain *why* women with
15 years of experience are less likely to be found in large law firms. Since these
large law firms typically fire associates who are not promoted to partners within
six to eight years, part of the explanation may be that women are less likely to be
promoted than their male counterparts. Consistent with this thesis, Spurr (1990)
reports a significant gender difference in promotion rates for a sample of large law
firms—although his study cannot control for billable hours or other measures of
output.

Wood et al. (1993) also report a feature of the labor market that is important
to our analysis—the large earnings penalty for women who work part-time to

care for children. After controlling for annual hours of work, law school performance, race, location of residence, family structure, years of experience, and number of jobs, working part-time to care for children reduces earnings 5.6% for each year worked part-time. To put this figure in perspective, a woman who worked part-time for three years would experience a 17% decline in her wages. In contrast, taking a leave of absence to care for children has no effect on earnings.

In law and medicine, wage differentials are a useful measure of occupational standing because it is unusual for men or women to exit these professions. In other settings, poor prospects may be reflected more in exit than in low wages. Preston (1993a; 1993b) reports that 20.1% of female scientists and engineers employed in 1982 had left their profession by 1989. For men, the comparable figure was 10.7%. Even after controlling for age, job, and occupational characteristics, women are significantly more likely to leave their profession for reasons other than promotion. In order to learn more about gender differences in occupational exit, Preston (1993b) conducted a series of follow-up interviews with women and men who graduated with a science or engineering degree from SUNY–Stony Brook. She found that the struggle to manage the dual responsibilities of family and career leads many women to compromise their career prospects. For Ph.D.s these compromises involve reducing the number of early career job changes. A Ph.D. typically works at two or three postdoctoral appointments before taking a permanent position. This first permanent job may last only six years if the scientist is not granted tenure. More important, each of these job changes may involved a substantial move. The female Ph.D.s Preston interviewed often narrowed the geographical scope of their job search to accommodate their husbands' careers.

Explaining Gender Differences

If work setting and type of work experience are important determinants of success in professional careers, why should these differences be correlated with gender? Most of the academic literature on this question focuses on two, very different, causes: discrimination and human capital investments.

Some discrimination models posit that customers have preferences that lead firms to avoid hiring women. For example, if patients trust male doctors more than female doctors, health care providers will do better by hiring men. Models of customer discrimination are clearly limited to professional settings where patient contact is very important. It is hard, for example, to use these models to explain why specialties with little patient contact (e.g., surgeons) are overwhelmingly male.

An alternative model of discrimination focuses on the attitudes of employers rather than customers. Employers who undervalue the abilities of women will be reluctant to hire them. Once hired, gender prejudices cause supervisors to refrain from offering women the kind of guidance and mentorship needed for a successful professional career. The central theoretical problem with these models of employer discrimination is the fierce competition for progressional talent. Employers who regularly hire and promote men but not women will find themselves at a competitive disadvantage. Over time, market competition will severely limit the extent to which employers can indulge their discriminatory preferences.[8]

Gender discrimination by employers *could* persist in the face of competition if discrimination helped employers identify individuals with desirable traits. If, for example, elite employers spent substantial sums of money training their professional work force, they would find it more expensive to hire employees with short expected job tenure. No employers can predict with certainty the eventual job tenure of new hires. The typical life cycle of female college graduates from the 1950s and 1960s (work followed by a long absence from the labor force to raise children), however, would suggest that on average the employer would do better to offer special training to young men than young women. This type of discrimination is often called statistical discrimination because employers use the average behavior of gender groups to infer something about the likely behavior of individuals (Aigner and Cain, 1977; Lundberg and Startz, 1983). The incidence of statistical discrimination is severely limited by civil rights laws that expressly prohibit such practices. In addition, statistical discrimination makes economic sense only to the extent that the behavior of women as a group differs substantially from the behavior of their male counterparts. We have seen, however, that recent cohorts of college-educated women are pursuing family *and* careers simultaneously. As the labor market attachment of women converges with that of men, statistical discrimination in labor markets should decline in importance.

Where discrimination models explain gender differences in terms of restrictions on the options available to women, human capital models focus on why women would make different career choices than men. Since women are likely to have different preferences and abilities than men, it is natural to expect gender differences in careers. What human capital theories offer is an explanation for why the choices women make should lead them to career paths entailing lower earnings and status than those made by their male counterparts.

Human capital models of gender differences in careers rest on the assumption that women are better at nurturing family and children than men (Lazear and Rosen, 1990). Because women are more effective at these nonlabor market tasks, it is efficient for them to specialize in household production. Given this specialization, when family demands increase (e.g., when a new child is born), women will be more likely than their husbands to reduce effort and time devoted to their career—even to the extent of exiting the labor force. Knowing that women are more likely to leave the labor force, employers will be less likely to invest in the kind of firm-specific training that is often required early in a professional career. Even small differences in initial training investments can produce large differences in career outcomes because employers concentrate subsequent investments in training on employees who (by virtue of their large early investments) are less likely to quit the firm. In this way, efficient economic decision making can lead to substantial differences in the careers of men and women. These differences are not the result of women having fewer abilities and opportunities than men. Rather, it is men (who are poorly suited to home production) who have the more limited set of abilities and options.[9]

Human capital accounts of gender differences in career progressions have a compelling economic logic—but they are incomplete in two important ways. First, this view makes most sense when women were very likely to leave the labor force for long periods of time in response to marriages or the birth of a child. The case for gender differences in career progressions is therefore weakened by the strong labor force attachment of younger cohorts of professional women. The second problem with human capital models is establishing that the specialization of women in household production is the result of different abilities rather than a response to discrimination. This objection is especially salient given the degree of overt harassment and discrimination experienced by the first waves of women entering male professions (for a description of the experiences of women in law see Berger and Morello, 1986).

In the next section we develop a theory of work norms that focuses on work hours. We suggest that this account provides an alternative explanation for gender differences in professional careers. In contrast to the discrimination approach, our work-norms model applies even in settings where the incidence of discrimination is kept low by fierce competition for talent and/or civil rights laws. In contrast to the human capital approach, our work-norms account of gender differences in career progressions makes sense even in settings where women do not leave the labor force for long times.

An Economic Theory of Work Norms

The Textbook Model

According to textbook economic theory, hours of work are determined in much the same way as the color of cars.[10] When buying cars, consumers pay attention to the price of the car as well as to such nonprice attributes as car color. A customer whose heart is set on a sporty red convertible will pay a higher price for a red convertible than a blue one. Carmakers, therefore, have incentives to match colors as closely as possible to the preferences of customers. This does not mean that every customer will get precisely the color he or she wants. Increasing the variety of available car colors is costly. It is easy to imagine that the cost of adding a relatively unpopular color, like chartreuse, to the menu would exceed the amount that chartreuse lovers will be willing to pay for the color. Even though some colors will not be offered, the menu of car colors will be efficient in the sense that it includes all the colors for which the marginal benefit to customers exceeds the marginal cost to producers. This means that no customer or car company could be made better off by altering the list of available car colors.

Mechanisms analogous to those in the market for cars operate in the textbook model of labor markets to produce an efficient menu of work hours from which workers can choose. When looking for work, potential employees pay attention to both the wage and the nonwage attributes of jobs. An employee with demanding responsibilities at home would be willing to go to work for a lower wage in exchange for shorter (or more flexible) work hours. Employers competing for scarce talent therefore have strong incentives to match work hours as closely as possible to the desires of employees. This does not mean that every employee gets exactly the hours he or she wants or that every employer offers a full range of possible work hours. Rather, the menu of work hours available from different employers will be such that all hours levels will be offered so long as the marginal benefit employees get from working nonstandard hours exceeds the marginal cost to an employer.

Equal Sharing Rules, Work Hours, and Work Norms

The textbook model of the determinants of work hours abstracts from an important feature of professional labor markets: professionals often work together in firms or partnerships to exploit gains from cooperation. The significance of these groupings for the operation of labor markets depends on the way the surplus is distributed within the firm. To see the importance of distributional rules, it is helpful to consider two polar cases: equal sharing and pay for performance. Under pay for performance each group member is paid the surplus that he or she contributes. Under equal sharing, each professional contributes his or her earnings to a pool that is then equally divided among members of the group.

In many real world settings, the distributional rules in professional firms more closely resemble equal sharing than pay for performance. There are a number of reasons why equal sharing rules appear in firms composed of professionals. When people perform complex tasks in teams, it is often easier for participants to enforce a simple sharing rule than a complex pay for performance system. [11] This conclusion applies, a fortiori, in the coequal groupings of professionals found in partnerships, product development teams, and academic departments. Differences in relative pay that cannot be clearly linked to performance are likely to provoke strong negative reactions from group members. A rule mandating equal sharing reduces the drain of time and energy taken up by battles over the distribution of the surplus. In some cases, the gains from cooperation may be indivisible. For example, sharing is unavoidable in settings where the reputation of the entire group confers advantages to individual group members. In some partnership settings, the partners also share income as a means of offering some income insurance to other partners (Gilson and Mnookin, 1985; Lang and Gordon, 1994).

If all professionals in the labor market were identical the distribution of pay would be the same under pay for performance and equal sharing. When some professionals produce more surplus than others, however, the distributional rule becomes critically important. Under equal sharing rules, professionals who produce lots of surplus by virtue of long hours will end up subsidizing their less hardworking colleagues. For this reason, equal sharing rules cause professionals to seek out partners who work as least as many hours as incumbent members of the firm.

If the work propensities of every professional were easy to spot, then the best any individual could do would be to form a firm with others who are similarly motivated. An individual who produces $60 of surplus per hour and works eight hours per day would always *want* to form a partnership with an equally productive partner who works 10 hours—but the 10-hour professional would be very foolish to accept such an arrangement. In a two person firm with an equal sharing rule, a 10-hour worker would produce $600 worth of surplus in a day and get back only $540. The extra $60 would end up in the pocket of the eight-hour professional. This logic extends to every professional who wants to work more than eight hours, thus the best an eight-hour professional could do would be to form a firm with other eight-hour professionals (Farrell and Scotchmer, 1988).

Things are quite different, however, when work propensities are *not* directly observable. In this case, a 10-hour professional would need to take steps to keep eight-hour professionals from joining his or her firm. Direct questions put to job candidates are not likely to be revealing on this point. Once word gets out that claiming to be a hard worker helps for finding partnership positions, all prospective partners will present themselves accordingly.

The obvious problem with screening on the basis of direct questions is that talk is cheap. Screening that can effectively prevent bad matches must make use of indicators that are related to work propensities and, at the same time, costly to fake. One screening device that meets these criteria is a work norm in which all partners are required to work very long hours. A professional who normally works 10 hours would generally find it easier to put in a 12-hour day than would a professional who prefers 8 hours. Since the burden of additional hours falls more heavily on eight-hour then 10-hour professionals, firms can be assured of attracting only 10-hour professionals by imposing a work norm sufficiently in *excess* of 10 hours.[12]

Work Norms and the Long-Hours Trap

Firms using equal sharing rules will benefit from stringent work norms when the benefit of deterring short-hour professionals exceeds the cost. In the two-partner firm discussed above, the benefit of deterrence to a 10-hour per day professional is the absence of the $60 daily transfer to eight-hour colleagues. The cost of deterrence is the extra hours required.[13] Thus, if the extra hours needed to discourage eight-hour professionals reduces the welfare of 10-hour professionals less than $60, firms with long-hour professionals will adopt a work norm entailing excessive work hours.

An important feature of the work norms that arise under sharing rules is that they are likely to persist even as the fraction of short-hour professionals in the population increases. Indeed, stringent work norms may persist when conditions are such that all the professionals would be better off without them. This "long-hours trap" occurs because the incentives guiding the actions of individual firms differ from those that would prevail if all firms could act in a coordinated manner.

To see this, consider the example of an entire economy composed of two-person firms in which equal sharing rules prevail. Suppose that 50% of the professionals would prefer to work eight hours and the remainder prefer 10 hours. Maintaining the assumptions from above, each of these professionals produce a surplus of $60/hour. If no firm imposed work norms, the probability any current partner has of being paired with a short-hour individual is .5. Thus, each

10-hour worker has a 50% chance of giving away $60 per day to an eight-hour professional. If a 12-hour work norm was enough to deter eight-hour workers, then each 10-hour professional would impose such a norm provided the lost two hours of leisure was worth less than the $30 the norm saves them.

Now consider what happens if the proportion of short-hour individuals falls to 20%. In this case, the expected benefit to adopting stringent hours norms falls to $12 (0.2*$60). A savings of $12 may not be enough to make the work norm worthwhile for the 10-hour professional. Does this mean that all firms will abandon their work norm? Not necessarily. Any *individual* firm that dropped the 12-hour norm would find themselves inundated with eight-hour applicants. If the proportion of short-hour applicants at this innovating firm was sufficiently above the population average of short-hour professions (e.g., above 50%), no individual firm could profit by abandoning its work norms.

The logic of the long-hours trap is similar to the logic behind an "arms race." Rival superpowers devote "too many" resources to their arsenals in the sense that equal security could be achieved at lower cost if the nations could simultaneously reduce their stockpiles of weapons. Similarly, a long-hours trap requires "too many" hours in the sense that some would be made better off (and none worse off) by a coordinated reduction in work hours.

The long-hours trap persists because market incentives cannot ensure a *simultaneous* change by large numbers of firms. This coordination failure has important implications for public policy. It suggests that professional associations can, by influencing the actions of a number of firms, play an important and positive role in shaping how labor markets respond to changing workforce demographics.

The Distribution of Economic Opportunities and Outcomes

In our discussion so far, the presence of work norms need have no important consequences for the distribution of economic opportunities among short- and long-hour professionals. It might be that short-hour professionals are segregated into firms of their own, but the jobs in these firms are every bit as good as those in long-hour firms.

In many settings, however, professionals compete for access to privileged positions that offer a combination of income and hours that are clearly superior to those available elsewhere. If these elite positions are concentrated in long-hour firms, the process of screening on work hours will have the effect of disadvantaging short-hour professionals. It is often the case in economics that a sorting process that disadvantages one group of workers is justifiable on grounds of efficiency. In the case of work norms in professions, we cannot presume that the sorting on work hours is efficient. As our discussion of the long-hours trap indicates, sorting may persist long after it ceases to be efficient.

Access to privileged positions is often regulated by a promotion tournament. Promotion tournaments are incentive systems that award prizes in the from of valuable promotions to employees whose performance exceeds that of others in a comparison group. Many professional partnerships in law, accounting, and management consulting run an "up-or-out" variant of promotion tournaments. In the "up-or-out" system, professionals are hired as associates for a 6–10-year period. At the end of this period, the best relative performers are rewarded with an equity partnership position. The competitors who are not promoted are fired and must find employment elsewhere. "Up-or-out" systems also prevail in academic departments, with the reward being tenure rather than an equity stake in the organization.

The distribution of economic outcomes produced by a promotion tournament is always more unequal than the distribution of economic opportunities. In Garrison Keillor's fictional Lake Wobegon, *all* the children are above average. Everywhere else, the practice of rewarding the best relative performer requires that only a fraction of participants can win promotion. Since the probability of winning the tournament is less than one, a firm will only attract professionals if the value of the partnership is greater than other alternative positions. Thus, even if the expected value of all professional jobs were identical, promotion tournaments will produce an unequal distribution of economic outcomes. Those fortunate or skilled enough to win the promotion tournament would receive salaries greater than those found elsewhere.

If firms use excessive work norms to screen short-hour associates out of promotion tournaments, then long-hour professionals will be disproportionately found in the high salary partnerships, while short-hour professionals will be found in relatively low-paid alternative jobs. This inequality of outcomes may have important implications for the sociology of professions, though by itself it does not indicate inequality of economic opportunity. If, however, work norms deter short-hour professionals from entering promotion tournaments with the highest expected value, then the distribution of economic opportunities is shifted in favor of long-hour associates.

Summary

When professionals work together, they often distribute the gains from cooperation through some sort of equal sharing rule. Sometimes these sharing rules are explicitly specified. Other times, the sharing occurs because membership in the group enhances the reputations of all its members. Whatever their origin, sharing rules create incentives for professionals to work in groups that are homogeneous with respect to the work propensities of individual members. In particular, groups will take action to screen out new employees who prefer shorter hours than the incumbents.

We have argued that the incentives inherent in equal sharing rules leads firms to impose stringent work norms as a means of screening out professionals wanting to work short hours. These work norms will typically require hours that are excessive—even from the point of view of professionals who are willing to work long hours. Perhaps more significantly, work norms will also be rigid. Increases in the number of short-hour individuals in the profession will typically not lead to a reduction in the number of hours required to satisfy the norm. Indeed, the rigidity in hours can be so severe that the work norms will persist even when all firms and employees would be better off without them. Escaping from this "long-hours trap" typically requires an agency to coordinate the actions of employers. Professional associations can fill this role by persuading a number of firms to simultaneously introduce short-hour paths to partnerships.

Work norms also have implications for the distribution of economic opportunities and economic outcomes. If work norms prevail in elite positions, then professionals wanting short work hours will be disadvantaged in terms of economic opportunity. If work norms are important in deciding the outcome of promotion tournaments, short-hour professionals will be disadvantaged in terms of economic outcomes—even if economic opportunities are identical across all professionals.

The theory of work norms we develop differs in important respects from a discrimination approach to analyzing gender differences in professional careers. Consistent with the discrimination literature, we acknowledge that firms can adopt human resources practices that systematically disadvantage women. Unlike most discrimination models, however, our work norm theory predicts significant differences in economic outcomes by gender even in settings where civil rights laws and competition for talent preclude discrimination based on gender. Indeed, if firms could rely on an observable characteristic like gender to prevent short-hour professionals from entering long-hour firms, work norms might be an unnecessary screening device.

Our work norm approach differs in two important ways from explanations based on human capital theory. First, as we demonstrate in the case of a long-hours trap, the process of matching employees to job characteristics can be sluggish and inefficient. Second, work norms can lead to gender differences in career outcomes even when women do not exit a firm or the labor force when they marry and have children.

Finally, our model suggests that work norms can be expected in any setting where the following three criteria hold: (1) the members of a group benefit from the productive activity of other group members; (2) the output of the group can be significantly influenced by the work effort of individual members; and (3) members of the group have the ability to establish work norms. Criterion 2 suggests that work norms may be particularly likely in groups where complementarities among employees are such that small differences in an individual's level of performance can generate large differences in the value of output produced by the group.[14] Teams of professionals developing new products with short product life cycles (e.g., software engineers) may therefore be especially likely to be characterized by excessive work norms. These norms might also appear in the competition for managerial positions in hierarchical settings where the actions of managers high up in the hierarchy have a multiplicative effect on output through their influence on employees lower down in the hierarchy (Rosen, 1982).

Evidence for Work Norms

This section reports the results of two empirical investigations of work norms. The first investigation focuses on large law firms. The second focuses on a large business consulting firm. The goal of each of these studies was to determine whether work norms of the sort described in the preceding section exist in actual organizations.

Results from A Survey of Large Law Firms

Large law firms are a convenient vehicle for studying work norms[15] because virtually all of these firms have the same, simple structure. There are two important classes of lawyers: associates and partners.[16] Associates are hired for a fixed period—usually between six and 10 years. At the end of this time, they are either promoted to "equity partner" or dismissed.

As an empirical matter, large legal partnerships almost always allow for some income sharing among partners (Gilson and Mnookin, 1989; Lang and Gordon, 1994). If work norms matter in professional labor markets, they should therefore be found in law firms. Since large law firms rely on the lengthy associate period to screen potential partners, our investigation of work norms focuses on the work hours and promotion prospects of associates.

The defining feature of work norms is that individuals are required to work *more* hours than they would otherwise desire at the going wage. It is therefore possible to identify work norms by asking associates whether they would like to change their hours given their current wage. In practice, however, implementing this empirical strategy is problematic. When stringent work norms are present, a question about hours reduction at the current wage requires respondents to consider an option that was not available to them in the past. Since the respondents could not anticipate the opportunity to reduce hours, they may have made consumption plans on the basis of the high incomes associated with their excessive hours. These consumption plans may entail financial commitments (e.g., mortgage payments, car loans, and school tuition payments for children) that preclude a downward adjustment in work hours at the current wage.

For these reasons we adopted an alternative approach to identifying overwork. Rather than asking how associates would adjust hours given their current wage, we asked how they would adjust hours in response to a small wage increase. Specifically, associates were asked to pick from three choices: (1) decrease hours by 5% with no change in accompanying income over the coming year; (2) keep hours the same over the coming year with a 5% increase in income; or (3) increase hours by 5% over the coming years with a 10% increase in income.[17]

Data for this study were collected in a survey of associates and partners at two major law firms in a large northeastern city.[18] The surveys asked all associates on a partnership track about their work hours, billable hours, and attitudes toward work hours. A total of 216 surveys were distributed and 133 were returned for a response rate of 62%. A simultaneous survey questioned the partners at these firms about the decision to promote associates to partners. We distributed 188 surveys and received responses from 64.4% of the partners in our sample.

The results of the work hours question are reported in Table 8–1. We found

Table 8-1. How Associates Would Choose to Use
a Hypothetical 5% Wage Increase

Choice	Percentage Choosing
Reduce billable and nonbillable work hours by *5% with no change* in annual salary	65.41% (87 associates)
Continue working *the same number* of hours with a *5% increase* in annual salary	25.56% (34 associates)
Increase billable and nonbillable work hours by 5% with a *10% increase* in annual salary	9.02% (12 associates)
Total Responses	133

that 25.56% of respondents wanted to keep their hours unchanged and enjoy a 5% increase in income. Nearly two-thirds (65.41%) of the associates indicated that they would prefer *reducing* work hours and keeping income unchanged over the coming year. This pattern is what we would expect if associates are working under the sort of stringent work norms predicted by our screening model.

Table 8–2 presents descriptive statistics for associates wanting to reduce, keep the same, or increase hours of work. The "reduce hours" and the "keep the same hours" associates looked very similar and in no case were the differences in the means across these groups statistically significant. Particularly noteworthy is the finding that the annual salaries across these two groups were the same (row 7). This is important because the magnitude of the income change implicit in the work-hours questions was likely to be the same across groups.

The "increase hours" group is a little bit different from the other two. In general they tended to have less legal experience prior to joining the current firm and therefore slightly lower average salaries. It is possible that associates in this group were trying to "catch up" to other associates in the firm by accumulating more experience. In any case, there were only 12 associates in the "increase hours" group.

If the high incidence of overwork recorded in Table 8–1 is indeed the result of the processes described by our screening model, we should also find that work hours are an important indicator in the promotion to partnership decision. To address this issue we asked each attorney in the firm to indicate the importance of billable hours and other factors in determining promotion to partnership. We then asked each attorney the importance of hours billed as an *indicator* of qualities that the firm might look for in partners.

Factors Important in Promotion   Respondents were asked to evaluate the importance of 12 different factors that were likely to play a role in the promotion process in these law firms. Importance was measured using a 5-point scale where

Table 8-2. Characteristics of Associates by Hours Preferences

Characteristic	Associate Would Choose to Use 5% Wage by:		
	Reducing hours 5%	Keeping current hours	Increasing hours 5%
(1) Percent male	52.9%	64.7%	66.7%
(2) Mean year graduated law school	1989	1989	1990*
(3) Mean age (years)	32	31.8	29.8**
(4) Mean tenure (years)	3.1	3.0	2.2
(5) Percent married	73.6%	58.8%	83.3%
(6) Percent with children	30.2%	38.2%	33.3%
(7) Mean annual salary	$80,264	$80,053	$72,645*
(8) Mean hours worked per month	198	199	204
(9) Mean hours billed per month	164	160	169
(10) Percent working part-time	5.8%	8.8%	8.3%
(11) Weekend days worked: average week	0.5 days	0.4 days	0.6 days
(12) Weekend days worked: busy week	1.3 days	1.3 days	1.4 days

*difference from column 1 significant at 5% level; **difference from column 1 significant at 10% level

1 was not important, 2 was slightly important, 3 was moderately important, 4 was very important, and 5 was of the utmost importance. Table 8–3 lists the fraction of respondents who claimed that a factor had an importance of 4 or 5. Column 1 presents the results for associates and column 2 presents the results for partners.

It is clear from inspection that associates and partners had similar views about which factors were important in the promotion process. The correlation coefficient between the two columns in Table 8–3 is 0.99. The vast majority of associates (90%) and partners (99%) clearly viewed the quality of work product as important in promotion decisions. Willingness to work hard was also considered important by large numbers of associates (96%) and partners (89%). In contrast the number of hours billed to clients was seen to be important by a much smaller proportion of associates (68%) and partners (52%). Indeed, billable hours ranked 7th in importance for both associates and partners.

Hours as an Indicator Quite a different picture emerges when attorneys are asked about the importance of billable hours as an *indicator* of other traits and achievements relevant to the partnership decision. Respondents were asked to evaluate the importance of billable hours as an indicator for 5 of the 12 factors listed in Table 8–3. Attorneys who believed that billable hours are an important indicator and who also believed that the factor itself was important in promotion were assigned a value of 1 and zero otherwise.[19] Thus 46% of associates reported that the quality of work product was very important in promotion decisions *and* that partners assigned much importance to billable hours as an indicator of work product quality. The comparable figure for partners was 39%. Inspection of the two columns in Table 8–4 reveals that similar proportions of associates and

Table 8-3. Associates and Partners Who Consider the Following Factors
Very Important for Promotion to Partnership*

Factor	Associates (%)	Partners (%)
The quality of work product	90	99
The number of hours billed to clients	68	52
The mastery of an important area of specialization	67	75
Contribution to administration or recruitment	08	01
The development of good working relationships or mentoring relationships with senior lawyers in the firm	68	51
The development of a good working relationship with clients and peers	76	81
The potential for bringing new clients and business to the firm	75	69
Demonstrated ability to bring new clients and business to the firm	48	19
A willingness to work long hours when required	96	89
Loyalty to the firm	69	71
A willingness to pursue the interests of clients aggressively	76	76
Ambition for success in the legal profession	67	51
Total Observations	130	118

*Respondents were asked to rate factors on the following 5-point scale: 1 = not important;
2 = slightly important; 3 = moderately important; 4 = very important; and 5 = of the utmost
importance. The table lists the percentage of respondents who rated the factor 4 or above.

partners viewed hours as an important indicator of underlying associate abilities
and accomplishments. The correlation coefficient between rows 1–5 of columns
1 and 2 is 0.94. Consistent with our model of income sharing among partners, a
large minority of associates (92%) and partners (78%) viewed billable hours as an
important indicator of a willingness to work long hours when required. The
signaling value of work hours was *not* limited, however, to work propensities. In
our sample of associates, the median number of important factors for which
billable hours was also an important indicator was 3. The median for partners
was 2.

The importance of work hours as a signal in promotion is also reflected in a
nationally representative survey of attorneys conducted by the American Bar
Association. In this survey 59.3% of respondents believed that reduced-hour or
part-time employment limited opportunities for advancement including partnership (American Bar Association, 1990, p. 27).

Alternative Interpretations Of The Results

Can Respondents Be Working Optimal Hours?   The results of the work-hours survey can be reconciled with conventional theory if individuals always work their

Table 8-4. Percentage of Associates and Partners Who Considered Billable Hours an Important Indicator of a Factor Viewed as Important for Promotion*

Factor in the Promotion Decision	Associates (%)	Partners (%)
Ambition for success and respect in the legal profession.	46	39
A willingness to pursue the interests of clients aggressively.	48	37
A willingness to work long hours when required.	92	78
Degree of loyalty to the firm.	5	28
The ability to produce high quality work product.	32	32
The ability and willingness to bring new clients into the firm.	16	20
Median number of important factors for which hours are an important indicator.	3	2
Total Observations	130	117

*Respondents were asked to rate the importance of billable hours as an indicator for six different factors in the promotion process. A five-point scale was used to record responses. In this scale: 1 = not important; 2 = slightly important; 3 = moderately important; 4 = very important; 5 = of the utmost importance. Billable hours were seen as an important indicator when two conditions held. First, respondents gave billable hours a score of 4 or 5 as and indicator. Second the factor that was being indicated by billable hours was given an importance rating of 4 or 5 in the previous table.

preferred level of work hours and their preferred level of work hours falls sharply when wages rise. When preferred work hours fall in response to wage increases individuals are said to be on a backward bending labor supply curve.

If preferred hours fall with wage increases, then we should also find longer work hours for associates earning lower wages. In each of the firms we study, wages increase with job tenure—but we find no evidence that work hours change with tenure. The plausibility of a backward bending labor supply curve explanation is also called into question by the magnitude of the desired reduction in hours. The response of preferred hours to a 5% wage increase is much larger than has been observed on other empirical studies of the effect of wages and work hours. The respondents who wanted to reduce hours, indicated that they would reduce work hours 5% in response to a 5% increase in wages. This choice implies an elasticity of hours with respect to wages of −1. This elasticity is roughly 10 times that usually reported in the literature (Pencavel, 1986).[20]

Fixed Employment Costs   The results of Table 8–1 could be consistent with the conventional economic model of work hours if there are substantial fixed employment costs. Consider, for example, a firm that spends a large amount of money training associates. With the same training, a part-time associate would cost the firm much more per hour than an associate working 60 hours per week. Since firms pay the fixed employment costs, they will require hours that seem excessive to employees. This might produce the results in Table 8–1 and 8–2.

The fixed employment cost explanation is harder to reconcile with Tables 8–3 and 8–4. The presence of fixed employment costs should not lead firms to use work hours as an indicator of important, but hard to observe, characteristics.

Long Hours as a Commitment Device   Our discussion has so far assumed that firms demand long work hours to screen out associates who have predetermined work propensities. An alternative explanation is that firms require long hours from associates in order to *commit* associates to long hours.

One possible commitment mechanism is discussed in social psychology as the *over-sufficient justification effect* (Fiske and Taylor, 1991). This term refers to a process in which individuals attribute to themselves motivation for behavior that cannot be the result of external pressures. Performing a task for insufficient external rewards leads individuals to conclude that they must be motivated by intrinsic interest. In the context of law firms, subjecting associates to hours longer than they otherwise would choose produces a reaction such as: "I couldn't have done it for the money, so I must have done it because it was important to me." (Fiske and Taylor, 1991, p. 46). The result is that associates will come to place a greater value on their work than would otherwise be the case.

Cognitive dissonance is a closely related psychological process that might also produce a commitment to excess hours. The term "cognitive dissonance" refers to the conflict or anxiety resulting from an inconsistency between beliefs and actions. To reduce anxiety, individuals may revise their beliefs and resolve the inconsistency. In economics, cognitive dissonance has been applied to analyzing workplace safety. Workers who are exposed to dangerous situations learn to cope by revising their assessment of risk (Akerlof and Dickens, 1982). Similarly, professionals subjected to stringent work norms may adjust their hours preferences in order to reduce the inconsistency between actions and beliefs.

The keys to applying both the over-sufficient justification and the cognitive dissonance mechanisms to overwork are the twin assumptions that: (1) preferences or beliefs are malleable at some early state and (2) at some later state these preferences or beliefs are persistent. An alternative mechanism for creating a commitment to long hours focuses on hard-to-reverse investments in the infrastructure required to support long hours. An associate who has spent six to 10 years working evenings and weekends invests in numerous adaptations to long hours. For example, the associate may have married someone who likes having a spouse who works long hours and earns a large income. Once made, these accommodations may be hard to undo. The result is that the associates who enter a firm with one set of behaviors emerge years later with another set of behaviors that simply aren't going to change.[21]

Commitment mechanisms might also be important for explaining the long hours associates work. The data we have, however, do not offer much support for models in which associates adapt to long hours as a result of their experience with strict work norms. If individuals acclimatize to long hours over the course of the employment relationship, we should find that hours are the same across tenure groups, but that the degree of satisfaction with hours increases with job tenure. In our data, work hours do not change with increased job tenure but neither do the preferred hours of associates. This can be seen in Table 8–2, where the average tenure of associates who want to reduce hours is the same as the average tenure of associates who want to keep their current level of work hours.

Long Hours as an Adjustment to High Salaries   Lawyers and observers of the legal profession have noted that the salaries of associates in large firms increased dramatically through the 1980s. Sander and Williams (1989) report that the starting salary of associates increased (in constant 1985 dollars) from $33,890 in 1973 to $38,000 in 1986. For elite New York firms, the comparable salaries in 1985 dollars were $44,000 in 1985 and $63,733 in 1986. To put these numbers in perspective, the real incomes of starting associates in small firms fell during this period—as did the income of solo practitioners. Couldn't the long hours we observed in 1993 simply be a way for law firms to reduce the per-hour cost of their associates?

Good time-series data on the work hours of associate lawyers are not generally available. The American Bar Association (1990) did, however, survey a sample of associates in 1984 and 1990. We have analyzed the monthly hours worked by associates in large firms (those with 60 or more attorneys) and found no change in the distribution of hours during this period of rapid growth in associate salaries. Qualitative reports suggest that the capacity for sustaining long hours was a desired trait in partners long before the boom of the 1980s. Galanter and Palay (1991) quote the following description of the sort of attorney elite law firms were seeking in the 1960s. In addition to academic qualifications, law firms want associates who ". . . are graduates of the 'right' schools, have the 'right' social background and experience in the affairs of the world, and are endowed with tremendous stamina."

Looking Outside of Law Firms

Work norms of the sort we observe in law firms should also appear in similarly structured partnerships operating outside the legal profession. Many large consulting firms take the form of "up-or-out" partnerships. This section presents a brief description of work norms in one such consulting firm.[22]

The management consulting firm we study is a very large, nationally known partnership. In order to protect the identity of the firm, we will refer to it by the fictional name Target Consulting. Entry level consultants in Target pass through four levels before being promoted to equity partner. At each stage in the process, those who are not passed to the next level must leave the firm. The entire process, from initial hiring to promotion to equity partner, takes between 8 and 13 years.

Thirty to forty percent of the new consultants hired by Target Consulting are women. This hiring rate has been pretty stable for the past 10–12 years, but the promotion rate of women into equity partnership positions remains low— currently in the neighborhood of 10%. The relative lack of success in promoting women to partnership positions is a cause of concern within Target. All the partners we interviewed agreed that meeting its aggressive growth targets will require Target to do a better job of retaining talented women. Concern over the retention problem at high levels in the firm is manifest in a recent decision to form a nationwide task force to improve the retention and advancement of women by changing the nature of work.

Exit interviews that Target conducted with women who left over the past year indicate that family concerns (such as having time for children or balancing the demands of two-career families) play a key role in decisions to quit. These exit interviews suggest that the problem of retaining women can be traced to undesirable working conditions—particularly long hours combined with rigorous travel demands. Although these issues surfaced in exit interviews conducted with women, the partners we interviewed believed that similar concerns are likely to become increasingly important for male consultants.

The hours required of Target consultants are both long and variable. As one partner put it "hours are like a roller coaster" with 50 hours per week at the bottom and peak hours being much higher. These peak-hour periods could last for a day or a month, depending on the nature of the deliverable coming due. The long hours are made more difficult by rigorous travel demands. Clients are often located in different cities, states, or countries. The expectation at Target is that "all employees are to go where they are needed . . . and with a smile." Saying "no" to a job because it involves travel can be interpreted as indicating a lack of commitment on the part of the consultant. Another partner, responding to a description of our research on law firms, wondered whether "travel is Target's screening criteria" in deciding whom to consider for promotion to partnership.

The culture of long hours, variable hours, and frequent travel is reinforced by some of the criteria used in deciding promotion to equity partner. In addition to having excellent performance ratings and a certain minimum amount of experience at the firm, a consultant cannot be considered for promotion to equity partner unless he or she is "chargeable" for more than 60% of his or her work time. This means that at least 60% of the hours in a standard work year must be taken up with work that can be charged to a job. In addition, the consultant must demonstrate a good track record in drumming up new business. The time spent developing new clients is not counted as chargeable.

In response to pressures to reduce turnover, Target is looking for ways to alter its work norms. It appears, however, that changing these norms is not easy. What follows is a brief description of the initiatives currently under consideration or underway at Target.

One device for helping consultants balance the demands of work and family is to allow for leaves of absence. Target offers the federally mandated 12 weeks of family leave plus any leave arising from a pregnancy-related disability. Target also allows for additional unpaid leave and this time is not counted as time toward partnership.[23]

Unpaid leave seems to be relatively easy to incorporate into Target's current system. Leave policies, by themselves, however, do not address the concerns of consultants once they return to work. For working consultants, Target is considering offering services ranging from emergency child care to a concierge service that will run errands for consultant who are out of town. Target is also considering small changes in travel rules. For example, Target has dropped the requirement that consultants on distant jobs be at their client's office by 8 A.M. on Monday. Allowing consultants to show up at noon gives them more opportunity to go home and spend time with family and friends over the weekend.

A more fundamental change to Target's human resources system would be to set up a career track in which consultants progress toward equity partner while working reduced hours. The partners we interviewed had considered such a change, but were concerned about a number of potential problems. One worry is that consultants measure their progress in the firm relative to others in their entering cohort. These comparisons make it hard to get ambitious people to participate in a short-hours track that also entails slower progress toward equity partner.[24] A related worry about a short-hour track is that it will become the "female" track and will therefore be avoided by ambitious men and women who might otherwise want reduced hours.

Allowing for part-time partners appears to be even more controversial than allowing part-time consultants into the partnership track. Under the current rules, income is determined by the number of shares a partner "owns." All consultants enter the partnership with the same number of shares. New shares are allocated each year and additional shares are given to reward exceptional performance by individual partners.

Under the current system, the partner who works reduced hours would get a substantial subsidy from his or her colleagues. A policy allowing for part-time partners would therefore require a renegotiation of partnership agreements. These negotiations could be costly and divisive—especially if many partners decided to work part-time. A common rationale for resistance to reduced-hour partners is "if we do this for women, we would have to do it for men." As one partner explained it, the typical salary for a partner is measured in the hundreds of thousands of dollars per year. There is a deep fear that if the partnership allowed it, many partners would be happy to work half the time at half the salary. After all, most people can live very well on half of a $500,000 annual salary. Partners who want to reduce hours as they age pose many of the same problems as partners who want to reduce hours to care for children. Target avoids short hours at the tail end of careers by offering partners substantial financial inducements to retire at age 56.

Even if reduced hours are not viable for partners or for consultants on the partnership track, Target could still retain talent by allowing reduced hours for other consultants who will not be considered for partnership positions. At Target, consultants at the level just below equity partner can be taken off the partnership track and retained as permanent consultants. These permanent consulting positions were originally introduced as a means of retaining consultants who have valuable specialty skills but who do not offer sufficient promise to be promoted to partner. In recent years, however, some of these permanent positions have been filled by women wanting to work part-time. One partner worried that these permanent consulting positions will become a dumping ground for senior women who, by virtue of ability, should be in the partnership.

Part-time jobs are sometimes created for consultants at lower levels in the organization, but these are idiosyncratic arrangements and do not reflect a formal policy or program. Similarly Target consultants who leave the firm in search of shorter hours and less travel are occasionally hired back to work as subcontractors. These subcontractors are paid a per diem rate. The terms of the agreement between Target and the subcontractors can limit the amount of travel as well as evening and weekend work that can be asked of the subcontractor. The subcontractor is also free to provide similar services to other companies subject to various restrictions.[25]

The findings we report for Target parallel in interesting ways our findings at law firms. Target Consulting, like the law firms we studied, relies on an up-or-out promotion tournament as a means of awarding lucrative partnership positions. Sharing rules among partners create important incentives for partners to screen for associates willing to work long hours and, as a result, stringent work norms are applied to associates. A notable difference between Target and our elite law firms is the role of travel. Travel is much more important in the life of a business consultant than in the life of a lawyer. Long business trips are, if anything, more disruptive of family life than long and irregular hours. If heavy travel is simply an inescapable feature of business consulting, than introducing shorter work weeks may not do much to help solve Target's retention problems. If, on the other hand, the consulting firms have used travel as an indicator of underlying work propensities, then the travel components of jobs may be excessive in the same sense that hours may be excessive.

Summary

In an empirical study of associates at large law firms we find that: (1) associates work more than the optimal number of hours; (2) both partners and associates believe that work hours are an important indicator in the promotion process. These results are consistent with our theory of work norms in professional labor markets and they are hard to reconcile with the conventional economic model of hours determination. A qualitative study of a large business consulting firm suggests similar processes may be at work in professional firms outside the legal profession.

Work Norms and The Distribution of Economic Rewards

In the preceding section, we reported evidence on the use of work norms to screen out professionals who may prefer short work hours. The fact that this screening occurs at elite firms raises the prospect that the distribution of economic rewards favors professionals with a propensity to work long hours.

In this section, we consider the effect that screening in large firms may have on the distribution of economic outcomes and opportunities in the legal profession.[26] Our argument is straightforward. The two law firms discussed above are similar in structure to large corporate law firms found throughout the United States. We thus expect that screening on work hours prevails at many other large, corporate law firms.[27] If large law firms offer greater economic rewards than other firms, it follows that the work norms we uncover disadvantage short-hour attorneys.

Are Positions In Large Law Firms More Valuable
Than Other Positions?

Histories of the origins of large law firms suggest that these firms reached their current size because they occupy (by virtue of their reputation and connections) a privileged position in the market for legal services (Galanter and Palay, 1991). Until recently, however, data did not exist that allowed for a systematic comparison of the economic returns from positions in large and small firms.

In 1984, the Young Lawyers Division of the ABA conducted the first, nationally representative survey of lawyers in the United States. Rebitzer and Taylor (1995) used these data to compare the earnings of partners in large and small firms. Table 8–5 presents the basic results. Column 1 of Table 8–5 should be read as follows: All else being equal, if the partners in the ABA sample were to find themselves working in a firm with two lawyers, their average predicted income for 1983 would be $55,514. In contrast, if these same partners were in firms with 15 lawyers then, ceteris paribus, their average predicted annual incomes in 1983 would be $92,025. If all the partners worked in the average-sized firm in the top-size category (i.e., in firms having 228 lawyers), the average predicted income in 1983 would be $161,422. Thus, the move from the lowest to the highest firm-size categories increases the earnings of equivalent partners by $105,908 in 1983. These estimates do not control for differences in ability, human capital investments, or working conditions across firm-size categories. They should therefore be interpreted as "upper bound" estimates of the firm-size effect on the earnings of partners.

Column 2 of Table 8–5 presents estimates of earnings by firm size after introducing variables that control for differences in individual ability, investments in human capital, hours, and working conditions (see Rebitzer and Taylor, 1995, for a complete description). Ceteris paribus, if all the partners in the ABA sample worked in firms with two lawyers, their predicted 1983 incomes would be $60,778. However, if firm size were increased to 228 lawyers, the predicted income of the partners would increase to $127,286. Thus the move from the smallest to the largest size category increases partners' annual earnings by $66,508. This is 63% of the increase calculated in column 1. Put differently, the additional variables added to the second equation in Table 8–5 can account for only 37% of the effect of firm size on earnings.

Based on the figures in Table 8–5, the additional income received by partners in big firms is quite substantial. Let us assume that an associate in a large firm who is not promoted to partner immediately finds subsequent employment as a partner in a firm of two lawyers. From column 2 of Table 8–5, the annual income of partners in large firms is roughly $66,000 greater than that of equivalent partners in small firms. Under the assumptions that this income differential persists over 25 years and that lawyers have a discount rate of 5%, the discounted present value of the wage premium accruing to a newly promoted partner in a large firm is $930,200 in 1983 dollars.[28] If the probability of promotion to partnership in a large firm is as low as 10%, and the associate period lasts six years (Galanter and Palay, 1991), then the expected discounted present value of winning the tournament to a newly entering associate is $69,413 in 1983 dol-

Table 8-5. Average Predicted Partners Incomes Under Hypothetical Firm Sizes in 1983*

Firm Sizes	Predicted salary	
	{1}	{2}
2 Lawyers	$55,514	$60,778
15 Lawyers	$92,025	$84,799
228 Lawyers	$161,422	$127,286

*These estimates are taken from salary equations estimated in Rebitzer and Taylor (1995). Data are from a nationally representative survey of the legal profession described in American Bar Association (1990). Column 1 is predicted income in different firm sizes holding the level of hours at the mean of the sample. Column 2 is predicted income in different firm size holding constant a large number of additional covariates measuring quality of schooling, LSAT scores, law school achievement, location, type of practice, experience, and tenure.

lars.[29] To put this figure in perspective, the median annual salary of associates in large firms in 1983 was between $40,000 and $54,000.

The reward for winning the contest for promotion to partner may be great, but if the odds of victory are small, then the opportunity to work as an associate in a large firm may be no more valuable than the opportunity to work as an associate in a smaller firm. We can infer something about the expected value of entering the promotion tournaments in large and small firms by comparing the earnings of *associates* in large and small law firms. In order to interpret these comparisons, it is first necessary to consider the economics of promotion tournaments in more detail.

Promotion tournaments are structured to create work incentives for associates. In order for the associates to be properly motivated, the firm must, at the margin, set the expected reward from working hard and wining the tournament equal to the cost to the associate of working hard. For similar attorneys doing similar work, the rewards from working hard in the promotion tournament must be the same.[30] This means that the *expected value* of the partnership must be the same at both firms. If the expected value of partnership is the same at both firms, then a finding that similar associates doing similar work are paid more in the larger firm would be proof the promotion tournaments in the large firm has a greater expected value than the analogous promotion contest in the small firm.[31]

Estimates of the firm size effect on associate wages are presented in Table 8–6 (taken from Rebitzer and Taylor, 1995). The results in column 1 mean that if all the associates in the sample were employed in firms having two lawyers, the average salary would be $25,889. If the same group of associates were employed by the average-sized firm in the largest firm-size category (228 lawyers), their annual incomes would increase to $45,018.

Column 2 of Table 8–6 presents estimated earnings by firm size after controlling for measured differences in productive ability, investments in human capital, hours, and working conditions. The average annual predicted income of

Table 8-6. Average Predicted Associates Incomes Under Hypothetical Firm Sizes in 1983*

Firm Sizes	Predicted salary ($)	
	{1}	{2}
2 Lawyers	25,889	28,967
15 Lawyers	32,593	33,246
228 Lawyers	45,018	40,085

*These estimates are taken from salary equations estimated in Rebitzer and Taylor (1995). Data is from a nationally representative survey of the legal profession described in American Bar Association 1984. Column 1 is predicted income in different firm sizes holding the level of hours at the mean of the sample. Column 2 is predicted income in different firm size holding constant a large number of additional covariates measuring quality of schooling, LSAT scores, law school achievement, location, type of practice, experience, and tenure.

associates employed in firms of two attorneys in 1983 is $28,967. If they were employed in the largest firms, the average annual predicted income of this group of attorneys would increase to $40,085. Results presented in Rebitzer and Taylor (1995) show that a substantial firm-size earnings differential for associates persists when estimates are further corrected for unmeasured, productive characteristics of individuals.

Summary

The presence of stringent work norms would have few distributional consequences if jobs in the large law firms studied were as desirable as other jobs in the legal profession. Evidence from a nationally representative survey of attorneys indicates, however, that partnerships in large law firms pay considerably more than alternative jobs—even after controlling for differences in experience, talent, quality of legal education, and tenure. On this basis, we conclude that work norms may shift the distribution of economic outcomes in favor of attorneys wanting to work long hours. Evidence of a positive firm-size effect on associate earnings suggests that the expected value of being hired at a large firm exceeds that of being hired at smaller firms. This finding implies that work norms in large law firms also reduce the economic opportunities for short-hour attorneys. We suspect similar outcomes pertain in other professional firms. If a larger proportion of women than men in professions desire short hours, then these work norms will, on average, limit female access to elite jobs.

Conclusion

Many predominantly male professions are experiencing an unprecedented influx of women. This change in demographics creates pressures to alter established human resources practices. Much of the pressure for change concerns work hours. Women pursuing professional careers while raising families will not be able to work as many hours as earlier cohorts of men. The prospects for equality of economic opportunities across genders in these professions depends critically on how firms respond to the increasing number of prospective employees wanting short-hour jobs.

This chapter puts forward a new framework for understanding the determination of work hours in professional firms. We have argued that professionals often work in groups, teams, or partnerships in which all the members of the group share in the product of other group members. These sharing rules create incentives to adopt stringent work norms as a means of screening out those who want to work reduced hours. Once in place, these work norms tend to persist, even when they no longer serve the best interests of the individuals involved.

Our model of the determinants of work hours suggests that professional labor markets may become trapped in a long-hours equilibrium characterized by an insufficient number of short-hour jobs. It will often be impossible for individual firms to escape this long-hours equilibrium on their own. Coordinated change by a number of firms at the same time may be needed to introduce substantial numbers of short-hour jobs.

The evidence reviewed in this chapter indicates that work norms are important in elite law firms and consulting firms. This finding suggests that, at least in these two professions, work norms are likely to shift the distribution of economic opportunity in favor of individuals who can tolerate long hours. Further research is required to see if these conclusions also hold for professional partnerships in medicine and accounting. Academic departments often function like partnerships and also may rely on implicit hours norms to screen candidates for tenure.

The long-hours trap in professional labor markets may also have important implications for family structure. Professionals working excessive hours early in their careers may choose to delay child rearing. In the case of elite law and consulting firms, women often emerge from the associate period at an age where it becomes increasingly difficult to conceive and bear children. The combined effect of work norms and fertility constraints on the career prospects of female professionals is an important area for further research.

The theory of work hours developed in this chapter also suggests a connection between the sociology of professions and the operation of professional labor markets. If the long-hours trap results from an inability of markets to coordinate the activities of firms, then professional associations might improve labor market efficiency by persuading a number of employers to simultaneously introduce short-hour partnership tracks. The ability of professional associations to undertake this task depends, of course, on the actions taken by influential and powerful members. In the case of law, partners in large firms have considerable influence over the activities of bar associations, but the work norms we have analyzed suggest that access to these influential partnership positions is limited to those willing to tolerate excessive work hours early in their careers. This selection process may give leadership positions to those individuals who are personally least well equipped to understand and react to the shifting demographics of the legal profession. The consequences of this selection pressure on the distribution of power and influence within professions may be quite important for understanding the economics of professional labor markets.

Notes

1. These figures are weighted averages calculated by the authors from a merged file of outgoing rotation groups in the *Current Population Survey* for the years 1979 and 1991.

2. This discussion of the historical changes in the importance of college education for women relies on Goldin (1992).

3. For those born around the turn of the century, the ratio of female to male college graduates was roughly 70%, compared to 56% for those born in 1930 (who therefore were in college after the war) (Goldin, 1992).

4. Goldin (1992) estimates that the economic return college-educated women received from higher income marriages was at least as large as the labor market benefits of college.

5. The rapid introduction of short-hour jobs is all the more remarkable when compared with the slow rate of innovation observed for other features of human resources systems. It has, for example, proven difficult to introduce high-performance human resources systems in many firms, even though the potential benefits of these systems appears large (for a review of this literature see Levine, 1995, and Osterman, 1994).

6. In Coleman and Pencavel, hours worked at all jobs are calculated as the product of weekly hours and weeks worked over the preceding year. Weeks worked included weeks of paid vacations and sick leave. The sample was limited to wage and salary employees with positive earnings and weeks worked in the year prior to the census. The hours trends described above appeared in a regression that controlled for changes in real GNP, cohort size, and average hourly earnings.

7. Pfeffer and Davis-Blake (1987) similarly find that the wages of college administrators are systematically lower in colleges where the fraction of college administrators who are female is high. This pattern of men working in different (and more remunerative) settings than women is not limited to professional occupations. Reskin and Roos (1990) examined a number of previously male, nonprofessional occupations in which women had made strong inroads. They conclude that men and women were concentrated in different jobs within these occupations and that men retained most of the more desirable jobs.

8. This objection applies less forcefully to discrimination in professional schools. Even here, however, the competition for talent will lead employers to pressure professional schools to admit and graduate talented women.

9. A further implication of this model is that women employed in a given position will be on average more able than men. This difference is not the result of discrimination—but rather due to efficient specialization. Since women are more efficient at home production than men, only more able women will find it worthwhile to forgo home production for firm-specific human capital (Lazear and Rosen, 1990).

10. The discussion in this section is adapted from the formal model of adverse selection in work hours in Landers, Rebitzer and Taylor (1996).

11. Baker, Jensen, and Murphy (1988) argue that these factors also limit the extent of pay for performance in many white-collar and blue-collar employment relationships.

12. This describes a "separating" equilibrium—so called because the firm's offer separates types of workers. For a discussion and proof of the existence of this equilibrium in a partnership setting see Landers et al. (1994).

13. The costs of deterrence are modeled in this way for the sake of analytical conve-

nience. In a richer model where talent differed across professionals, a firm may prefer a high quality eight-hour attorney to a 10-hour, low-quality attorney. In this setting, an important cost of work norms would be the failure to attract talented short-hour attorneys.

14. Kremer (1993) argues that this type of technology, which he calls "O-ring" production technology, is ubiquitous and can account for a very long list of otherwise anomalous features of labor markets.

15. The results discussed in this section are taken from Landers et al. (1996).

16. Some law firms hire a small number of so-called permanent associates. Typically, these attorneys have important technical skills but lack the full complement of skills required to succeed as partners.

17. The surveys also included a table describing what a 5% change in work hours would mean for associates working different hours. For example, an associate working 200 hours per month would learn from the table that a 5% change in hours would imply an increase or decrease of one eight-hour day per month or 12 eight-hour days per year.

18. The survey was conducted during the summer of 1993. Three waves of questionnaires were distributed at Firm 1 and, on the advice of management, two waves were distributed at Firm 2. The ultimate response rates at the firms were nearly identical.

19. The importance of hours as an indicator was measured by the same 5-point scale described in the previous paragraph. Hours were classified as an important indicator whenever the respondent indicated that they were *very important* (4) or of the *utmost importance* (5).

20. Most studies examine the response of actual hours to wage changes. Kahn and Lang (1991) find that the elasticity of actual hours with respect to wages is nearly identical to the elasticity of desired hours with respect to the wage.

21. We are grateful to Claudia Goldin for raising this issue in a personal communication.

22. This case study is based on interviews with two managing partners and two equity partners.

23. Candidates for promotion to equity partner must have at least 60 months of experience—not including time off for family leave.

24. Presumably a short-hour track that did not entail a longer path toward partner would be seen as unfair by the remaining consultants.

25. One contract that we saw prohibited the subcontractor from providing similar services to three competing consulting companies. Other clauses in the contract restricted the subcontractor's use of confidential information acquired in the course of the assignment.

26. The analysis in this section comes from Rebitzer and Taylor (1995).

27. This expectation is also supported by informal discussions with partners at other leading firms.

28. If the alternative employment for lawyers not made partner were in firms of 15 lawyers, then the discounted present value of promotion to partnership in a large firm would be $598,809 in 1983.

29. A *Wall Street Journal* report indicates that the probability an associate hired in the classes of 1981, 1982, or 1983 would have made partner by 1992 was .10 at the 30 largest New York law firms. This is likely to be a lower bound promotion probability. First, promotion rates in 1992 were depressed by the cyclical downturn in the legal services industry (Woo, 1992). Second, these 30 New York firms have the reputation of being among the most difficult firms in which to make partner in the whole country.

30. If the marginal returns to similar effort were different, one of these firms is either offering an insufficient work incentive or an excessively generous work incentive.

31. Rebitzer and Taylor (1995) offer an extensive discussion of this point together with a proof that the conclusion holds under very general assumptions.

References

Aigner, Dennis, and Glen G. Cain. 1977. "Statistical Theories of Discrimination in Labor Markets," *Industrial and Labor Relations Review* 30, no. 2 (January), 175–87.

Akerlof, George. 1976. "The Economics of Caste and of the Rat Race and Other Woeful Tales," *Quarterly Journal of Economics* 90 (November): 599–617.

Akerlof, George A., and William T. Dickens. 1982. "The Economic Consequences of Cognitive Dissonance," *American Economic Review* 72, no. 3 (June): 307–319.

American Bar Association, Young Lawyers Division. 1990. *The State of the Legal Profession,* Chicago: American Bar Association.

Baker, Laurence. 1993. "Narrowing the Gap: Evidence on Male- Female Earnings Differences Among Young Physicians." Working Paper (November) Princeton University.

Baker, George P., Michael C. Jensen, and Kevin Murphy. 1988. "Compensation and Incentives: Practice vs. Theory," *Journal of Finance* July 43 no. 3 (July): 593–616.

Berger Morello, Karen. 1988. *The Invisible Bar: The Woman Lawyer in America: 1638 to the Present* Boston: Beacon Press.

Blackburn, M., Bloom, David E., and R. B. Freeman. 1991. "Changes in Earnings Differentials in the 1980's: Concordance, Convergence, Causes and Consequences." *NBER Working Paper #3901.*

Blank, Rebecca M. 1990. "Are Part-Time Jobs Bad Jobs?". In *A Future of Lousy Jobs?.* Gary Burtless, ed., 123–165. Washington, D.C.: The Brookings Institution.

Blau, Francine, and Lawrence M. Kahn. 1992. "Race and Gender Pay Differentials," Working Paper no. 4120 (July) NBER.

Coleman, Mary T., and John Pencavel. 1993a. "Changes in the Work Hours of Male Employees Since 1940," *Industrial and Labor Relations Review* 46, no. 2 (January): 653–676.

———. 1993b. "Trends in the Market Work Behavior of Women Since 1940," *Industrial and Labor Relations Review* 46, no. 4 (July): 653–676.

Farrell, Joseph, and Suzanne Scotchmer. 1988. "Partnerships," *Quarterly Journal of Economics* May 103, no. 2 (May): 279–298.

Fiske, Susan T., and Shelley E. Taylor. 1991. *Social Cognition,* 2nd ed. New York: McGraw-Hill.

Galanter, Marc, and Thomas Palay. 1991. *Tournament of Lawyers: The Transformation of the Big Law Firm.* Chicago: University of Chicago Press.

Gilson, Ronald, and Robert Mnookin. 1985. "Sharing Among the Human Capitalists: An Economic Inquiry into the Corporate Law Firm and How Partners Split Profits," *Stanford Law Review* 37:313–392.

———. 1989. "Coming of Age in a Corporate Law Firm: The Economics of Associate Career Paths," *Stanford Law Review* 41:567–595.

Goldin, Claudia. 1990. *Understanding the Gender Gap: An Economic History of American Women.* New York: Oxford University Press.

———. 1992. "The Meaning of College in the Lives of American Women: The Past 100 Years." Working Paper no. 4099 (June), NBER.

Juster, Thomas F., and Frank P. Stafford. 1991. "The Allocation of Time: Empirical Findings, Behavioral Models, and the Problems of Measurement," *Journal of Economic Literature* June 29, no. 2 (June): 471–522.

Kahn, Shulamit, and Kevin Lang. 1988. "The Effects of Hours Constraints on Labor Supply Estimates." Working Paper no. 2647 (July) NBER.

———. 1991. "The Effects of Hours Constraints on Labor Supply Estimates," *Review of Economics and Statistics* 73, no. 4 (November): 605–611.

Kremer, M. 1993. "The O-Ring Theory of Economic Development." *Quarterly Journal of Economics* 108 (3): 551–576.

Landers, R., Rebitzer J., and Taylor, L. 1996. "Rat Race Redux: Adverse Selection in The Determination of Work Hours," *The American Economic Review* (June).

Land, Kevin, and Peter-John Gordon. 1994. "Partnerships as Insurance Devices: Theory and Evidence." Working Paper (July 7) Boston University.

Lazear, Edward P., and Sherwin Rosen. 1990. "Male-Female Wage Differentials in Job Ladders," *Journal of Labor Economics* part 2 (January): S106–S123.

Leete-Guy, Laura, and Juliet Schor. 1994. "Assessing the Time Squeeze Hypothesis: Estimates of Market and Non-Market Hours in the United States, 1969–1987," *Industrial Relations* 33, no. 1 (Winter): 25–44.

Levine, David. 1995. *Reinventing the Workplace.* Washington, D.C.: Brookings Institution.

Lundberg, Shelly J., and Richard Startz. 1983. "Private Discrimination and Social Intervention in Competitive Labor Markets," *American Economic Review* June 73, no. 3 (June): 340–347.

Osterman, Paul. 1994. "How Common is Workplace Transformation and Who Adopts It?" *Industrial and Labor Relations Review* 47, no. 2 (January): 173–188.

Pencavel, John. 1986. "Labor Supply of Men: A Survey." In *Handbook of Labor Economics.* Orley Ashenfelter and Richard Layard, eds. Amsterdam: North-Holland.

Pfeffer, Jeffery, and Alison Davis-Blake. 1987. "The Effect Of the Proportion of Women on Salaries: The Case of College Administrators," *Administrative Science Quarterly* 32 (March): 24.

Preston, Anne. 1993a. "Why Have All the Women Gone: A Study of Exit of Women From the Science and Engineering Occupations." Working Paper (March).

———. 1993b. "Occupational Departure of Employees in the Natural Sciences and Engineering." Report to the Alfred P. Sloan Foundation, (June).

Rebitzer, James B., and Lowell J. Taylor 1995. "Efficiency Wages and Employment Rents: The Employer Size Wage Effect in the Job Market for Lawyers," *Journal of Labor Economics.* 13, No. 4 (October) 1995 p. 678–708.

Reskin, Barbara F., and Patricia A. Roos. 1990. "Explaining the Changing Sex Composition of Occupations." In *Explaining Job Queues, Gender Queues: Explaining Women's Inroads into Male Occupations.* Barbara F. Reskin and Patricia A. Roos, eds. Philadelphia: Temple University Press.

Rosen, S. 1982. "Authority, Control and the Distribution of Earnings." *The Bell Journal of Economics:* 311–323.

Sander, Richard H., and Douglass E. Williams. 1989. "Why are There So Many Lawyers? Perspectives on a Turbulent Market," *Law and Social Inquiry* Vol. 14 p. 431–79.

Spurr, Stephen J. 1990. "Sex Discrimination in the Legal Profession: A Study of Promotion," *Industrial Labor Relations Review* 43, no. 4 (April): 406–417.

Statistics Canada. 1985. "The Survey on Work Reduction: Microdata Documentation and Users Guide," (December).

Woo, Junda. 1992. "Climb to Top is Steeper at Big Law Firms" *Wall Street Journal* June 15,
   p. B8.
Wood, R. G., M. E. Corcoran, et al. 1993. "Pay Differences Among the Highly Paid: The
   Male-Female Earnings Gap in Lawyers' Salaries." *Journal of Labor Economics* 11(3):
   417–441.

Index